Strategy for Successful Development of Business Information Systems

Michael M. Gorman

Whitemarsh Information Systems Corporation
2008 Althea Lane
Bowie, Maryland 20716
Tele: 301-249-1142
Email: Whitemarsh@wiscorp.com
Web: www.wiscorp.com

Designations used by companies to distinguish their products are often claimed as trademarks. In all instances where Whitemarsh Press is aware of a claim, the product names appear in initial capital or all capital letters. Readers, however, should contact the appropriate companies for more complete information regarding trademarks and registration.

This publication is designed to provide accurate and authoritative information in regard to the subject matter covered. It is sold with the understanding that the publisher is not engaged in rendering legal, accounting, or other professional services. If legal advice or other expert assistance is required, the services of a competent professional person should be sought. FROM A DECLARATION OF PRINCIPLES JOINTLY ADOPTED BY A COMMITTEE OF THE AMERICAN BAR ASSOCIATION AND A COMMITTEE OF PUBLISHERS.

ISBN 978-0-9789968-1-9

Printed in the United States of America

Table of Contents

Figures

Tables

Preface

A government agency needed a project management system: Not Microsoft Project, but a business information system[1] to manage their functional projects. The overall scope included projects, staff, deliverables, assignments, status reports, travel and expenses, client organizations and their staff, and the like. So the agency hired a contractor to come in and do a requirements analysis, and build a business information system. The requirements analysis was standard fare: meet with management, meet with functional experts, and meet with technical staff. Everybody was interviewed and the requirements document filled several volumes. Everyone was happy.

The contractor took the requirements document away and implemented the business information system. After about a year of detailed design, coding, unit testing, and system testing, the business information system was delivered to the government agency. The government agency shrieked in horror. What had the contractor done? That is not what the agency had said. Not what they had wanted. How could this happen? So the contractor was promptly fired.

Since this clearly had to be an aberration, a new contractor was hired. The new contractor met with management, met with functional experts, and met with technical staff. Everybody was interviewed and the requirements document filled several volumes. Everyone was happy.

The contractor took the requirements document away and implemented the business information system. After about a year of detailed design, coding, unit testing, and system testing, the business information system was delivered to the government agency. The government agency shrieked in horror. What had the contractor done? That is not what the agency had said. Not what they had wanted. How could this happen? So the contractor was promptly fired.

Since this clearly had to be an aberration, a new contractor was hired. Now to save the readers time, just go to back to the start of this cycle and read it again: twice more.

---

[1]. In this book, a business information system is a set of application-specific software that created, manipulates, evolves or deletes data–most commonly–from a database through a database management system in support of some mission area of the enterprise. A business information system is class of information system, and it is distinguished from other classes such as a computer's operating system, or "systems software" information system such as telecommunications management, database management systems, and end-user security management.

An epiphany then happened to the government agency. Since all the contractors were using the same data processing and implementation technology infrastructure to build the business information system, it had to be the fault of the underlying technology infrastructure. The next step was to try to terminate and/or replace the underlying technology infrastructure. At that point, the technology vendor brought in a consultant to completely evaluate the situation. The cycles of requirements through failure were examined to determine what went wrong. A classic methodology was used, and so it was presumed that there would be a classic result. Actually, there was.

After the study, a meeting was called by the consultant with the government agency's heads. The agency was eager to know not only what went wrong but who to blame. The answer was a shock. It was the agency that was at fault, not the contractors. Of course the agency angrily protested the findings. The consultant carefully went through the requirements-failure cycles and showed that during every cycle the perception of what the problem was and therefore what the solution should be had changed.

It was not a case of whether the contractor got the requirements right. Rather it was a case of the government agency not knowing what requirements it actually wanted. When the contractor talked to different government staff, the answers were different not just from one staff member to another, but from previous answers provided by the same government staff member over the different cycles. The objective, a successfully developed business information system, was impossible to achieve.

What to do? It was suggested to the government agency that they create their own detailed specification of what needed to be accomplished. The agency countered, "that's the contractor's responsibility!" The consultant indicated that if four different contractors couldn't create the "just right" specification, it was not the contractor's fault. The agency asked what it should do. The consultant suggested that a week-long workshop be conducted with agency staff to derive the requirements. The agency agreed. The consultant asked the agency head for the names of the staff that absolutely were too important to be on the team. A list was immediately produced. The consultant said, "these are the names of the individuals that must participate." The agency head's response was not "printable."

The final agreement was this. A workshop would be conducted that would cause the creation not only of the specifications of the business information system to be produced, but also a prototype as the specification's proof. Further, the specifications were to be stored in an early version of the Whitemarsh Metabase[2] so that the repository could be used in the subsequent full implementation contract as the key reference point for the specification of what needed to be implemented. Finally, the process was required to iterate the requirements via the prototype demonstrations until complete.

The workshop was conducted over five full days. There were four agency teams of four individuals each along with one information technology person per team. Each team lead had to be a functional expert. Additionally, the team lead was instructed that the information technology person was to act solely as the team's scribe in creating the metadata. If the information technology person got out of hand, it was suggested to the team lead that they could to use duct-tape to silence the information technology person. A stick was also provided.

At the end of the week, the specification, the metadata, and a high-level prototype were complete. The agency's information technology department took the result and increased it with one or two more levels of detail, including evolving the prototype. The full implementation contract was let and the system was developed, tested, and accepted by the agency.

This book is all about how to create this kind of environment. That is, functional experts employing a CASE/Repository tool to create valid requirements, the use of business information system generators by these same individuals to create a prototype of the requirements, and the iteration of the prototype until all the requirements have been teased out of the functional experts and have been properly reflected in the overall specification that is demonstrated via the prototype.

The CASE/Repository tool employed to illustrate the overall process in this book is the Whitemarsh Metabase. Hereafter, the terms CASE and metadata repository will be referred to by the single term, Metabase, because

---

[2]   Metadata is a generic term that identifies all classes of information technology specifications across the enterprise. Hence all data and process specifications are metadata. All requirements could also be considered metadata. A metadata repository is a database within which all metadata is stored. A metadata database is a metabase. Whitemarsh has employed the term, Metabase, in this context since 1982. A metadata repository system is a software system that captures, stores, reports, and manages all metadata. The system that manages the Metabase is the Metabase system. Sophisticated metadata repositories are multi-user and support the capture and reporting of metadata in a non-redundant, integrated manner across the enterprise.

it was designed to be both a CASE tool for database and systems engineering, and a metadata repository for all in the enterprise to employ. Readers can go to the Whitemarsh website (www.wiscorp.com) and download the Metabase. Once installed all the computer windows in this book can be seen via the Metabase system.

Whitemarsh started using the term, Metabase, in 1982 as a way to signify a metadata database [3]. An early production-class version of the Whitemarsh Metabase was implemented by Hartford Insurance in 1979 with great success and with an enterprise[4] scope. Another Metabase was implemented by Whitemarsh for the U.S. Army in 1984. The Army Metabase enabled the manufacturing of both specifications and software to such an extent that the per-system cost was reduced from about $400K to less than $40K.

Today, the term, metabase, has become very popular. A recent "Google search" identified almost one million hits. However, whenever this term, Metabase, is used in this book it refers to the Whitemarsh Metabase. Metabase has been used on almost every Whitemarsh project. The result has always been the same: More for less in a shorter time, at higher quality and lower risk. Over the years, the Metabase has been implemented through different database management systems such as CSC's Manage, Computer Associate's IDMS, Cincom's Supra, Information Busilder's Focus, and SoftVelocity's Clarion. The Clarion version is both the most recent and the

---

[3] In this book and in all Whitemarsh materials, database and DBMS are very different terms. A database is meant to imply an organized collection of business data that conforms to rigorous semantics and high levels of standardization and integrity. Databases come in different classes such as original data capture, data warehouses, and subject areas. DBMS, meaning database management system is a software system created by vendors to define and manage databases. Oracle is a DBMS vendor and its DBMS is called Oracle. Oracle is thus not a database vendor because it does not create, sell, and maintain databases. Rather, it creates, sells and maintains DBMSs. Confusing database with DBMS is like confusing passengers with vehicle.

[4] As defined within this book, an enterprise is merely a term to relate to a collection of organization units that have common collections of data, processes, activities within a business or a company and sometimes beyond corporate affiliations as in the case of data interchanges. An enterprise is therefore not just a synonym for business or a company. Rather, it is intended to convey a common data, process, and activity view across the organizational units sharing that view.

most sophisticated. Finally, a CSC Manage version of the Metabase was also used in the Workshop described in this Preface.

Additionally, all the software examples in this document were implemented through Clarion (www.SoftVelocity.com). Clarion was chosen because it, based on Whitemarsh's experience, alone fulfills the minimum essential requirements for the high quality, cost effective business information system generator that is essential for prototyping and iterating business information systems requirements specifications. The metadata et al for the case study in this book is available through the Metabase's demo database which can be obtained from the Whitemarsh website. The example data is from the Movies example Metabase database instance. The Movie Rental Corporation is a "nom de plume" for the largest movie rental business in the United States.

Clarion is also well suited for production class database applications on Microsoft operating system environments. All of Whitemarsh's production class software products are implemented through Clarion. The underlying databases currently operate either through Clarion access methods or through ODBC to standard SQL server-based engines.

Recently, Whitemarsh had the opportunity to create a large scale membership management business information system for an international association. Upon completion, the database and business information system was sized to be 6600 function points. By industry standards, a function point costs $400. Thus, under traditional methods, the database and application should have cost $2.64 million and taken more than 12 staff years. But through the use of this book's principles, Metabase, and Clarion, the business information system cost the Whitemarsh client only about $350 thousand, and took less than two staff years. That's an 87% reduction in cost and more than six times improvement in staff productivity. The implemented application has been running now for about six years. No changes have been needed.

Notwithstanding this ringing endorsement of Clarion as a client-side development environment, Whitemarsh has engineered its software and the underlying databases such that they can be implemented through other client-side development environments. The key "take-away" here is not that Clarion should be purchased and employed (although that's a highly recommended idea), it's that the process of iterative design-prototype development is the right strategy to employ so as to:

- Avoid wasting the time and resources of information technology.

- Accelerate the creation, evolution, and deployment of information technology solutions

- Maximize the precious time of functional experts

If these are key goals in your organization, this book is for you and your organization. Act on these goals. Increasing production, lowering cost, increasing quality, and reducing risk will be your result.

This book is not however just about one-off business information systems development. It also addresses the need for business information systems planning, at a high level, across the enterprise. It does not serve the enterprise well if competing organizations implement conflicting solutions characterized by different definitions for the same data, different processes for the same functions, and redundant business information systems. Such redundant efforts are a profound waste of time and resources. Not only is the time to create the redundant and conflicting solution a waste, so also is the effort to intersect these ill-conceived solutions, to ultimately dismantle them, and to then replace them. Added to this waste is the opportunity lost to accomplish the "real" missions of the enterprise.

This book addresses the need for having business information system projects (regardless of sponsor or author) integrated within one project management environment so that maximum efficiency can be achieved.

There needs to be an integrated approach to data within the enterprise so that some organizations can use the data created by others. This is important. There is more than enough data within enterprises. What is scarce are integration, non-redundancy, and semantic harmonization.

A significant quantity of today's key infrastructure data is already captured and managed by "ERP" (Enterprise Resource Package) systems. Consequently, most new business information systems are ancillary or supplementary to key functionality that is already automated.

Currently, most organizations have a mixed technology environment. That is, some legacy batch processing, some client-server, and other environments that are Internet based. The reason why this book and the approach illustrated herein is independent of implementation strategy is because this book is not about implementation. Rather, it is about the creation of an implementable set of business information system specifications that are inherently valid. Then comes implementation.

This book has been years in the making because it has evolved through many cycles of actual use within projects starting back in the late 1970s. During this time, the Metabase has been implemented a number of times under a myriad of DBMSs for clients in many different industry and government sectors. This implementation of the Metabase is within Clarion (www.SoftVelocity.com), which is by far the most sophisticated business information system generator that exists today.

Along the way, there have been key contributors to this effort. Thanks therefore goes to Herman Koester of St. Louis who challenged me to put the entire approach into one of those infamous "12-step" plans. Sorry, there are only 9-steps. Thanks goes to Hank Lavender, who, for almost 10 years, has been a constant and relentless reviewer and inquisitor. Gratitude also goes to Bruce Haberkamp who read a mid 1990s manuscript of this book and encouraged me to incorporate its key points into the process that is now part of Army policies, AR 25-1 and the DA PAM 25-1-1. Thanks also goes to Peter Rush who, despite work, home, and personal pressures found the time to make very cogent and insightful comments. Finally, thanks goes to my wife Maxine and my son, Matt who listened attentively, and asked critical questions that sent me back into my rewrite cave.

1

The Problem

Many, if not most, information technology projects exhibit these characteristics: over budget, under specified, delivered late, and unable to meet organizational expectations [5] [6] [7]. In one of the studies by The Standish Corporation, 31% of a class of client/server systems efforts failed outright; another 53% were challenged (late, greater than budgeted, and fewer features than promised), and only 16% were delivered on-time, within budget, and with features as promised.

In the Chaos study by Standish, the top three reasons uncovered for successful business information systems were:

- User involvement.
- Executive management support.
- Clear statement of requirements.

And, the three top reasons cited by executives for business information systems failures were:

- Incomplete requirements.
- Lack of user involvement.
- Lack of resources.

[5] The Standish Group. *CHAOS: 1998: A Summary Review*: 1999. The Standish Group International, Dennis, MA 02638.

[6] Matson, Eric. Speed Kills (the Competition). Fast Company (August 1996). Page 1. Web: www.fastcompany.com/online/04/speed.html.

[7] Strassmann, Paul A. *40 Years of IT History*: 1997. Page 6. Web: www.strassmann.com/pubs/datamation1097/index.html

All the Standish studies have been updated almost every year. While there has been some improvement, there has not been a dramatic change. The failure or challenge percentages are relatively the same and the reasons for success and failure remain almost constant.

The United States Government's General Accountability Office (GAO) has been studying information technology projects for a number of years. A review of United States General Accountability Office (www.gao.gov) studies of why business information systems fail shows that new requirements so commonly crop up during the business information systems development phase that this must be considered intrinsic to the software development life cycle as currently practiced. This phenomenon is the root cause of a preponderance of these GAO identified reasons for failure.

The new problems that arise when new requirements are uncovered during development fall into two categories: Database design changes and software changes.

Significant database design changes often result from an insufficiently data-driven methodology through which the database is initially designed. Experience has shown that very high quality database designs created through a data-driven methodology commonly return many times their design cost in reduced software development and evolution costs.

Software changes result from database design changes and also from process logic changes. Database design changes can be largely eliminated through the use of a quality database design methodology. The onerous effects of process logic changes, can be dramatically affected through the use of object-oriented analysis, design and programming techniques employed within the environment of business information system generators.

A key strategy to minimize the negative impact of software changes is "code-generation," that is, through a business information system generator. It is a software system that takes in metadata specifications that have been created through the Metabase or other tools such as data modeling tools, and outputs the actual production-ready business information system. Business information system generators have evolved greatly in the last 20 years and should be used in almost all situations. Clarion is a business information system generator.

A review of eight GAO studies mentioned above clearly shows that the main reasons why business information systems fail has nothing to do with information technology [8] [9]. Rather, the failures reside outside the sphere of information technology control. Nevertheless, information technology must work with the enterprise in the creation of a knowledge worker environment that enables information technology to be successful. Such an environment would be Win-Win all the way around. In support of that goal, this book presents the following:

- A description of the essential prerequisites for information technology success.

- The nine-step approach to business information systems development.

- A strategy for developing, executing and maintaining enterprise-wide business information systems and to identify the right accomplishment sequence for these business information systems.

- An overview of enterprise-wide project management that enables the nine-step projects to be completed on-time, within budget, and delivering what is promised.

Before presenting this 9-step approach in any detail, a fundamental objection to this entire approach must be addressed. It has become painfully clear that some organizations try to avoid the problem of underdeveloped or immature requirements by buying COTS. COTS, that is Commercial Off the Shelf Software, if improperly procured, may exacerbate this problem, not solve it.

When COTS is purchased, what is actually being procured is software based on somebody else's requirements analysis. Was that analysis sufficient? Was it comprehensive? Did it match the organization's real needs? If any of the answers is no, then buying COTS could produce a bad result for four reasons.

---

[8]   Gorman, Michael M. Knowledge Worker Framework: 1999. Web: www.wiscorp.com

[9]   United States Government Accounting Office. Managing Technology: Best Practices Can Improve Performance and Produce Results,: 1997 (GAO/T-AIMD-97-38). Washington, D.C. (web: www.gao.gov)

- Any business information system built on top of inadequate requirements causes an unsuitable COTS system to be selected and installed. The software will have been purchased. Staff will have been trained. Hardware will have been procured. Data will have been converted. Only after production use has begun will it be known that it was the wrong solution. Fixing that problem requires either abandoning the purchase, training, hardware, and data conversion, and beginning the process all over again, or convincing the users that their real requirements, which are only starting to be discovered through system use, aren't all that important or necessary. The first alternative is very expensive, and the second is quite unacceptable.

- Changing COTS installed software ranges from difficult and expensive, to impossible. Once changed, some COTS becomes custom software, which subsequently, is both difficult and expensive to change to the next COTS version.

- How would you know if the COTS system is based on inadequate requirements if a thorough requirements analysis hasn't been performed? Without doing this book's 9-step approach, the probability of having the right requirements will be very low. The risk will be very high.

- Because the acquired software is COTS, the procuring organization now lacks both the capabilities and the tools to make its own software modifications. Rather, the organization's mission is accomplishable only when and if some outside vendor changes the COTS system. If the initial requirements analysis either wasn't done or was done in a cursory manner, the organization's mission accomplishment may be fatally impacted.

If an organization wishes to purchase COTS, it is because of the four reasons cited above that the 9-step approach, albeit modified, is even more essential. During Step 8, instead of actually "building" the software, the organization takes the five critical elements that result from this approach, that is, Missions, Organizations, Functions, Database Design, and validated Prototype and wraps all five into a Request for Proposal and issues it to a potential set of vendors. What will be given to the potential vendors is a highly refined and validated set of requirements, and what will come back from the vendors will be a COTS proposal and software system that matches the "real" requirements.

1.1 Organizational Environment for the Nine Step Approach

This book presents a nine-step process that addresses many of the Standish and GAO information technology findings. The nine steps are:

- Develop missions.
- Design the database.
- Generate the prototype.
- Evolve the specification through prototyping.
- Create the request for proposal.
- Evaluate the vendor responses.
- Award the contract.
- Manage the contractor.
- Test conformance to prototype.

This book presumes that many requirements development organizations[10] do not contain sophisticated information technology development organizations and have no interest in establishing them. Rather, this book presumes that requirements development organizations prefer to specify information technology needs through some sort of central design authority, and, through the business information systems development organizations, procure, install,

---

[10]   In the context of this paper, a requirements development organization is one that possesses significant functional knowledge of a business area that is to undergo automation or an automation upgrade. In contrast, an information systems development organization is one that possesses the skill necessary to transform a requirements document into a highly efficient computer system.

    While the knowledge areas of these two groups may overlap, they are largely non-intersecting. Finally, both organizations may be in the same or different enterprises. They deal with each other through formal memorandums of understanding, or even legally binding contracts. In the former case, they would be two different agencies within some government organization, large industry, or university setting, and in the later case they would be separate corporate entities.

employ information technology solutions that are both functionally acceptable and conformance tested to ensure common functionality across requirements development organizations.[11]

Whenever requirements development organizations take on full development including complete business information systems development, operation, evolution and maintenance, that is, all nine steps, they commonly fail to achieve optimum results. While there can be many reasons for this, the GAO studies show the most common to be:

- Failure to meet initial end-user expectations.

- Inability to continuously infuse advances in technology in the deployed information technology environments.

- Inability to break from the long-standing tradition of individual autonomy, that is, stove-pipe development.

This last reason, autonomy, prevents the effective deployment of business information systems based on a unified business information system's design and implementation strategy across a group of requirements development organizations because:

- One size does not fit all.

- Requirements development organizations often require slightly different functionality one from the other.

- The cost of evolving business information systems through old technologies and approaches is neither cost effective nor viable.

A solution that does work is one that capitalizes on the strengths of both the requirements development organizations and business information systems development organizations, while avoiding their weaknesses. The proposed approach consists of a three-part paradigm:

---

[11] Strassmann, Paul A. *Outsourcing IT: Miracle cure or emetic*: 1998. Web: www.strassmann.com/pubs/outsourcing.shtml

- A requirements development organization to define, validate through prototyping, and maintain functional requirements.

- A business information systems development organization that creates production class business information systems from the prototype.

- Conformance tests and testing by the requirements development organization that ensures that the developed business information system conforms to the essential functionality contained in the prototype and the Metabase.

Even though this nine-step approach is optimum for large, heterogenous hardware environments across multi-site requirements development organizations, this approach can be simplified to accommodate homogenous and/or single-site requirements development organization environments.

While all nine steps are the responsibility of requirements development organizations, the bulk of the actual work to actually implement the business information system, that is, Step 8 would be accomplished by a business information system organization, with oversight, of course, from the requirements development organization.

All of these "Whitemarsh" tool-based examples are fundamentally based on just good information technology common sense. Hence every tool-presented window should be able to be accomplished by any number of tool suites. The reason why the Whitemarsh tool suite was employed was to eliminate any objection to the use of the book's strategies. That is, that the book is just a collection of theories. Clearly these are not just theories. Rather, this book represents the best practice of tens of thousands of users around the world.

1.2 Problem Summary

Inadequate responses to the problem addressed by this book, that is, how to successfully create "requirements" in advance of business information system development are endemic. Information technology 's traditional solution to this problem has however been quite unique. It has been to demand something that is not only impossible but is never done in almost any other discipline.

Information technology 's demand is that the requirements document be complete and comprehensive, unchanging, and near absolutely correct before any prototyping, coding, or other development activities are begun. If all the requirements are either not present or imperfect, there will be cost overruns, and excessive time spent correcting the "mistakes" of the functional users.

In virtually every other complex discipline, models and prototypes are developed and iterated a number of times so as to "tease out" the true nature, design, and desired behavior. Over the years, the need for prototypes has been trumpeted loud and clear. Everyone gets excited, but then nothing seems to happen. That's because there's been no information technology methodology specifically engineered to create the prototypes; no Metabase environment to capture, store, and iterate the prototypes; and no integrated code-generation environment that can quickly create the prototyped business information systems in a form that is sufficiently real to enable the real requirements to surface. Finally, no strategy exists to iterate a given requirement from initial inclusion within the Metabase through prototype environment and recycle.

This book presents a methodology for prototyping. Further, it points to the Metabase tool that can be downloaded and employed for a sufficient amount of time to fully demonstrate the prototyping solution. Finally, this book points to an integrated code-generation environment, Clarion, that fully supports prototyping.

1.3 Remainder of this Book

Chapter 2 of this book presents a description of the essential prerequisites for business information system development success, and states why having this environment returns many times its cost. It shows that the use of the tools described in this book can reduce business information systems development costs by about 66%. In this chapter, the discussion of the Knowledge Worker Framework identifies the different major classes of activities and products that have to be created in support of enterprise database, and business information systems development.

This chapter also shows the allocation of the U.S. General Accountability Office's "Reasons for failures" that occur when the activities and products identified in the Knowledge Worker Framework are not accomplished. The most surprising part of the allocation of failure is that 95% of all business information systems fail for reasons outside the domain of information technology.

Addressed in this chapter are the steps of a methodology specially designed to advance the quality of the very requirements that must be present for successful databases and business information systems. The chapter identifies the characteristics of business information system generators that need to be present to accomplish prototyping, the key characteristics of the Metabase, and CASE tools.

This chapter addresses the need to reorient from a stove-pipe project-based mentality to a "release" mentality to enable capabilities across multiple business information systems to advance in a coordinated fashion.

Finally, the chapter identifies key metrics and work environment factors that dramatically affect both the quality and the timeliness of database and business information system accomplishment.

Chapter 3 presents the nine-step approach through screen-shots from the Metabase and the Clarion environment that illustrate how to accomplish each of the key steps. The key surprise of this 9-step approach is that the first seven steps require only business users and functional experts, and that only the last two steps require the involvement of an information technology organization. Step 8 is the step within which the business information systems development organization creates the business information system. Step 9 is the conformance testing step wherein the requirements development organization certifies that the created business information system meets the requirements.

The main objective of Steps 1-7 is to enable functional users to advance their awareness of their information technology requirement and to evolve this awareness through prototyping until it is then ready for information technology to implement: one time and correctly.

Chapter 4 presents an overview of the Whitemarsh Business Information Systems Plan process. It does no good to know how to implement business information systems well if you do not know which ones to implement and in which sequence.

Over the past 10 years, starting in the late 1990s, there has been a dramatic increase in the use of Enterprise Resource Packages (ERP). These are comprehensive database and business information system implementations across broad functional areas. Consequently, many of the newly created database and business information systems are derivative business information systems, not one-off business information systems that start from blank slates. Because of this very significant change, enterprise-wide database and business information systems plans are more important than ever, and the very metadata created during the development of these plans needs to be stored in the Metabase so that impact analyses can be quickly developed and accomplished.

As a direct consequence of ERPs, there have been fewer large scale business information system implementations, and many more moderate to small business information system efforts. This increases the need for enterprise-wide information systems plans to integrate and interrelate the data from the more numerous decentralized and distributed database and business information system development. Many of these are building discordant stove-pipes of semantics, data models, process models, and the like. An enterprise-wide information systems plan can help identify and manage efforts to deconflict and eliminate redundant databases and business information systems.

Chapter 5, Whitemarsh Project Management presents an overview of the Whitemarsh approach to project management. This too is illustrated through screen-shots from the Whitemarsh project management system.

The Whitemarsh project management approach is different from traditional time-management approaches because it manages deliverables rather than expended time through work plans, and it enables enterprise-wide project management through the use of project, deliverable, and task templates coupled with person-based skill inventories and work environment factors. Thus, while every project is different, each is built from commonly found (define once, use many times) building blocks. The entire Whitemarsh environment meets one of the Software Engineering Institute's critical success factors: Self-correction. The Whitemarsh approach to project management is especially important because it is set within the context of other enterprise metadata and all the projects that are identified, in development, in production, or in maintenance across the enterprise.

Chapter 6, Summary, brings forth the features, advantages, benefits, conclusions and future actions that flow from adopting this approach to database and business information systems development. There is no downside to adoption. The overall information technology organization, and the functional organizations that are supported by information technology, are more productive, less costly, of higher quality, and lower risk because more work is done in a non-redundant, integrated manner. More work products are able to be reused. Data semantics can be harmonized, which then eliminates whole classes of data transformation and reloading business information systems and logic. Again, there is no downside to doing more, faster at a lower cost and risk.

1.4 Questions and Exercises

1. Have you been involved in situations like the one in the Preface? What was the most common set of reactions? Was the root causes similar to those cited in the Preface? If yes, how did you resolve the situation. If no, what were the root causes and what did you do?

2. Have you used a CASE tool? What were its good and bad features? If it's no longer used, why did it fail? Did it have an explicit ODBC accessible database? Was or would that have been good?

3. Have you used a data and/or process modeling tools? What were its good and bad features? If it's no longer used, why did it fail? Did it have a explicit ODBC accessible database? Was or would that have been good? Were you able to integrate the data and process metadata? If not, what did you do? Was data a slave to process or vice versa? What's good or bad about that? Did these tools have an explicit ODBC accessible database? Was or would that have been good?

4. Have you used a Metadata Repository such as Rochade? What were its good and bad features? If it's no longer used, why did it fail? Did it have an explicit ODBC accessible database? Was or would that have been good?

5. Would a metadata management tool that combines, CASE, data and process engineering, and a metadata repository be of value? What should its features be? Should it have an open database schema architecture such that it could be accessed through ODBC via commercial report writers and 3GL programming languages?

6. Do you agree or disagree with the Standish reasons for business information system success or failure? Explain. What other reasons come to mind? Which ones are "app killers?"

7. Do you fundamentally agree or disagree with the 9-steps as a way to engineer and deploy business information system correctly and for the first time? Explain. What steps are missing and what's the effect of their being missing?

8. Given that you have a practical way to do prototypes, how key are they in the overall business information system development success especially as a way to evolve and validate requirements?

9. Can you successfully avoid the "requirements problem" by just buying a commercial off the shelf (COTS) package?

10. How should the 9-step approach be modified to work with package purchasing? What steps are not really needed or should be modified?

11. If the 9-step approach is followed and a COTS procurement produces no-bidders, why might that be a good result? What's been the cost? What's possibly been saved? What then are your options?

12. What's your definition of a stove-pipe? How can COTS be or not be a stove-pipe? How can stove-pipe development be avoided? How would a Metabase tool help avoid stove-pipes?

13. Are requirements changes a sign of failure or a sign of unfolding reality? Is it possible to discover all requirements up front? How will prototyping help discover new requirements?

14. How has Enterprise Resource Planning (ERP) packages affected the ability to have enterprise-wide data and process semantics and integration? Given that you have an ERP package, how do you integrate it with other database and business information systems and with other ERP packages?

2

Essentials for Business Information System Development Success

This chapter presents the essentials for business information system development success and describes why having such essentials returns many times the cost. It shows that through the use of these essentials, business information systems development costs can be reduced by about 66%.

While business information systems can be implemented without these essentials, they cannot be accomplished in an integrated, non-redundant, and cost effective manner without them. The essentials for business information system development success are listed and described in Table 1. Each is described in sections that follow.

Essentials for Business information system Development Success	
Essential	**Description**
Knowledge Worker Framework	The Knowledge Worker Framework is an overarching framework within which all work products that are key to the development of business information systems are organized and categorized. The framework provides a well-ordered column and row structure, along with work product integration, non-redundancy and inter-cell relationships. This enables a do-once, use many times environment that saves time, money and promotes understanding and exchange.
Data-driven Methodology	A data-driven methodology for business information systems development is essential for success because it has been shown that the data-driven approach reduces the quantity of items that have to be developed through information technology. Coupled with the Knowledge Worker Framework, there is certain knowledge of what needs to be specified, and in what sequence to reduce or eliminate duplication, and to reduce or eliminate semantic conflict.

Essentials for Business information system Development Success	
Essential	**Description**
Database Object Classes	Database Object Classes are highly-engineered and well formed collections of data and embedded processes that relate to business-defined states along a highly engineered life cycle. Business information systems almost always focus on the database objects within one or a few Database Object Classes. Database Object Classes are critical to business information system specification and development as a way to achieve non-redundant, integration, and semantic conflict elimination. It is important to have Database Object Class encapsulated in database management systems wherever possible to eliminate the need to have them redundantly defined in different business information systems. This saves time, reduces cost, improves productivity, and dramatically increases the consistency of process execution.
Data Architectures	Data architectures have two dimensions. The first, database architecture classes, are the different types of databases implemented across the enterprise. There are five discrete database architecture classes. Examples include those that originally capture data such as order processing systems, and data warehouse databases that supports longitudinal analysis of customers, product lines and sales, and the like. The second dimension are data model generalization levels. There are five levels, from enterprise-wide data elements down to operating database data models and views. These generalization levels enable enterprises to engineer data definitions and semantics that are integrated, non-redundant and semantically harmonious. Data definitions and semantics not so engineered give rise to stove-pipe databases which, in turn, result in stove-pipe business information systems. Elimination of stove-pipes is essential to a well ordered and managed information technology environment.
Business Information System Generators	A business information system generator imports the database's design and creates a first-cut business information system that has menus, browse lists, and update windows. The first-cut business information system is in a design-metadata form that users can "tune-up" without compromising the ability to generate the actual program code that gets compiled, linked and bound into an executing module. Business information system generators dramatically improve programmer productivity, and enable these tools be used in prototyping. Whole systems can be created in a week or two. Iterations can be created in just days. This is ideal for prototyping. Prototyping is the critical ingredient for iterating towards valid database and business information system requirements.

Essentials for Business information system Development Success	
Essential	**Description**
Metabase Environment	The Metabase is a metadata database surrounded by a metadata management system that is able to be used by knowledge workers as they accomplish all phases of their requirements development, business information system generation, and maintenance tasks. The Metabase environment is a combination of the features from Computer Aided Systems Engineering (CASE) systems, and metadata repository systems. A quality Metabase system can be employed by whole teams and organizations. It enables databases and business information systems to be integrated, non-redundant, and based on harmonious semantics across all their project domains. The Metabase environment contributes to the effort by ensuring that there is minimal redundancy definition and maximal reuse of all Knowledge Worker Framework work products.
Discrete and Release Development Environments	Business information system projects can be accomplished through traditional one-off project management methods such as water fall or spiral methodologies. Once the overall set of business information system projects is completed, the organization must transform itself from a one-off project development environment to a multi-project, multi-database, and multi-business information systems environment that generates many changes across a broad database and business information systems topology to maintain an overall level of organization and management across the involved systems. The alternative to waterfall or spiral environment is called a release environment. Both environments are needed.
Metrics and Work Environment Multipliers	Metrics and work environment multipliers are needed along with standard work breakdown structures for database and business information system projects. Through standard work methods and metrics, the whole database and business information systems environment can be transformed from a custom-developed environment to a manufacturing environment. This increases quality, increases productivity, reduces cost, and reduces risk.

Table 1. Essentials for Business information system Success.

In this chapter, the material on the Knowledge Worker Framework identifies the different major classes of artifacts or work products that need to be created to support enterprise, database, and business information systems development.

Also shown via the Knowledge Worker Framework is the allocation of the U. S. General Accountability Office's "reasons for failure" that were distilled from many GAO reports. Failures occurred when the Knowledge Worker Framework artifacts were not created, made non-redundant, or were not integrated. The most surprising part of the allocation of the "failure reasons" is that 95% of all business information systems fail for causes outside information technology.

The nine step approach, set out in Chapter 3, presumes the existence of the supports listed in Table 1.

All these supports exist today, and when employed, their cost is *negative* because of the time and money savings in the first several projects, if not the first project, in which these information technology supports are employed.

2.1 The Knowledge Worker Framework

A knowledge worker is someone who primarily works with information and abstract concepts. Another type of worker is the real product worker. White collar workers such as clinicians and clinical support personnel are knowledge workers because they develop care plans, provide treatments, and record results. Alternatively, workers on a manufacturing line, and for example, food service personnel, are not knowledge workers because they are primarily focused on the creation and/or assembly of real products.

Both knowledge workers and real product workers share common characteristics including plans, schedules, estimates and result assessments. Notwithstanding, the fundamental work methods and environment that underlie the knowledge worker and the real product worker are different at the core. Trying to make one a clone of the other is both frustrating and invalid.

Due to the abstract nature of their work, information required by knowledge workers can best be stored, assimilated and used as objects, which are encapsulations of data and processes. To most effectively support knowledge workers, the enterprise should strive to create object-oriented environments.

These two concepts, knowledge worker and object-oriented environments are brought together into technology architectures since both uniquely characterize the ideal working environment.

The knowledge worker's environment involves both automated and non-automated activities. Some non-automated activities involve the use of automation, for example, once a patient receives a treatment from a clinician's (non automated activity), the characteristics of the treatment, and the clinicians observations about the patient's reaction to the treatment are typically recorded in some automated system. A knowledge worker's framework must therefore address manual and automated activities.

Knowledge workers perform groups of functions to accomplish their designated job or to accomplish some aspect of the enterprise's mission. Knowledge workers may perform these function-groups in different combinations depending on the enterprise's organization. For example, if an organization is highly distributed into multi-functional units, there may be staffs that perform diverse groups of functions. Conversely, a highly centralized organization may have certain staff devoted to specific and highly specialized functions. The knowledge worker is therefore a complex multi-faceted person who performs diverse functions of different complexities for one or more organizations.

Knowledge workers need a framework within which all their work products are created, stored, and interrelated. All the architectures are thus set within the Knowledge Worker Framework.

The Knowledge Worker Framework's products are completely defined, integrated and non-redundant. They are supported by an indepth methodology, books, other papers, workshops, seminars, and of course the Metabase system that stores, interrelates, updates, and reports all Knowledge Worker Framework products through a multi-user SQL database.

To be successful, information technology must reside within a complete framework. That is, one that addresses the needs of the knowledge worker, not just the information technology worker. This is obvious, as the cause of 95% information technology reasons for failure lie outside information technology. The enterprise must have a framework that addresses the complete set of needs of its knowledge worker.

The Knowledge Worker Framework, summarily presented here, provides the overall context for the activities that ultimately lead to implemented-correctly-the-first-time business information systems. The Knowledge Worker Framework is portrayed in Table 2. This table shows the full set of artifacts (all the cells) that affect the knowledge worker. The columns that are directly addressed by this book are Mission, Database Object Class, and Business Information System. The brief definition of the columns are:

- The Mission column sets out the essential descriptions of the enterprise and also the policies which govern its operation.

- The Database Object Class column defines the overall data for the enterprise including database types and data model generalization levels. Database object classes themselves are defined within one of the data model generalization levels. Data, in the Knowledge Worker Framework, is defined within the context of missions.

- The Business Information Systems column defines the business software systems deemed necessary to capture, transform, manipulate, and report business data. Business information systems are defined within the context of the databases and data models of the Database Object Class column.

- The Business Organization column defines and represents the organizational constructs, jobs, and the like that have to be performed in the enterprise to accomplish its mission.

- The Business Function column represents the human processes of the enterprise. These are performed across and/or within the context of business organizations. The Business Function and Business Organization columns are strictly "human" in their orientation.

- The Business Event column is the interface between the two "machine" columns and the two "man" columns. All Business Events are set within the context of business calendars and business cycles.

Knowledge Worker Framework						
		Man-machine Interface				
		Machine		**Interface**	**Man**	
Deliverables	**Mission**	**Database Object Class**	**Business Information System**	**Business Event**	**Business Function**	**Organization**
Scope	List of Business Missions	List of Major Business Resources	List of Business Information Systems	List of Interface Events	List of Major Business Scenarios	List of Organizations
Business	Mission Hierarchies	Resource Life Cycles, Data Elements, Specified Data Model	Information Sequencing and Hierarchies	Event Sequencing and Hierarchies	Business Scenario Sequencing and Hierarchies	Organization Charts, Jobs and Descriptions
Business Information System	Policy Hierarchies	Database Object Class Models	Business Information System Designs	Invocation Protocols, Input and Output Data, and Messages	Best Practices, Quality Measures and Accomplishment Assessments	Job Roles, Responsibilities, and Activity Schedules
Technology	Policy Execution Enforcement	Implemented Data Model	Business Information Systems Application Designs	Presentation Layer Business Information System Instigators	Activity Sequences to Accomplish Business Scenarios	Procedure Manuals, Task Lists, Quality Measures and Assessments
Deployment	Installed Business Policy and Procedures	Operational Data Model	Implemented Business Information Systems	Client & Server Windows and/or Batch Execution Mechanisms	Office Policies and Procedures to Accomplish Activities	Daily Schedules, Shift and Personnel Assignments
Operations	Operating Business	View Data Models	Operating Systems	Start, Stop, and Messages	Detailed Procedure Based Instructions	Daily Activity Executions, and Assessments

Table 2. Knowledge worker framework.

The term, *business*, is employed in combination with "organization" here not to signify a commercial enterprise versus a scientific enterprise, but to imply *bureaucratic* versus some other class of usage such as the *organization* of a computer program or business information system.

In contrast to the overall nature of the columns, the rows provide an indication of the formal orientation of the cells with respect to the column's title.

The brief definition of the six rows are: The Scope row discovers, enumerates, interrelates, and, at a high level sets out the enterprise's Missions, Database Object Classes, Business Information Systems, Business Event interfaces, Business Functions, and Business Organizations.

The Business row details the objects that have been discovered and presented in a high-level way in the scope row. In addition to being more detailed this row sets the missions, organizations, and functions within hierarchies.

The Systems row is the first row devoted to a "systems perspective." It presumes that the artifacts created for this row will be employed during the creation of a system. Not all systems are to be information technology systems, however. Some systems are just a systematic set of policies that guide the accomplishment of a highly engineered set of human activities, that is, functions.

The Technology row, is similar to the Systems row in that it represents a detailing and a new set of artifacts needed to support either policy specification, Business Organization, and Business Function specification, or a furthering of the efforts in support of IT.

The Deployment row presumes that the new environments, from Mission through Business Organizations are ready to be deployed prior to operations. Essentially this overall row is a roll-out of all the artifacts so that they can be employed.

The Operations row represents the new operating environment. The mission cell would be the operating business. Feedback mechanisms would occur from every set of organization-based functions. This will then enable a feed back cycle at least one row above. There would be a similar set of operations for the Business Functions and the Business Organizations.

All the artifacts from the cells in the Knowledge Worker Framework form an integrated, non-redundant collection of metadata across the enterprise. Essentially, the total collection of metadata across the Knowledge Worker Framework represents a model of the enterprise.

A more complete explanation of the Knowledge Worker Framework is provided in Attachment 1. This explanation provides a row by row, and column by column description of the cells, and how the work products of the cells contribute to the successful development of business information system.

A high-level enterprise architecture results from an analysis of the knowledge-worker products represented in the Scope and Business rows of the Mission, business Function, and Organization columns from the Knowledge Worker Framework.

If the knowledge workers' products identified within these rows and columns already exist, are accurate, and are current before an information technology project begins, the process of requirements gathering and evolution is relatively easy.

A most critical feature of the Knowledge Worker Framework is that the cells can be seen as belonging either to the environment within which Information Technology exists (the outer 24 cells), or to Information Technology itself, that is, the inner 12 cells. Table 3 shades the "outer 24." Table 4 presents the "inner 12."

The failures cited in the GAO studies were allocated to the cells and the counts are shown in Table 5. As can be clearly seen from Table 5, when a business information system fails, it is almost always never the fault of the information technology implementors.

For an enterprise to be successful, the need is obvious: first define and optimize the work products that occur in the "outer 24" cells. A review of the GAO failure reasons provides a close match to the reasons cited in other studies of information technology failures.

The most important benefit of using the Knowledge Worker Framework to allocate the reasons for information system failure is the identification of the cells within which the failures occur. The allocations by percent are provided in Table 6. These, also set out in a summary fashion in Table 7, are:

- First, 41% of the reasons for failure occur because of problems in the first two rows, that is, scope and business. Said another way, every if everything else was done perfectly, only 59% of the reasons for failure would have been addressed. There wasn't sufficient identification and/or analysis of the enterprise's missions, organizations, or functions. It was impossible to succeed because the problem space was not sufficiently understood. That often occurs because there is too much emphasis on database and business information systems design.

- Second, 29% of all the reasons for failure occur because of improper analysis and configuration of just the Mission, Organization, and Function columns within these same Scope and Business rows. This is just a subset of the first above. If these three areas are insufficiently identified, analyzed, and reviewed, the analysts do not understand what the enterprise is, how it is organized, or what it does.

- Third, 50% of all the reasons for failure occur in the eight cells that are between the System and Operations rows of the Business Function and Business Organization columns. These errors occur because organizations and functions are not properly reconfigured subsequent to a database and/or business information system implementation. Continuing the old processes, policies, procedures, organizations, and methods of work in the face of new supports from databases and business information systems is a recipe for disaster.

- Fourth, only 5% of all the reasons for failure occur within the information technology cells. That is, within the Database Object Class, Business Information System, and Business Event columns that are between the System, Technology, Deployment, and Operations rows. Or to put it another way, 95% of all the reasons for failure lie outside information technology.

Knowledge Worker Framework						
		Man-machine Interface				
		Machine		Interface	Man	
Deliverables	Mission	Database Object Class	Business Information System	Business Event	Business Function	Organization
Scope	List of Business Missions	List of Major Business Resources	List of Business Information Systems	List of Interface Events	List of Major Business Scenarios	List of Organizations
Business	Mission Hierarchies	Resource Life Cycles, Data Elements, Specified Data Model	Information Sequencing and Hierarchies	Event Sequencing and Hierarchies	Business Scenario Sequencing and Hierarchies	Organization Charts, Jobs and Descriptions
Business Information System	Policy Hierarchies	Database Object Class Models	Business Information System Designs	Invocation Protocols, Input and Output Data, and Messages	Best Practices, Quality Measures and Accomplishment Assessments	Job Roles, Responsibilities, and Activity Schedules
Technology	Policy Execution Enforcement	Implemented Data Model	Business Information Systems Application Designs	Presentation Layer Business Information System Instigators	Activity Sequences to Accomplish Business Scenarios	Procedure Manuals, Task Lists, Quality Measures and Assessments
Deployment	Installed Business Policy and Procedures	Operational Data Model	Implemented Business Information Systems	Client & Server Windows And/or Batch Execution Mechanisms	Office Policies and Procedures to Accomplish Activities	Daily Schedules, Shift and Personnel Assignments
Operations	Operating Business	View Data Models	Operating Systems	Start, Stop, and Messages	Detailed Procedure Based Instructions	Daily Activity Executions, and Assessments

Table 3. Knowledge worker framework: 24 information technology environment cells.

		Knowledge Worker Framework				
		Man-machine Interface				
		Machine		Interface	Man	
Deliverables	**Mission**	**Database Object Class**	**Business Information System**	**Business Event**	**Business Function**	**Organization**
Scope	List of Business Missions	List of Major Business Resources	List of Business Information Systems	List of Interface Events	List of Major Business Scenarios	List of Organizations
Business	Mission Hierarchies	Resource Life Cycles, Data Elements, Specified Data Model	Information Sequencing and Hierarchies	Event Sequencing and Hierarchies	Business Scenario Sequencing and Hierarchies	Organization Charts, Jobs and Descriptions
Business Information System	Policy Hierarchies	**Database Object Class Models**	**Business Information System Designs**	**Invocation Protocols, Input and Output Data, and Messages**	Best Practices, Quality Measures and Accomplishment Assessments	Job Roles, Responsibilities, and Activity Schedules
Technology	Policy Execution Enforcement	**Implemented Data Model**	**Business Information Systems Application Designs**	**Presentation Layer Business Information System Instigators**	Activity Sequences to Accomplish Business Scenarios	Procedure Manuals, Task Lists, Quality Measures and Assessments
Deployment	Installed Business Policy and Procedures	**Operational Data Model**	**Implemented Business Information Systems**	**Client & Server Windows And/or Batch Execution Mechanisms**	Office Policies and Procedures to Accomplish Activities	Daily Schedules, Shift and Personnel Assignments
Operations	Operating Business	**View Data Models**	**Operating Systems**	**Start, Stop, and Messages**	Detailed Procedure Based Instructions	Daily Activity Executions, and Assessments

Table 4. Knowledge worker framework: 12 information technology cells.

Deliver-ables	Mission	Machine		Inter-face	Man		Row Totals
		Database Object Class	Business Information System	Business Event	Business Function	Organization	
Knowledge Worker Framework							
Man-Machine Interface							
Scope	13	5	6	1	8	10	43
Bus-iness	12	6	6	1	15	14	54
Business informa-tion system	8	6	5	0	28	18	65
Tech-nology	3	0	0	0	18	14	35
Deploy-ment	1	0	0	0	12	11	24
Oper-ations	1	0	0	0	8	8	17
Col. Totals	38	17	17	2	89	75	238

Note: Some of the GAO errors were assigned to multiple cells. Hence the ~120 rose to ~238

Table 5. Allocation of GAO information technology failure causes to the cells of the knowledge worker framework.

		Knowledge Worker Framework						
		Man-Machine Interface						
		Machine		Inter-face	Man			
Deliv-erables	Mis-sion	Database Object Class	Business Infor-mation System	Bus-iness Event	Bus-iness Fun-ction	Organ-ization	Row Totals
Scope	5	2	3	1	3	4	18
Business	5	3	2	1	6	6	23
Business Informa-tion System	3	2	2	1	12	8	28
Tech-nology	1	0	0	0	8	6	15
Deploy-ment	0	0	0	0	5	5	10
Oper-ations	0	0	0	0	3	3	6
Col. Totals	14	7	7	3	37	32	100

Note: All numbers expressed as Percent allocations of errors to cells. The 12 Gray cells are information technology Cells

Table 6. Percent Allocation of GAO information technology failure causes to the cells of the Knowledge Worker Framework.

U.S. General Accountability Office Reasons for Information Technology System Failure	
Percent	**Reasons for Failures Description**
41%	A lack of proper identification, analysis and configuration of enterprise architecture Scope and Business Rows across all six of the columns. That is, Missions, Database Object Classes, Business Information Systems, Business Events, Business Functions and Business Organizations.
29%	A lack of proper identification, analysis and configuration of enterprise architecture Scope and Business Rows of just the Missions, Business Functions and Business Organizations columns.
50%	A lack of proper re-engineering of the business functions and organizations as a consequence of re-engineered databases and business information systems.
5%	A lack of proper engineering and development of databases and business information systems.

Table 7. Summary of U.S. General Accountability Office Reasons for Failure

All of this leads to one and only one conclusion. Organizations that fail to get missions, organizations, and functions correct within the first two rows are almost certain to fail. These cells are the sole provinces of enterprise or subject matter experts, not information technology experts. Information technology experts should not participate, but if they do, they are likely to jeopardize success. That is because information technology experts are likely to see these cells only from an information technology perspective.

Enterprise and subject matter experts do not need information technology to accomplish the first two rows that represent 41% of the reasons for failure, nor the 50% error cells. There needs to be a good methodology, the Metabase system, and business information system generators, so that the enterprise and subject matter experts can get the requirements as accurate as possible before the information technology staff begins any database design or business information system development.

Another point is that to get information technology systems "right" there must be attention paid to the metadata inferred by the Knowledge Worker Framework. Finally, all the metadata from all the frameworks should be integrated (or at least federated) and non-redundant.

The Mission column of the Knowledge Worker Framework represents the rationale or basis for the enterprise within this knowledge worker environment. The first cell, Scope, presents the missions. The set of missions represent the basis of the enterprise. If a mission is missing, then so too is an important aspect of the business. Missions are either external or internal. External missions are those that support the income of the business. Internal missions are those that employ the business's income to operate the business in support of its external missions. For example, if the external mission of the business is to sell a specific product line, the internal missions are those that support sales, that is, human resource management, research and development, manufacturing, inventory and distribution, sales management, and the like.

Missions are mechanisms for analysis and design partitioning. Once the missions are listed, they become the criteria for including or excluding entries in the remaining cells. Additionally, once missions are delineated, one or more missions can be chosen as the basis of partitioning the framework. For example, one partition in this book's case study could be Finance Management, while another mission could be Product Distribution Management. Each mission-based partition might be pursued by different analysis and design teams, one for finance and the other for product distribution.

Partitioning by mission could lead to developing stove-pipe systems for each such partition. To counter this, there must also be horizontal integration across the work products that may be common across the partitions. A preferred approach is to complete the top two rows (scope and business) prior to partitioning the work into separate teams. If this is done, the end result will be integrated more easily.

The risk of partition-based stove-pipes is further mitigated because Knowledge Worker Framework artifacts across the columns, as implemented in the Metabase, are interrelated in a many-to-many manner. That means that Missions are related to one or more Database Object Classes, and a Database Object Class may be related to one or more Missions. As a result of this many-to-many approach, a single, unified set of metadata artifacts within the Metabase is used across the enterprise. The Metabase was built this way because reality is built this way. Sadly, reality is seldom reflected in the representations exemplified in most other tools available today.

The six columns of the Knowledge Workers' framework are all represented in the Metabase. This enables knowledge workers to identify, retrieve, track, and update all related data.

The next essential, data-driven methodology, is clearly the preferred approach to business information system engineering because it optimizes the creation of artifacts that need ultimately to be implemented.

2.2 Data-Driven Methodology.

During the 1970s and through the mid 1980s, there were endless debates concerning data-driven versus process-driven methodologies. Each side had their proponents. During the mid 1980s, two different business information systems projects were undertaken through both techniques.

This was not a formal experiment. It was undertaken because the government agency imposed a process-driven methodology on a contractor, which, when followed, resulted in overly complex and completely opaque requirements specifications. Like the example in the Preface, by the time the requirements-based process models were complete, the agency had changed its mind as to what it wanted. After two tries, the government agency was about to cancel the contract. Again, a consultant was brought in. In just three weeks, but this time through a data-driven approach, a completely new set of specifications were created and submitted to the government agency. The result was accepted and the follow-on implementation contract was awarded to the contractor. As an aside, a different metadata tool, University of Michigan's PLS/PSA, was used. This serves to reinforce the fact that the tool is not the silver bullet. Rather, the data-driven, highly engineered, integrated and non-redundant work products are the silver bullet.

After this requirements phase was completed, there was an examination of the metadata data tool's database. Precise counts were able to be obtained of the quantity of the work products that were expected to be built during the implementation phase. The difference between the process-driven approach and the data-driven approach was stark.

Table 8 presents the results of the critical counts. From these two projects it is very clear that there are fewer components (i.e., view, tables, processes, and data elements) that need to be developed when the effort is accomplished through a data-driven approach than with a process-driven approach.

Critical Quantities	Project "A"		Project "B"	
	Process First	Data First	Process First	Data First
Views	125	20	146	59
Tables	110	20	150	59
Processes	29	29	66	47
Data Elements (actually columns)	172	84	245	118

Table 8. Critical Counts of artifacts from process-first versus data-first approaches.

The use of Objects Class based tools, and techniques such as Rapid Application Development (RAD), Extreme Development and its successor, Agile Development, etc., have a natural tendency to reinforce the process-driven approach over the data-driven approach.

Process-driven environments tend to be dynamic, ever changing, and the like, while data-driven environments tend to be static, seldom or slow to change. This results, as is shown in Table 8, in increased the quantity of work products to be implemented. The process driven environment, most recently characterized by the Agile community requires that the data-driven environment be as dynamic and as the process-driven environment.

The most critical characteristic of any RAD/Code-generator-based methodology is that it be data-driven, not process-driven. Table 8 shows that a data-drive approach greatly reduces the quantity of artifacts that have to be turned into business information systems components. Additionally, a well-engineered database design, expressed through the SQL data definition language (DDL), can be the sole "input" to a business information system generator which, in turn, actually creates a first-cut business information system.

Data is executed policy. Therefore, database designs are really policy designs/architectures. Data modelers are thus policy makers. There are also procedures. This results in a Policy-and-Procedures pair. Procedures are what carries out policies. The consequence of the execution of policies, is data. Data then becomes the "proof" of policy execution. Collections of automated procedures are business information systems.

Policies should be rooted in enterprise missions because missions should be engineered without regards to Who, How, or Technology. If done so, missions are essentially timeless and apolitical.

Database designs should be based on missions. Hence, database designs, like missions are Who-less, How-less, and Technology-less. Thus, database designs are time-less and apolitical.

An organization that changes its procedures all the time in order to meet new styles, technologies, emerging opportunities, functions, and organizations is likely to be considered dynamic. Conversely, organizations that are unable to change on a dime are likely to be called "out of business."

But given that data is executed policy, and policy should be the most stable component of an enterprise, and finally, that databases designs should be rooted in mission-based policy, what can be said of an organization that dynamically changes its database designs all the time? Data warehouses, for the main, would have to excluded here as their purpose is more to match business analyses, which are a form of business processes. Wouldn't these dynamic database design organizations really be just chaotic messes? If these organizations are constantly fiddling and/or changing their database designs, aren't these same organizations changing their underlying policies and given that policy follows mission, they're changing their underlying missions? Wouldn't such organizations soon be "out of business" because there is no stable organization, control, and direction on which the customers can depend?

There is a difference between policy and procedure at the very heart of the process-driven versus data-driven debate. The process-driven community is clearly on the "procedure" side of information technology. The data-driven community is on the "policy" side. Each side is so different that neither should be a slave to the other.

When the data-driven community indicates that a programmer should have one "hand on the process adjustment knob" and another "hand on the database design adjustment knob," they (or he) just doesn't understand the intrinsic and critical differences between "policy and procedure."

If the data-driven community demanded "stability and no change" by the process-driven community, that is just as non-sensible as the process-driven community to demand "dynamic database designs" from the data-driven community.

Further, databases (that is, policy architectures) are in a fundamental 1-to-many relationship with business information systems (that is, procedures). If the policy-architecture is dynamically changing in response to requests from every procedure-change request, there will be real chaos within the process-driven community.

What about new databases and new business information systems? Shouldn't both be more dynamic? Yes, of course, but should this dynamic state be caused by a data-driven or process-driven approach? The data-driven communities asserts, data-driven. Not only is that the right choice, the statistics shown in Table 8 show that data-driven methodologies produce 4.6 TIMES fewer total artifacts, including the process-artifacts, that have to be implemented than if the methodology is "process-driven." It thus makes anti-chaos and economic sense to accomplish efforts through a data-driven approach. This is not a matter or religion; it's a matter of science and fact.

How then should business information system development proceed? Whitemarsh holds that it should be via "business information system generators," rather than legions of custom programmers. Custom programmers cost $400 per function point to create business information systems. Smartly engineered business information system generators cost $50 per function point to create business information systems. As an aside, through the capture of statics related to function points and the quantity of database tables in databases, there's about 80 function points of total effort for every database table. Some have fewer function points and others have a whole lot more. But on average, 80 will do. So, for any 100 table database, the total quantity of function points is 8,000. If through custom programming efforts, the cost is then $3.2 million. But through business information system generator efforts the cost is $400,000. Not a small difference.

Given the dramatic difference in costs, business information system generators are also very valuable for prototypes. Prototypes are valuable because nobody can set down the full set of requirements up front. Such impossible-to-accomplish efforts are known as the big design up front, or BDUF. One of the Agile communities biggest points is that BDUF is really just a BSUF. In this example, S = suicide. If business information system generators are driven through the input of a database's design, then doing the database design first is critical for the following reasons:

- Database design should be mission based.

- Database design represents the policy domain.

- Data-driven (aka the database's design) produces 4.6 times fewer artifacts to implement.

Given six weeks to develop a mission document and to create a 1st-cut database design, and then two weeks to create the first generated system, that's just 8 weeks altogether. For sure, that's no BDUF.

Thereafter, in two week increments, a prototype can be demonstrated and feed back can be obtained quickly to modify both the database's design to reflect the discovered "new or revised policy" and finally, to regenerate the prototype. Suppose this is done six times. That makes the data and process design, version 7, without having to have spent any considerable resources.

At the end of these seven cycles, the Mission, Database Design, and Process Model design will exist because the operational prototype represents at the very least the level of detail that would exist in any process model design of a BDUF. All in all, given a team of just three staff, "this" way of doing the BDUF only takes (3 * 8) + (3 * 6 iterations * 2 weeks per) = 60 total staff weeks. At $3K per staff week ($150K per year) that's just $180K. When has anyone done a version 7 BDUF for just $180K. Additionally, the 9-step approach has an operational prototype, quite unlike the traditional BDUF approach.

If this data-driven prototyping approach is contrasted with the process-driven approach there are dramatic differences. Under the Agile approach, the project is started with just a quick-requirement sketch, and then iterated through process engineering and re-active database design and modification. Suppose there are 5 working teams. It's a well known statistic that there's at least 5 process modules per table. So, given 100 tables, that's 500 process modules. Suppose a process module can be accomplished in two weeks. In that two weeks, the process module's requirement is discovered, it's design is created, it's coded, and at the very least it's unit tested. Computed out, that's 1,000 staff weeks. Suppose there's only one week of re-work needed because all the dynamic changes to the underlying database design. that adds another 500 staff weeks. So, the total is 1500 staff weeks. Total cost is $4.5 million under the process-driven approach. It is only after the expenditure of $4.5 million that you can see and demonstrate what can be seen for $180K under the data-driven approach.

This $4.5 million does not take into account the 4.6 times increase in artifacts because of a process-driven design. Thus, for the process-driven approach, the estimate is for the "best-case" for two reasons. First, it is presumed that the quantity of designed and constructed artifacts are as few as with the data-driven approach, and second, that two cycles of re-work are all that is necessary.

The next "essential" is Database Object Classes. Well engineered business information systems are almost always formed around one or a few Database Object Classes. Each Database Object Class is semantically whole. When it is properly designed and encapsulated, there exists highly cohesive data structures that are supported by embedded processes that transform the database object from one business-recognized state to another. Database Object Classes are the next logical data-based building block step after the formation of the Knowledge Worker Framework missions.

2.3 Database Object Classes

Starting in 1992, the ANSI INCITS Technical Committee on Database Languages, H2, began the definition and insertion of "object-oriented" facilities into the SQL language.

Database object classes are defined within the context of database schemas independent of any particular DBMS. Hence, Whitemarsh has defined database objects classes within the Database Object Classes column of the Knowledge Worker Framework, and specifically in the data model generalization level, Implemented Data Model. This keeps database object classes within database schemas but independent of any particular DBMS just as the SQL:1999 standard requires.

The result was SQL:1999, which created row-based object class structures. Each object, a row from a database schema table, consists of traditional single-valued columns, and also columns that represent complex data structures. Within complex data structure columns there can be arrays (e.g., nicknames), groups of contained elements (e.g., address), repeating groups (e.g., multiple addresses), and nested repeating groups (e.g., addresses with telephone numbers). There is no standards-based limit to the depth or breadth of the complexity of the data structures within an SQL:1999 table.

Within Database Object Classes, as defined within an SQL:1999 table , hierarchical data structures can exist. There also may be factored references from within a SQL:1999 database object table column to columns from different tables. For example, if the Customer table has an Orders column, and within this column, there is a nested structure for Order-Line-Items, then each Order-Line-Item might have a contained substructure that has a reference to the Product, which is accessed along with each Order-Line_item.

There is a clear need for Database Object Classes independent of whether the SQL DBMS has implemented SQL:1999 nested data structures or not. For example, there may be a table for Customer, but related to customer there may be 5-15 subordinate tables that all have Customer-Id as the high order column in the table's primary key. Collectively, these 5-15 tables are the data structure of the Customer database object class. Another example would be Orders where the data structure consists of Order with Order Detail. Business information system developers almost always craft their application systems in terms of tightly organized functional groupings of data. In the first example, there would be a Customer Management business information system. In the second example, the business information system would be Order Management. In this particular example there would be a relationship between the two database object classes because Customers are the source for Orders.

With the advent of client-server computing, database-oriented application logic was moved from the client to the sever and embedded within the domain of the DBMS. For example, that EmployeeGender can only be M, F, or U. Or that Birthdate must be less than or equal to Death Date. Or finally that DepartmentSalary equals the Sum(EmployeeSalary). The implementation alternatives was to either put these constraints into every single computer program that used them, or to factor these constraints from the computers programs and install them into the DBMS as triggers and stored procedures. The later is certainly preferred. As the SQL:1999 standard progressed, these processes were linked to before and after actions of DBMS update commands.

Most of these facilities were put into the SQL draft standard's document that was progressing towards standardization in the middle 1990s. So, the next logical step was to make table structures more robust, that is, object oriented. Hence the addition of column based nested structures of arrays, groups, repeating groups, and nested repeating groups.

For the purposes of conceptual understanding, each SQL:1999 complex column is represented in this book as a stand-alone database table. In SQL:1999, a Customer table has an Orders column, and within this column, there is a nested structure for Order-Line-Items, and each Order-Line-Item has a contained substructure that has a reference to the Product, which,is included within a Orders-Line-Item access. This, book, instead, has separate tables for Customer, Orders, and Order-Line-Items. That way, once a requirement is fully specified, there can be a DBMS-based database design step that encapsulates some of the tables as column-based complex data structures inside other tables as would be the case of having an array of telephone numbers inside a Person table.

SQL:1999 added the ability to have encapsulated processes and many other object-oriented features. A full collection of these features is described on the Whitemarsh website, www.wiscorp.com. The SQL Standards link on the home-page goes to the SQL page with many SQL standards resources.

Database Object Classes, regardless of persistence, and regardless of whether single or multi-table, contain the same four-part composition:

- Database Object Structure: The set of data structures that map onto the different value sets of real world database objects such as all the data for an auto accident, or a vehicle, or an emergency medicine incident.

- Database Object Table Process: The set of processes that enforce the integrity of data structure fields, references between Database Object Classes and actions among contained database object tables, and the proper computer-based rules governing database object table insertion, modification, and deletion. For example, a database object table process would properly and completely capture, store and manipulate the data for an auto accident.

- Database object information system: The set of specifications and resultant business information systems that controls, sequences, and iterates the execution of various database object processes that, in turn, cause changes in database object states to achieve conformance to the requirements of business policies. For example, the reception and posting of data from business information system activities (windows, data edits, storage, interim reports, etc.) that accomplish entry of the auto accident information.

- Database Object State: The value-states of a populated database object that represents the after-state of the successful accomplishment of one or more recognizable business events. Examples of business events are auto accident initiation, involved vehicle entry, an involved person entry, and auto accident DUI (driving under the influence of alcohol/drugs) involvement. Database object state changes are initiated through named business events triggered by business functions. The business function, auto accident investigation, triggers the business event, auto-accident-incident initiation, which in turn, causes the incident initiation database object information system to execute, which in turn, causes several database object processes to cause the auto accident incident to be materialized in the database.

The descriptions of Database Object Classes above are for "real" Database Object Classes. First, there would be the data structures for an auto accident, or the vehicle, or the emergency medicine incident.

Second, there would be the database object table processes that store, delete, or modify the data for all the database object structures associated with the accidents, vehicles, or emergency-medicine incidents.

Third, there would be various states of an accident such as location, weather, personal injuries, property damages, adjudication, fault determination, and the like.

Fourth, and finally, the database object information systems that transform the database object data from one defined state to another. For example, changing the "identified accident" state to the "recorded accident" state, in which all the base data is now stored in the accident tables.

A Database Object Class is specified to the SQL DBMS through the SQL definition language (DDL). All four components of a Database Object Class operate within the "firewall" of the DBMS. This ensures that database objects are protected from improper access or manipulation by 3GLs[12], or

---

[12] A 3GL or a 4GL is a shorthand representation for a class of computer programming languages. GL stands for generation language. Machine languages (1's and 0's) is generally held out to be the 1st generation. Assembler (CLA – clear register and add <value> to register) is held to be the 2nd generation. Languages like Cobol, Fortran, Pascal, C, and Ada are all 3rd generation language. Example would be "CurrentTotal = CurrentTotal + LineItemPrice." This would increase the current total by the amount for the line item, that all takes place in a processing loop. Most if not all 3GLs are standardized by ANSI (American National Standards Institute). 4GLs are

(continued...)

4GLs. A DBMS that only defines, instantiates, and manipulates two-dimensional data structures is a simplified functional subset of the DBMS that defines, instantiates, and manipulates database objects. The benefits from using Database Object Classes include:

- Whole containment within SQL DBMS so that all the data parts of the Database Object Class are encapsulated and available to all business information system that need access.

- Access to both type and instance components in support of understanding Database Object Class metadata that would be stored in the SQL DBMS's schema information tables, as well as the database object, themselves.

- Complete expression through ANSI SQL syntax for both data and process, which makes the Database Object Class independent of operating system and hardware platform.

- Import and export of Database Object Class syntax-based specifications of both the Database Object Class's data structures, and encapsulated processes through ISO/ANSI standard SQL facilities so that Database Object Classes can be created, distributed, and changed within a federated/distributed database environment.

- Ability to be distributed and have consistent operations via all SQL compliant DBMSs.

- Independence from presentation-layer and system bindings.

Because Database Object Classes are wholly contained within an SQL DBMS, they can be centrally accessed and manipulated regardless of the end-user

---

[12](...continued)

>amorphous and have not been ANSI standardized. Most 4GLs are proprietary to a particular vendor. Examples are Clarion, MS/Access, Oracle's PL/SQL, and Visual Basic by Microsoft, and Focus by Information Builders. Language examples include for example a language stream to define a screen's format, position for field values, editing and validation, and the like.

---

language environment, that is, batch, on-line, stand-alone "fat" clients, "thin" clients, Internet, or traditional client/server.

SQL DBMS databases contain both type and instance data. Type-data is metadata. Instance data is traditional data. For an employee database, type data is the metadata definitions for tables, columns, integrity constraints, stored procedures and the like. Instance data are the actual employee records. For example, EmployeeName is type data, and "Phil Shaw" is instance data.

Type-data is critical for distributed databases because it can be queried to determine the exact semantics required for instance data access operations. For example, if there is a currency exchange data object on a server, a query can determine the arguments and data types of the required inputs. Transactions can then be formulated and successfully accomplished.

Database Object Classes are expressible as syntax, which enables SQL-compliant DBMSs to receive new Database Object Class syntax for inclusion in an SQL DBMS database type data (i.e., Schema Information Tables), and subsequently, the ability to delete Database Object Classes schema information tables and the database objects from the instance data.

A fundamental requirement of any compliant SQL DBMS is that it is able to import and export both type and instance data through standard SQL commands. This is similar to an application's ability to export or import data through standard character set strings. When a new computer is established, a central server can be activated to download command strings of syntax and standard reference data. Once down loaded and stored within the SQL:1999 DBMS, the Database Object Classes are immediately operational regardless of the DBMS brand, operating system type, hardware vendor, or 3rd or 4th generation language tools that access and manipulate the newly installed Database Object Classes.

Because of ISO and ANSI standards, Database Object Classes operate consistently regardless of the SQL DBMS, operating system, and vagaries of the different presentation layer facilities. Enterprises are able to have centralized semantics that control the fundamental operations of the business objects that are essential to worldwide, heterogeneous computing environments.

Finally, Database Object Classes are independent from presentation-layer and operating system bindings. This enables use of local language conventions within the confines of standard policy essentials. For example, in multi-cultural applications, true semantics can be shielded from local abbreviations and local names.

Additionally, local vendors may provide their own presentation layer facilities, report writers, formats, paper sizes, window formats, and the like that would translate/transform culturally independent data to culturally dependent data.

Given Database Object Classes, these localized peculiarities can be accommodated. Because the Database Object Class environment is DBMS-based, additional and localized Database Object Classes can be easily created and deployed with automatic integration into the standard Database Object Class environments essential for effective worldwide, heterogeneous environments. In summary, Database Object Classes:

- Are easy to specify, implement, use and maintain.

- Can operate on worldwide, heterogeneous hardware and operating system environments.

- Can behave consistently regardless of their host computing hardware environments.

Database Object Classes do not however exit in isolation. Each is defined within the context of one or more databases. The next "essential" section sets out the two data architecture dimensions. The first dimension is for types of databases, and the second dimension is for the various data model generalization levels needed by the enterprise to effectively define and manage in a non-redundant, integrated, and semantically harmonious manner.

2.4 Data Architectures

The previous section, Database Object Classes, set out the highest level specifications of the major policy-based data groupings in the enterprise. These data groupings are created, manipulated, and ultimately dissolved in the enterprise as its mission is carried out.

This section, Data Architectures, provides an overall approach to managing the enterprise's data models. One of these data models, the Implemented Data Model, is the data model class within which database object data structures are defined.

Data architectures relate only to the metadata about the data, not the real data itself. There are two dimensions to data architectures. The first dimension, database architecture class, represents the class of database that a given data model addresses. If an analogy helps, a database architecture class is like an automotive vehicle class, that is, truck, minivan, or car. Each has some similar functions, but they are for really different purposes.

The second dimension, data model generalization levels, relates to the named levels of generalization that exist independent of any database architecture class. Again, if an analogy helps, one such class might be the class of all vehicle parts within major categories, e.g., power trains, steering, exhaust, body, and frame. Another, but "lower" generalization class might be the engine assemblies, transmission assemblies, exhaust assemblies. Each such assembly is complete and engineered and might be used in multiple vehicle types within a particular vehicle class. Further, different such assemblies employ parts from a power train collection, and/or an exhaust collection. A even lower generalization class might be the Ford F150 truck, or the Volvo XC90. Each of these vehicle classes uses an engine assembly, and a transmission assembly. The most specific generalization level would be a specifically built Ford F150 that has just come off the assembly line and is ready to operate. That specific Ford truck has a drive train assembly that was composed of part assemblies from drive train, transmission, and exhaust, which in turn, consists of parts from the categories, power train, steering, exhaust, and the like.

Analogous to the automotive example above, there are five data model generalization levels that span from enterprise data elements and data models of concepts through to the models of the databases that actually execute on physical computers under specific operating systems. Each level is complete in its own right, but is more detailed and/or more specific at the next lower level, and finally enables a given lower level to be subseted and grouped by the higher level.

2.4.1 Database Architecture Classes

Figure 1 provides a diagram that shows the general topology across all the database architecture classes. The database architecture classes are:

- Original data capture.

- TDSA, that is, transaction data staging area.
- Subject area databases.
- Data warehouses (wholesale and retail).
- Reference data.

A more detailed description of these database architecture classes is contained in Attachment 2, Database Architecture Class Descriptions.

Data generally progresses from left to right. As data is created and stored in Original Data Capture databases, it should proceed through a process of standardizing granularity, precision, time, and other semantics such as value domains. Once the data is standardized, it can proceed onwards to the other database architecture classes such as the Subject Area Databases (sometimes called Operational Data Stores), and to the various classes of data

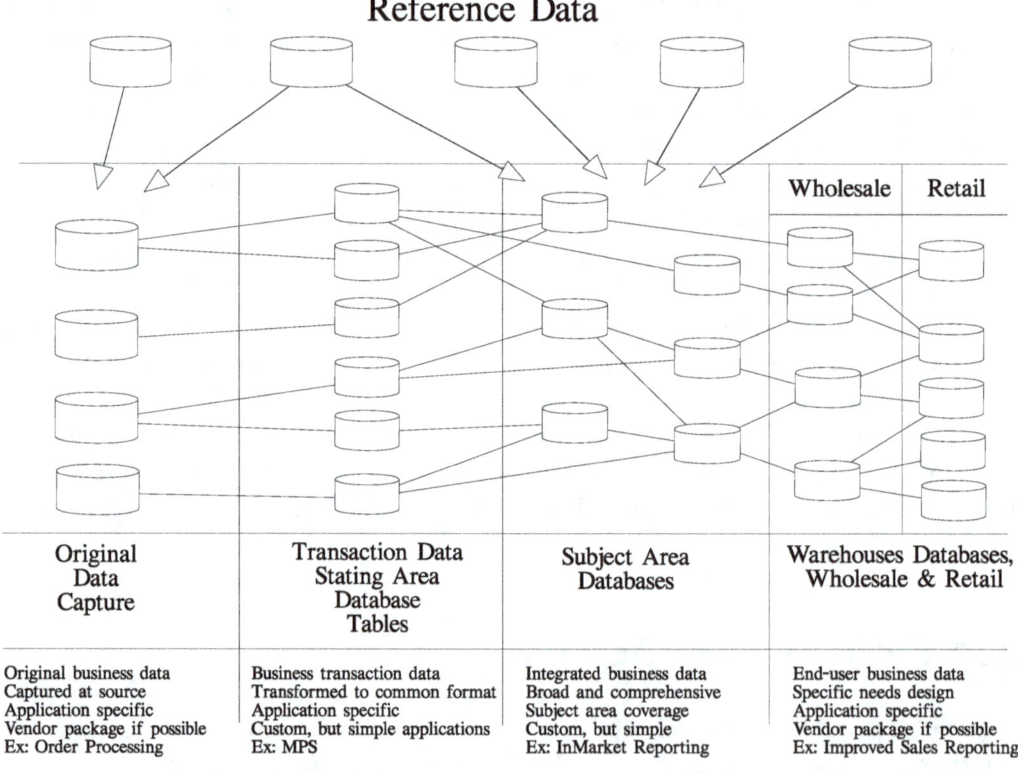

Figure 1. Database architecture classes.

warehouses.

The final database architecture class, Reference Data, is the sets of data that represent things like gender codes, city-state-zip triples, and the like. There may be specific databases within the Subject Area class that represent enterprise-wide definitive collections of value sets, for example, the definitive sets of employees, employee addresses, product names and descriptions, inventory, distribution and transportation routing networks, and the like. These subject area databases may be called Golden Source, Strategic Data, or most recently, Master Data.

2.4.2 Data Model Generalization Levels

The second dimension of data architectures is the data model generalization levels that exist across all classes of database architectures. The data model generalization levels and a brief description for each are provided in Table 9.

A common question to Whitemarsh is "What's this Data Element thing? Isn't it just a column of a table, or an attribute of an entity? And, why call the levels Specified, Implemented, and Operational as opposed to Conceptual, Logical, and Physical?"

The answer to all these questions is quite simple: To benefit the users, and because the names of the levels, while somewhat analogous to Conceptual, Logical, and Physical are quite different.

Most often, the names, Conceptual, Logical, and Physical relate to three different forms of the *same* data model. First, there is a database's conceptual form, which is sort of a fuzzy and not a completely thought out design. Then there is the logical form that is derived from its conceptual form, which is more precise, and is definitely in third normal form, but is not tied to any particular DBMS. Then there is the physical form, which is fully detailed, tied to a particular DBMS, and quite possibly not in third normal form to accommodate performance requirements. These definitions are the most common ones for the terms, Conceptual, Logical, and Physical. These three terms most often imply three stages of transformation of the same database. Because Whitemarsh has a different scope and purpose for data modeling, just transforming a given database's data model from the conceptual to logical to physical greatly shortchanges the data model management capabilities provided by Whitemarsh. In turn, enterprises would also be greatly shortchanged.

Data Model Generalization Classes	
Name	**Description**
Enterprise Data Elements	Data elements are enterprise-level business fact definitions independent of use within specific databases. Data elements are defined according to the requirements of ISO 11179 for data element metadata. Additionally, data elements include semantic and data use modifiers so as to enable automatic name construction, automatic definitions, and automatic abbreviations. There is a one-to-many relationship between Data Elements and Specified Data Models.
Specified Data Models	Specified Data Models are data models of concepts that are independent of use within specific databases. These Specified Data Models of concepts are defined as entities, attributes and relationships within specific subjects. Entities can be related across subjects. There is a many-to-many relationship between the Specified Data Model and the Implemented Data Model.
Implemented Data Models	Implemented Data Models are models of databases that are independent of any particular DBMS such as Oracle or DB2. Database object classes are included within Implemented Data Models because Database Object Classes are to be schema based and independent of any particular DBMS. The Implemented Data Models obtain their data structures from one or more Specified Data Models, and in turn provide these database data structures for use in the construction of data models of databases that actually operate under specific DBMS, and run on computers. Implemented Data Models are defined as tables, columns and relationships within schemas. Tables cannot be related across schemas. All the tables in this data model generalization level are in at least third normal form so as to ensure data model clarity and quality design. There is a many-to-many relationship between an Implemented Data Model and an Operational Data Model.
Operational Data Models	Operational Data Models are models of databases that conform to the requirements of a particular DBMS such as Oracle or DB2. Additionally, the database's design must conform to the expected processing requirements of a particular set of database applications supported by a particular database. Operational Data Model designs may vary because of many factors such as transaction volume, the host operating system, and the computer hardware size and throughput capabilities. Regardless, every variation of a component within an Operational Data Model database is related back to Implemented Data Model of the database. These Operational Data Models are defined as DBMS tables, DBMS columns and relationships within DBMS schemas. "DBMS" is employed here to signify that these data model components are tied to a specific

Data Model Generalization Classes	
Name	**Description**
	DBMS. There is a one-to-many relationship between an Operational Data Model and a View Data Model.
View Data Models	View Data Models are the business information system and Operational Data Model intersection mechanisms. View Data Models consist of views and view columns. They are also related to the business information systems that are the sources or targets of the database data. Views are specifically tied to specific DBMSs and view columns from a source view may be mapped to the view columns of a target view. Finally, view columns may be computed or derived.

Table 9. Data model generalization levels.

In addition to data-driven methodologies and Database Object Classes, data standardization techniques can affect enterprise-wide semantics. Table 10 presents the dramatic results from accomplishing data standardization in a highly organized manner. The difference between the two approaches is more than 30 times.

Activity	Quantity	Cost via technique for definition
Starting quantity of columns/fields	19,000	$6.75 million
Elimination of closely named columns and fields reduced the quantity to	3,000	$1.06 million
Elimination of same concept but very differently named columns and fields reduced the quantity to	560	$200,000

Table 10. Benefits from highly organized, standardized data.

Finally, the manner in which data standardization is accomplished is very important. While policy must be top-down, accomplishment can be bottom-up. Table 11 presents the problem that exists in many organizations. There is a desire to have data standardization. Hence it is centralized; so too is the accomplishment of data standardization. Centralization of accomplishment almost always results in paralysis. Under a centralized accomplishment model, the annual cost for data standardization as depicted in Table 11 is about $575K.

Required Per Year Costs for Centralized Data Standardization Staff					
Quantity of Projects	**Quantity of Names**	**Staff hours per project**	**Cost per project**	**Staff hours per year**	**Cost per year**
30 under development	500 names per project	240 hours	$18,000	7,200	$540,000
20 in production that need maintenance	900 names per year to maintain	23 hours of effort	$1,625	450	$32,500

Table 11. Costs involved in top-down data administration activities.

Under a decentralized implementation approach, the costs are close to zero because the work is accomplished by project staff members during their normal work effort. Eliminated is the effort required to document semantics in sufficient detail so that it can be explained to a centralized data administration (DA) staff member. Eliminated as well is the time required to present the need to the data administration staff, and then to review and revise the results produced by the DA staff. Finally, eliminated are the delays imposed onto the project's schedule because a DA staff member is not available. Simply put, while it is clearly preferred to have a top-down data standardization policy, it is much more preferred to have it accomplished in a highly distributed data modeling environment that has an enterprise viewpoint.

The next "essentials" section describes the very important role of business information system generators. Properly selected and employed, business information system generators dramatically reduce the quantity of work in the system's development life cycle. Business information system generators are the key accelerator to the nine-step process: It is the business information system "auto-writer." Business information system generators are all about business information system manufacturing as opposed to custom development. Code never written does not have to be designed, coded, debugged, document, or maintained. Given that this is a "no-brainer," acquiring and using business information system generators should be a "no-brainer" decision.

2.5 Business Information System Generators.

Business information system generators are an essential component of business information systems development. Generators like Clarion (www.SoftVelocity.com) can dramatically change the traditional nature of the business information systems development process.

The "input data" for the business information system generators should come from the Operational Data Model that is described in Section 2.4. The data model, expressed as DBMS tables, DBMS columns, DBMS keys, and relationships is all that a good business information system generator needs to create a first cut business information system.

Business information system generators play a critical role in prototyping and in design iterations. If a first-cut business information system can be created in an hour, and made ready to demonstrate in just a day or two, the resources required for prototyping can be dramatically reduced. Consider the following example for business information system life cycle costs.

In general, if the costs associated with requirements and design are $1, the activities associated with detailed design through initial business information system implementation costs another $4. That's $5 in total for a first implementation cycle.

Figure 2 illustrates the main phases associated with the traditional first implementation life cycle of an enterprise-wide business information system such as human resources, or accounting and finance. The scale on the bottom represents the quantity of months spent in each phase. The vertical scale that is not shown would be staff hours. The purpose of the chart is to show the relative quantities of staff hours expended across time. The curve clearly shows that the bulk of the effort (commonly about 70%) is expended before any demonstration is possible. Figure 2 shows that:

- About 70% of all effort is expended prior to the first real demonstration of a business information system. That is, before the

Operation and Maintenance parts of the last major phase shown in Figure 2. This percent may be much higher if requirements changes are discovered during System Test. Some multi-hundred million dollar efforts are scrapped because of requirements changes even before System Test.

- The 2nd and any subsequent versions require recycling of the first two phases (20-60%). That is, a repeat of part or all of Requirements Analysis and Design, and also Detailed Design, Coding, and Unit Testing.

The "problem" may have also significantly changed before the final solution arrives. This is the "hazzard" that GAO concludes is intrinsic to the very process. This can result in perpetual recycling of requirements without ever getting to System Testing.

Beyond the first-cycle implementation cost, the total life cycle expenditure for business information system revision cycles (not shown in Figure 2) commonly costs five times more. The total life cycle cost is thus, 30 times the design cost. The problem, however is not that requirements change. Rather, the real problem is that the effects of requirement changes that occur

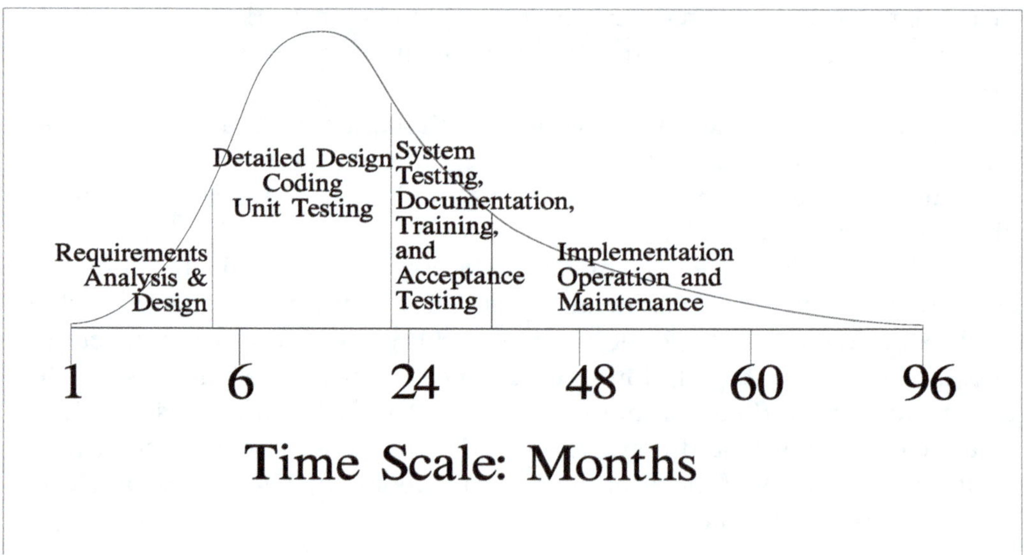

Figure 2. Phases for the traditional information systems development life cycle.

once System Testing et al are complete are too costly to reflect in the implemented business information system.

It must assumed as a given at the very start that requirements will change, even though this assumption is seldom folded into methodologies of today. Requirements changing can be especially fatal to procured software packages if these packages have not been designed for change from the very beginning.

Because $1 in requirements' changes causes $29 in additional life cycle costs, the exhortation is simple: Get the requirements right the first time because the cost of change is prohibitive. The reason the costs are so high and the time is so long is that:

- The tools that either dramatically shorten, or even eliminate steps have only recently become demanded.

- Traditional data modeling approaches are employed in preference to the data modeling coupled with prototyping and recycle approach that has been proven and is shown in this book.

Only by adopting the techniques and tools exemplified in this book can a reduction of 60% or more be realized.

For example, if a data-driven methodology is adopted and is supported by a quality business information system generator, the steps, shown in Figure 2, "Detail Design...," and "System Testing..." can be largely eliminated. If a quality Metabase environment is installed that stores and manages all the data models on an enterprise-wide basis, there can be an improvement in the first phase, Requirements Analysis and Design as well. Finally, if we implement only after four to six design iteration cycles of a prototype, a good bit of the last phase, Implementation, Operations, and Maintenance can be eliminated.

Quality business information system generators can import a database's design and generate a working business information system in a few hours. From that first generation, the generated business information system can be "electronically pruned" to a form that is suitable for demonstration. After several iterations of demonstration, modification, and regeneration, a quality specification can be created.

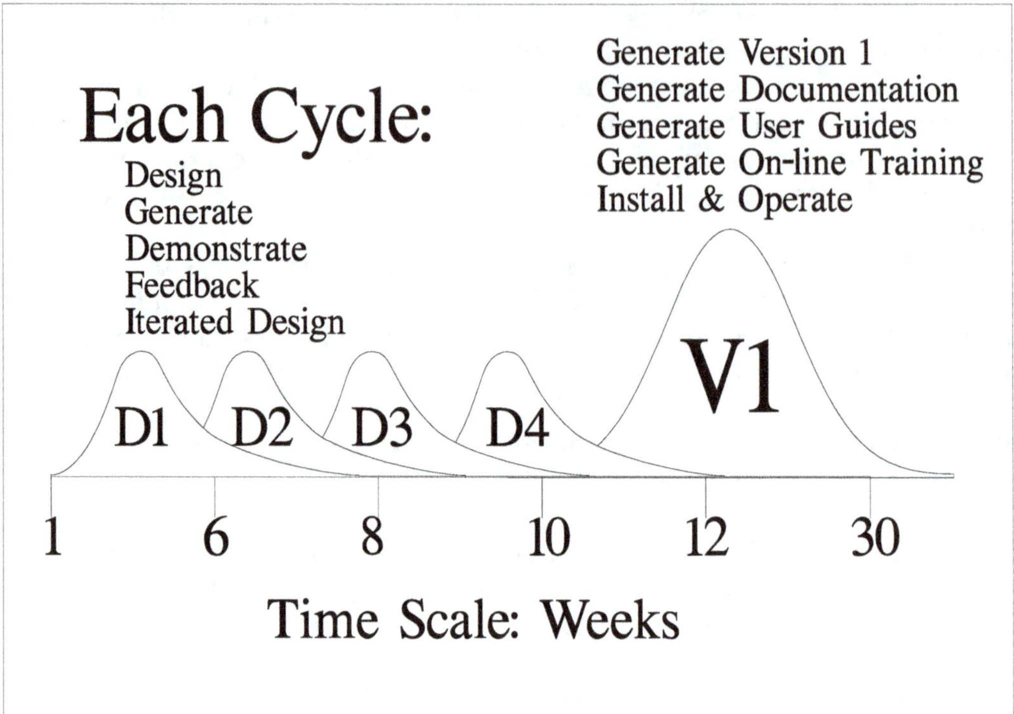

Figure 3. Iterative systems development life cycle.

The change to the process is illustrated in Figure 3. Shown are four prototype development cycles, and one full-implementation cycle. The first "D" (i.e., development) cycle contains the activities noted (that is, Design, ... , Feedback). Each subsequent "D" cycle is dramatically reduced because it only is focused on design changes, regeneration, and the next demonstration. The first cycle contains a requirements analysis and design step. But, that step is reduced to mainly producing the data model. To arrive at the prototype, the business information system generator takes in the data model's design and generates the first-cut business information system. A day or so is then spent to make it "pretty." Then, the prototype is demonstrated. In all, only about six weeks will have passed. Each "D" thereafter can occur in one or two weeks. Under this changed approach:

- "Real" business information systems are available to run at the end of every "D" cycle.

- Requirements are iterated until fully known, but are determined in a very condensed time-period.

- Full development occurs only after requirements are completely validated.

Under either case, the total life cycle cost is the cost of the first cycle plus five times more to account for revisions and extensions.

While over time, the subsequent revisions should cost less, several things happen to thwart that. First, as systems developed through traditional design and coding techniques get "old," their designs and program constructions degrade through the application of ad hoc patches and quick fixes. It takes much longer to accomplish maintenance work than new construction work. The result is the same volume of work.

Second, because of staff turnover, new staff have to relearn the system from scratch. That's almost a complete recycle of the Figure 2 processes. It is both painful and long. In addition, there's the "I'd never have done it that way syndrom" to content with. Every maintenance task seems to get transformed into a fix and enhance task. This naturally takes longer and the enhancement may actually install new bugs.

Third, as new features are required, some of these features are real design breakers. Because a production system has already been implemented, changes take much longer because of redesign, recoding, and the very tedious and error prone data conversion.

All the costing is shown in Figure 4. Under the traditional approach, if the first box costs $400,000, the total life cycle costs are 30x, that is, 5 + (5 * 5) or $12 million.

Faced with high costs, the high-pressure demand for immediate and visible results, the most common approach is to trim the first box. Suppose it was trimmed by one-half. In theory then, the total cost of the first business information system implementation cycle would be reduced to 2.5, that is, 0.5 + (4x 0.5). The total life cycle cost would only be reduced to 15 units, or $6 million. That's a 50% savings. Such savings are however false.

That's because the real requirements are still there. The only thing that has changed is that the analysis to discover the real requirements has been reduced by 50%. In short, 50% of the real requirements are undiscovered.

Now, if the requirements and design efforts are reduced by 50% from 1.0 to 0.5, and given the GAO error allocation of 41% of all information

Systems Development Life Cycle Costs

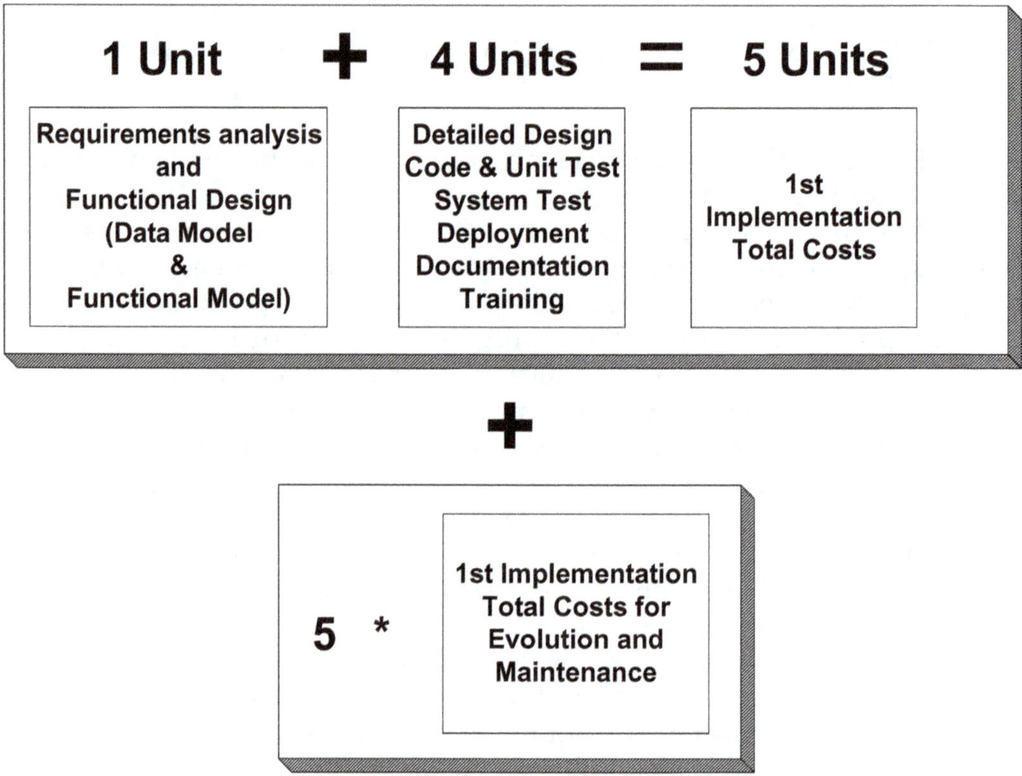

Figure 4. Cost structure of Systems Development Life Cycle.

technology errors if this step is underdone or done wrong, then the "4x" (the amount to accomplish what is really "required") is likely to be 12x. That is because it's done wrong, it has to be undone and then done right. Hence, three times the "4x" number. In that case, the 1st business information system implementation cycle cost is not the original 5 nor the 2.5, but is 6.5 (2.5 (done wrong) + 4.0 (now done right)). The overall life cycle unit quantity becomes 39, that is, 6.5 + (6.5 * 5). This is really a "pay me now, or pay me more later" situation. If a unit costs $400,00, the life cycle cost is now $15.6 million instead of the original $12 million. In short, a requirements analysis of design cut of $200K results in an overall cost increase of $3.6 million. Clearly, these savings are costly indeed.

For a real impact, the savings must be made to the 4x component (that is, Detailed Design,... , Training). If the 4x component is reduced to 2x, then the life cycle costs are reduced to $7.2 million, that is, 400K * 3 + (400K * 3) * 5. In addition, if due to the business information system generator approach, three of the major business information systems evolution cycles are eliminated, then the whole life cycle cost is reduced to $3.6 million, that is, 400K * 3 + (400K * 3) * 2. That represents dramatic savings of about 66% from the original $12 million. Now, in contrast to the $200K savings that cost $3.6 million, these are real savings.

Simply, this means that three business information systems can be implemented for the price of one, or that the productivity goes up by 300%. A compelling case. But can it be done? Yes, and this has been standard best practice for the data-driven Clarion community for the past 20 years. The steps for a quality business information system generator approach are these:

- Import the database design.

- Generate a first-cut application.

- Electronically prune the first-cut application metadata-based design to the desired behavior model.

- Generate the prototype for end-user evaluation.

Thereafter, present the prototype to users, gather changes, and repeat the steps above until the users say, "enough already." Then, and only then, create the production version.

Once the production version is created, there's the evolution and maintenance cycles. The code-generator approach dramatically affects maintenance as well. There were three reasons cited above that cause maintenance to either remain level or take more time under the traditional approach. In contrast to the traditional maintenance approach, under a quality business information system generator approach, many of the first type of evolution and maintenance problems are eliminated outright. The second type of evolution and maintenance problem is of course unavoidable, but because 90% or more of any business information system's code is generated, it does not have to be learned. In fact, because the ultimate program's code sort of doesn't really exist, it never has to be addressed at all.

Quality business information system generators operate at a meta-design level. The actual program code is generated from this meta-design level. Changes are made at the meta-design level as well. So, once the changes are made, the ultimate code is regenerated. If it wasn't necessary to deal with real code at first, there is no need now. Finally, the third type of evolution and maintenance problem largely disappears because there are four or more design iterations before first implementation. The five cycles of maintenance caused by an immature design are eliminated because the design has matured through prototyping before it is implemented.

The next "essential" relates to the Metabase environment. How are all the Knowledge Worker Framework work products captured? How are they interrelated? How are they stored, updated, and reported? All these questions are answered in the next section.

2.6 Metabase Environment.

The Metabase environment is a database and supporting metadata management system into which the artifacts from the Knowledge Worker Framework are stored. Whitemarsh has been designing, building and using Metabase systems since the early 1970s. In every project where the Metabase system has been used, the cost impact from designing and building the Metabase been negative. That is, the savings from using the Metabase on projects have always exceeded the cost of building it.

Included in these artifacts is the enterprise's architecture, that is, mission, organization, function, and database domains, and also the business information system and database analyses, design, implementation, maintenance and operations specifications. Metadata is not new. It has existed since there were architecture and engineering.

A Metabase system is really just a set of "document-loaded three-ring binders" in the form of an information technology database that is encapsulated in a metadata management system. What is unique about these "three ring" binders is that they can be queried, reported from, and easily updated.

The process of designing a Metabase database is the same process for designing a high-quality set of documentation: Nothing more, and nothing less. The process of implementing a Metabase database and its associated metadata management system is the same process for any database-centric

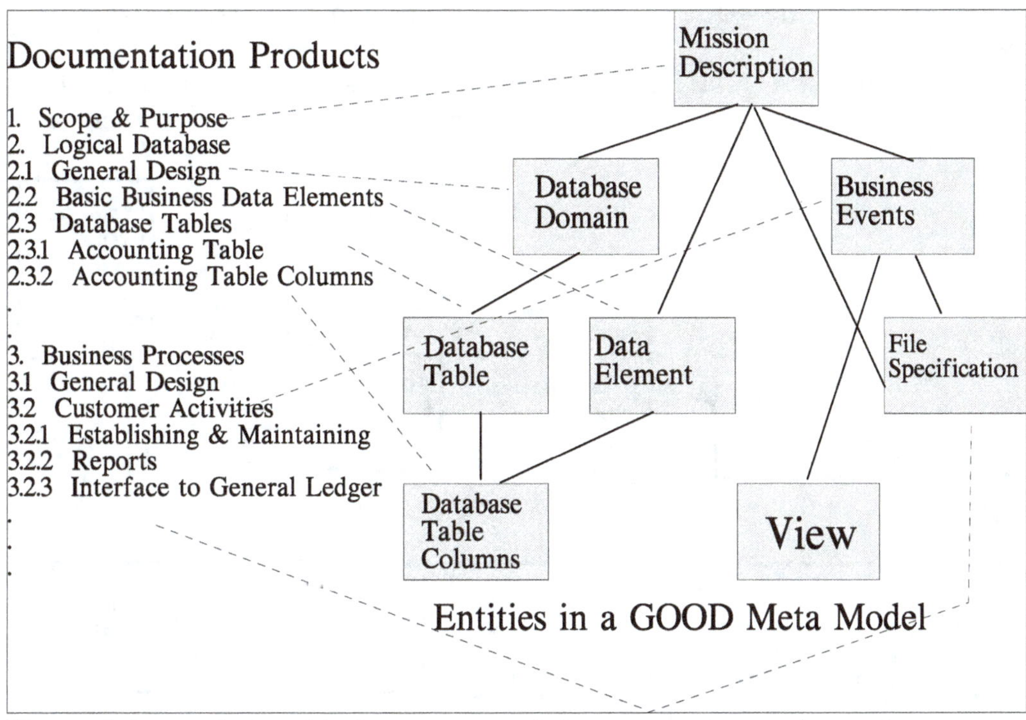

Figure 5. Interrelationship between good documentation and metadata repository meta entities.

business information system. Figure 5 presents the interrelationship between good documentation and the database tables from a Metabase.

If, for example, a finance database and business information system were created, its traditional documentation's table of contents might look like the Figure 5 product list on the left. Each entry would be a title relevant to the finance database and/or business information system. This list, however is just a transformation of the metadata model on the right. Each box on the right is really a Metabase database table that stores metadata. For example, in the mission description meta entity, the scope and purpose of the finance effort would be found. The accounting table from the left would become an instance of the metadata in the database table meta entity.

When Metabases are implemented through a DBMS, the "three-ring binders" become a database that can be integrated across all the meta objects, queried, updated, and reported. An additional quality of a Metabase database is that, like any other database, it may be available on an enterprise-wide basis.

The domain of data that is stored in the Metabase is the same as the "knowledge" that is employed by knowledge workers. Figure 6[13] presents a

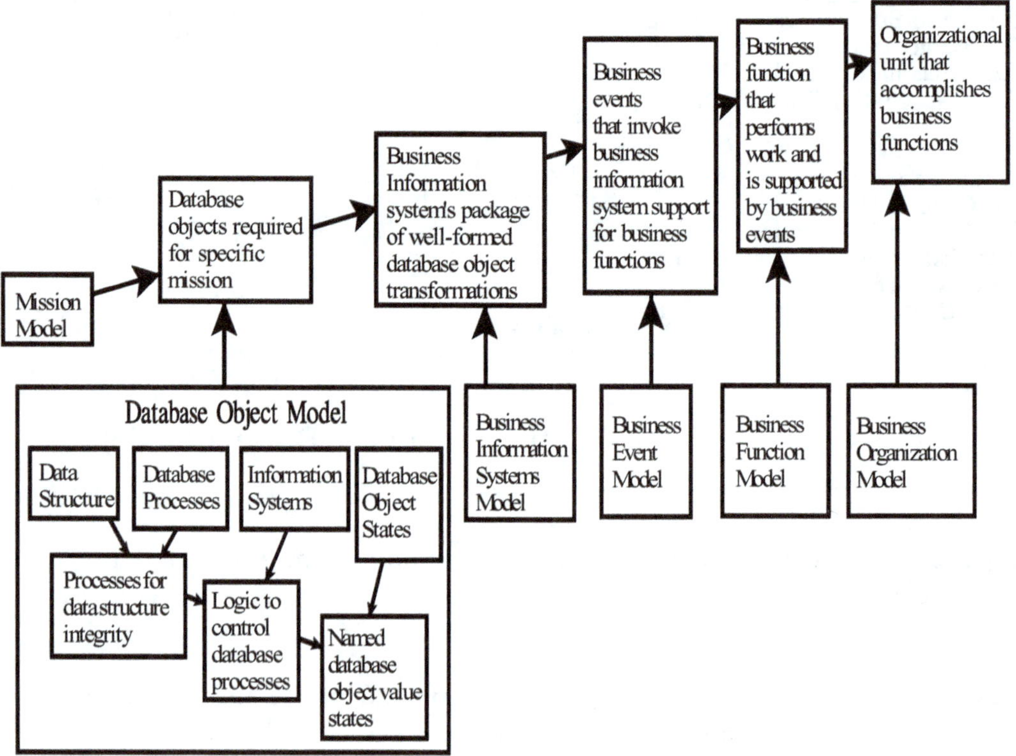

Figure 6. Interrelationship between Metabase meta models and Knowledge Worker Framework columns.

---

[13] Th rectangles in this figure are related to each other through one-to-many relationships. Throughout this book, the "line with arrow head" conventions are as follows: 1. A line from a component to itself with one arrow-head is a recursive relationship. Ex. From Figure 12, Mission contains mission. 2) A line between a component and itself with an arrow head on both ends of the line is a network relationship. Ex. From Figure 17, a concept can contain multiple concepts, and a concept can be contained in multiple concepts. 3) A line between two components with a single arrow head is a one-to-many relationship. Ex. From

(continued...)

diagram of the Whitemarsh metadata models (left to right rectangles) and how they are interrelated (diagonal of connected rectangles). The Database Object Class Model is shown in its own box, and is further subdivided. Note that the horizontally lined up rectangles (i.e., Missions through Business Organizations) are the same as the columns of the Knowledge Worker Framework.

The boxes that interrelate the Knowledge Worker Framework columns are textual expressions of the relationship between the columns. Each column, through this textual expression, is related to each other in a many-to-many relationship. The boxes in the Database Object Class Model are similarly related in a many-to-many relationship.

Essentially, this diagram indicates that missions are represented through one or more Database Object Classes. Database Object Classes are acted upon by one or more business information systems. Business information systems are "executed" within the context of events from the business. The business' events are invoked by one or more business functions, which, in turn, are performed by one or more business organizations. This tells the story of the enterprise.

A careful review of the diagram shows that the story can be also read in the opposite direction. That is, an organization performs one or more functions that, within the context of a business's events, invoke the execution of one or more business information systems which, in turn, cause value-based changes in one or more Database Object Classes that exist in support of accomplishing the missions of the enterprise.

A high level summary of the domain of the Metabase is presented in Figure 7. As illustrated in this diagram:

- Positions and assigned persons have information needs through their role within an organization perform functions in the accomplishment of enterprise missions.

- These information needs are satisfied by the state of certain enterprise resources such as finance, people, and products that are important to the enterprise.

---

[13](...continued)
Figure 12, Mission has zero, one, or more Database Domains..

- The Resource Life Cycle states are created through the execution of business information systems and the accomplishment of database object state transformations.

The domain of the Metabase is the same domain as the Knowledge Worker Framework. The artifacts of the Knowledge Worker Framework all have a "home" in the Metabase.

By generating, interrelating, and using all the work products in the Knowledge Worker Framework, business information system failures are prevented or resolved. These artifacts are stored in the Metabase in an

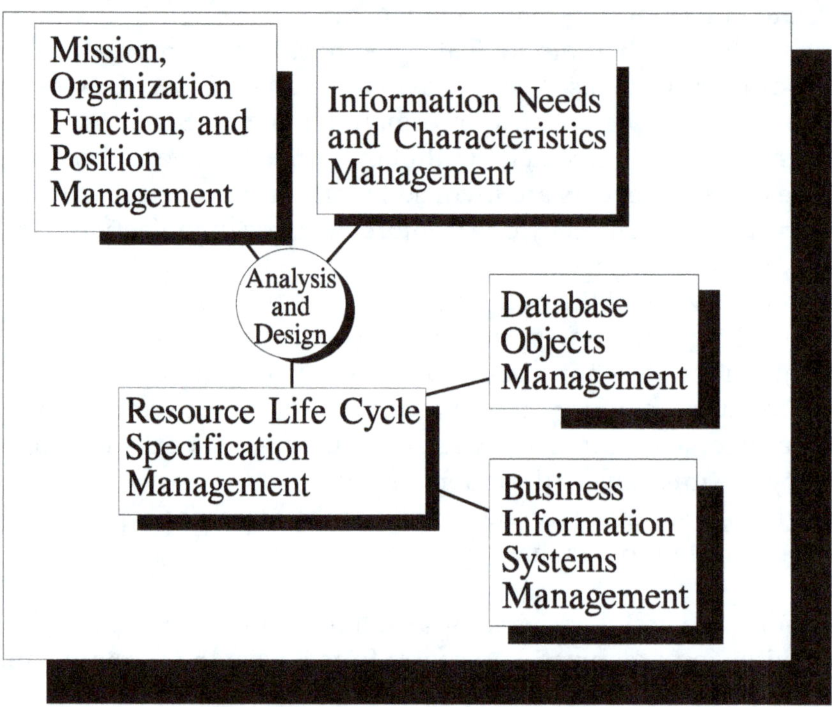

Figure 7. Whitemarsh metabase domain.

integrated and non-redundant manner such that they can be viewed and used across the enterprise. To have done anything different would have been illogical.

Finally, the Metabase generates the necessary metadata to feed the Clarion business information system generator, or other business information system generators that can read and use SQL-based database designs as the basis for their business information system code-generating platform. Again to have done anything different would have been illogical. The correspondence between the Knowledge Worker Framework and the Metabase's main metadata domains is set out in the multi page Table 12.

Metadata Domains Within the Knowledge Worker Framework						
	Knowledge Worker Domain					
Metadata Domains	Mission	Database Object Classes	Business Information Systems	Business Event	Business Function	Business Organization
Missions, which are: The essential missions that define the very existence of the enterprise, and that are the ultimate goals and objectives that measure enterprise accomplishment from within different business functions and organizations.	✔				✔	✔
Organizations, which are: The organizations that accomplish the aspects of missions with databases, business information systems and through functions	✔			✔	✔	✔
Functions, which are: The procedures that are performed by groups as they accomplish the various missions of the enterprise from within different enterprise organizations.					✔	

Metadata Domains Within the Knowledge Worker Framework						
	Knowledge Worker Domain					
Metadata Domains	Mission	Database Object Classes	Business Information Systems	Business Event	Business Function	Business Organization
Resource Life Cycles, which are: The resources, that is, the facilities, materiel, staff, etc. of the enterprise. How these resources are sequenced, interrelated, and how they are supported through databases and business information systems.		✔	✔			
Information Needs, which are: The information (a.k.a. query results or reports) needed by various organizations in their functional accomplishment of missions through databases and business information systems.			✔			
Databases, which are: The data needed by functional proponents, how it is defined within data architectures and databases and how and where those databases are deployed and then used by business information systems in support of mission accomplishment.		✔				

Metadata Domains Within the Knowledge Worker Framework						
	Knowledge Worker Domain					
Metadata Domains	Mission	Database Object Classes	Business Information Systems	Business Event	Business Function	Business Organization
Data Models, which are: The data models of the enterprise which consist of data elements, that is, the context independent semantic templates of data, which are configured into models of "real" data (the consequence of policy execution) determined to be needed by functional experts in support of enterprise missions. These data model specifications are then configured into implemented databases that ultimately operate within various organizations as they perform the functions needed by enterprise missions.		✔	✔			
Business Information Systems, which are: The Business Information Systems, including where they are, how they are related to mission, organization, function, and databases. Through which business and calendar cycle they are accomplished, and what the impact is on these business information systems when policy (a.k.a., data) is required or changed.			✔			

Table 12. Metadata domains set against knowledge worker areas.

Table 13 shows the distribution of GAO reasons for failure across the Knowledge Worker Framework grouped by major categories of work. That is:

- Enterprise architecture.

- Business Information Systems Planning.

- Mission changes post implementation. That is, the changes in policies required by the new database and business information system.

- Function and organization changes post business information system implementation. That is, the changes in procedures and work practices required by the new database and business information system.

- Database and business information system creation, deployment, and maintenance. That is, the actual creation, implementation, and maintenance of the databases and business information system that result from the requirements analysis of the first two rows, and the business information system planning of the third row.

Knowledge Worker Framework						
	Mission	Database Object Class	Business Information system	Business Event	Function	Organization
Scope	Enterprise Architecture (41% of failure reasons)					
Business						
Business information system	Business Information Systems Planning (9 % of less of failure reasons)					Function and organization changes to the enterprise to take advantage of new database and business information systems (50% of failure reasons)
Technology	Mission changes post implementation (1 % or less of failure reasons)	Database and business information systems creation, deployment, and maintenance (0% failure reasons)				
Deployment						
Operations						

Table 13. Distribution of metadata across the knowledge worker framework.

What is critical to notice here is the distribution of failure reason percentages. Almost none of the errors are involved in the actual information technology creation and implementation cells. These noted percents differ from Table 6 only because the cells for the business information system's row are now included in the Business Information Systems Planning efforts. The percent numbers are all accurate; it's just a different allocation.

Optimal use of the Metabase system accomplishes the following in the stated general order:

- Enterprise Architecture.
- Business Information Systems Planning.
- Information Technology.

Once these are accomplished then the post implementation efforts would start. That is:

- Mission changes post implementation.
- Function and organization changes post implementation.

When the Metabase is activated, its opening window, presented in Figure 8, is displayed. The top level menu shows the traditional Windows functions of File, Edit, Window, and Help. The details of each menu item is presented in the Metabase's Users Guide.

The figure shows the two submenus that are activated by pressing the "Metabase" and "Data Modeler" menu items. Any of the items on either of these two submenu browses can be pressed to start a particular Metabase module. The other menu item that can be activated is the Admin module. That can be employed only if the user has administrative authority.

Of especial interest here is that there can be multiple Metabase databases. Each Metabase module, that is, any of those listed on the two lists in Figure 8 can access different Metabase databases. For example, there might be a Metabase database in support of the combined set of enterprise infrastructure metadata such as Human Resources, Finance, Manufacturing, and Distribution, and another completely different Metabase database in support of an enterprise's external mission, that is, Customer Management, Marketing, and Products Sales. Metabase users can activate the same module

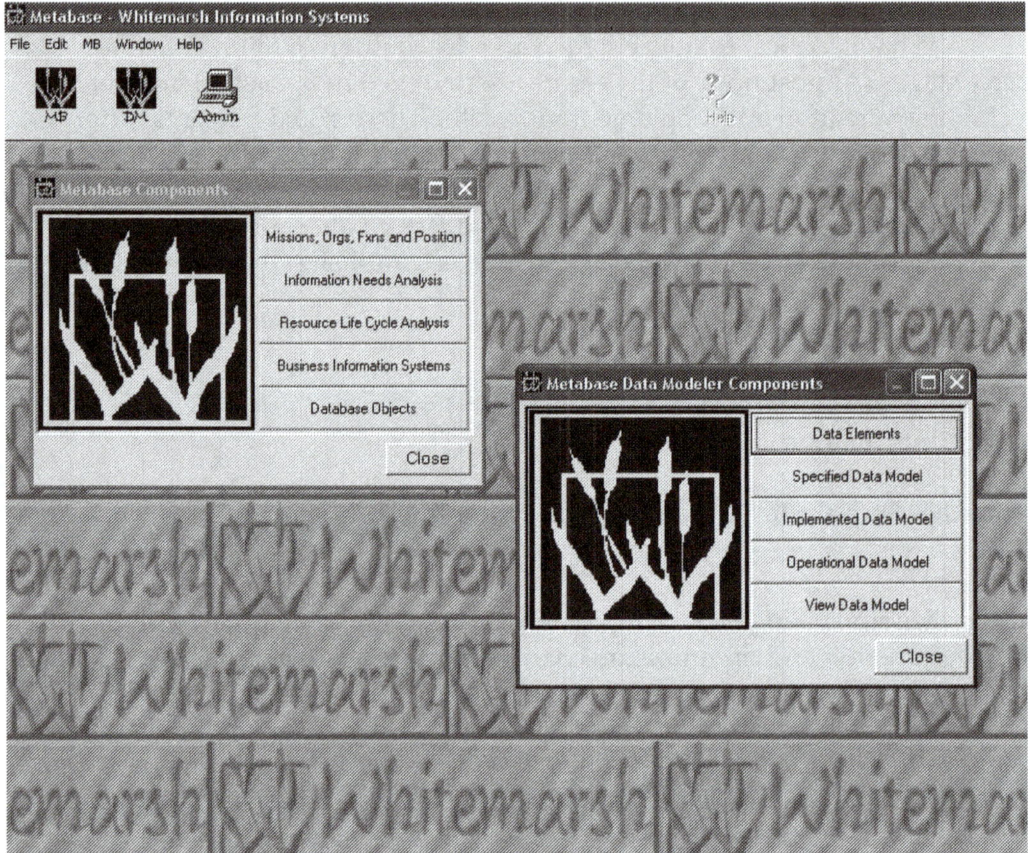

Figure 8. Opening window of the Whitemarsh Metabase system.

multiple times and select a different Metabase database within each. This enables metadata to be managed across Metabase database instances.

A particular Metabase database is selected by activating a functional module, then by providing a user name and password, and then by selecting the particular Metabase database to which access is allowed. The Metabase database instances and permission to access a particular Metabase database is established by the Metabase administrator.

Figure 9 shows the user name and password window that appears once a Metabase functional module is activated: for example, Mission-Organization-Function-Position. In this example, the user name is "YourName" and the password is "YourPassword." The Metabase database

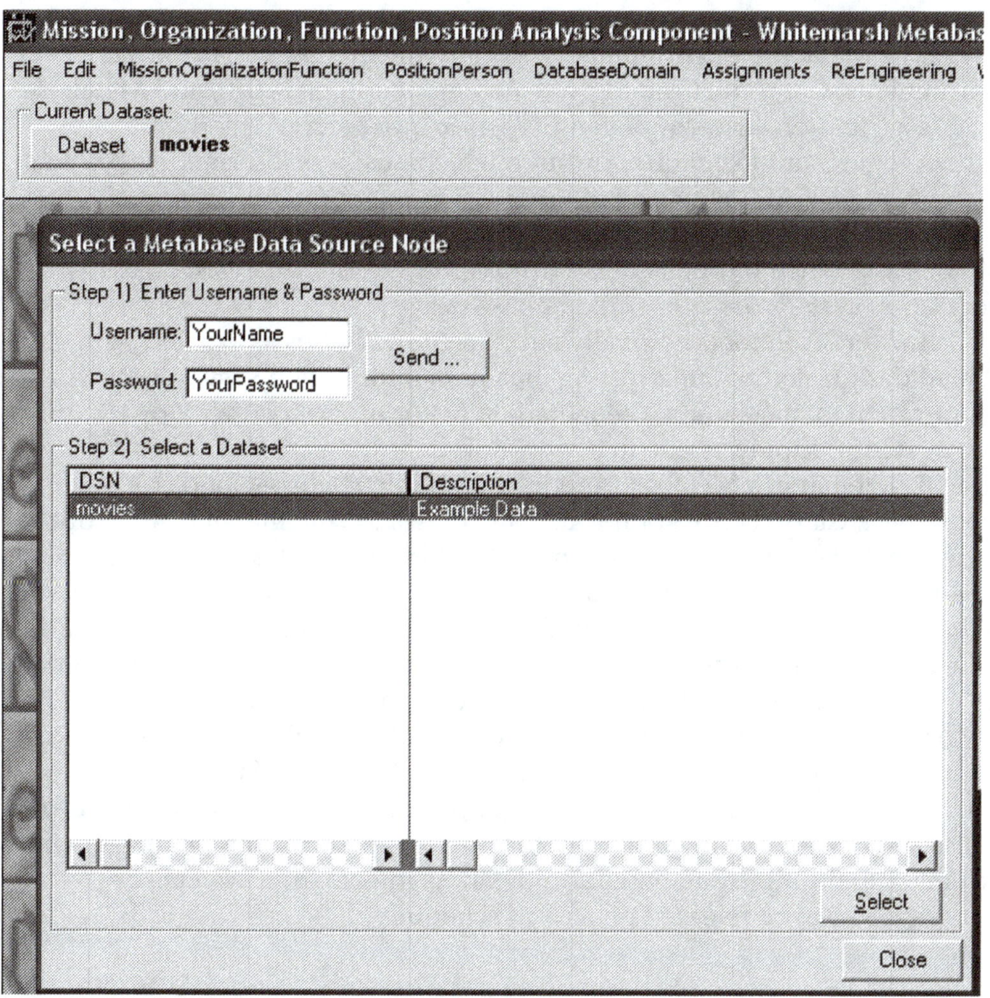

Figure 9. Selecting metabase database instance screen.

instance that was chosen is "movies." To select it, highlight it from within the "Step 2) Select a Data Set" browse, and press Select. At this point the Metabase functional module will only display data from that selected Metabase database. At any time the metadata database instance can be changed by pressing the data-set button, entering a new user name and password combination, and selecting a different Metabase database instance.

The Metabase environment is actually the merger of two earlier environments: Computer-Aided Systems Engineering (CASE), and Metabase. CASE is a common term employed to refer to a collection of software, methodologies, and techniques through which business information systems are engineered. CASE is commonly divided into UpperCASE, and LowerCASE (puns intended). UpperCASE tools generally support the activities associated with business information systems analysis, business information systems design, and database design.

LowerCASE tools generally support the activities associated with detailed design, coding, unit testing, business information system testing, and configuration management. The metadata resulting from either UpperCASE or LowerCASE should reside in a repository.

Whitemarsh's Metabase and its methodology corresponds to UpperCASE. Clarion corresponds to LowerCASE. Whitemarsh has separated the two so that clients can take the metadata products extracted from its UpperCASE product, Metabase, and feed these into different LowerCASE products like Clarion or those provided by Oracle, or Sybase. Clarion, as a business information system generator is illustrated in subsequent chapters.

The next "essential" relates to project development environments. New organizations without inventories of installed databases and business information systems operate under discrete, that is, one-off project development environments. Mature organizations should, however transform themselves to a release environment that enables planning and management of changes to multiple databases and business information systems by multiple teams to be released on a fixed schedule.

2.7 Discrete and Release Development Environments.

IT projects are accomplished within distinct development environments. The two most common are: discrete project and release. The discrete project environment is typified by completely encapsulated projects accomplished through a waterfall, or spiral methodology.

Figure 2 or 3 depicts this kind of environment. A project is established, it proceeds through a set of phases, one after the other, and the database and/or business information system is set into production. This is a traditional environment.

In contrast to discrete project environment is the release environment. In this environment, there are a number of different projects concurrently underway by different organizations and staff of varying skill levels in the same database environment. However, once a large number of projects are underway, the ability of the enterprise to know about and manage all the different projects, in a concurrent, coordinated, and interdependent manner degrades rapidly. At best, it's like herding cats. That is because the project management environments are most commonly geared to manage discrete encapsulated projects, not collections of concurrently executing projects against single or multiple databases and/or business information systems.

This problem can be solved with a continuous flow process that can manage project collections that result in simultaneous releases across a broad topology of databases and business information systems on a set time schedule. Figure 10 illustrates the continuous flow process environment that supports releases. The continuous flow process environment is characterized by:

- Multiple, concurrent, but differently scheduled projects against the same existing enterprise databases and business information systems.

- Single projects that affect multiple existing enterprise databases and business information systems.

- Projects that develop completely new capabilities, or changes to existing capabilities within existing enterprise databases and business information systems.

For enterprises that have transformed themselves from a one-off project environment to a multi-project, multi-database and multi-business information system release environment, Business Information Systems Plans can be created, evolved, and maintained on an enterprise-wide basis. This is essential to a high performing business.

There are four major sets of activities within the continuous flow process environment. The user/client is represented at the top in the small rectangular box. The Metabase system is shown in the center and is accessible by all four of the major continuous flow processes. Each of the ellipses represents a process targeted to a specific need. The four basic needs are:

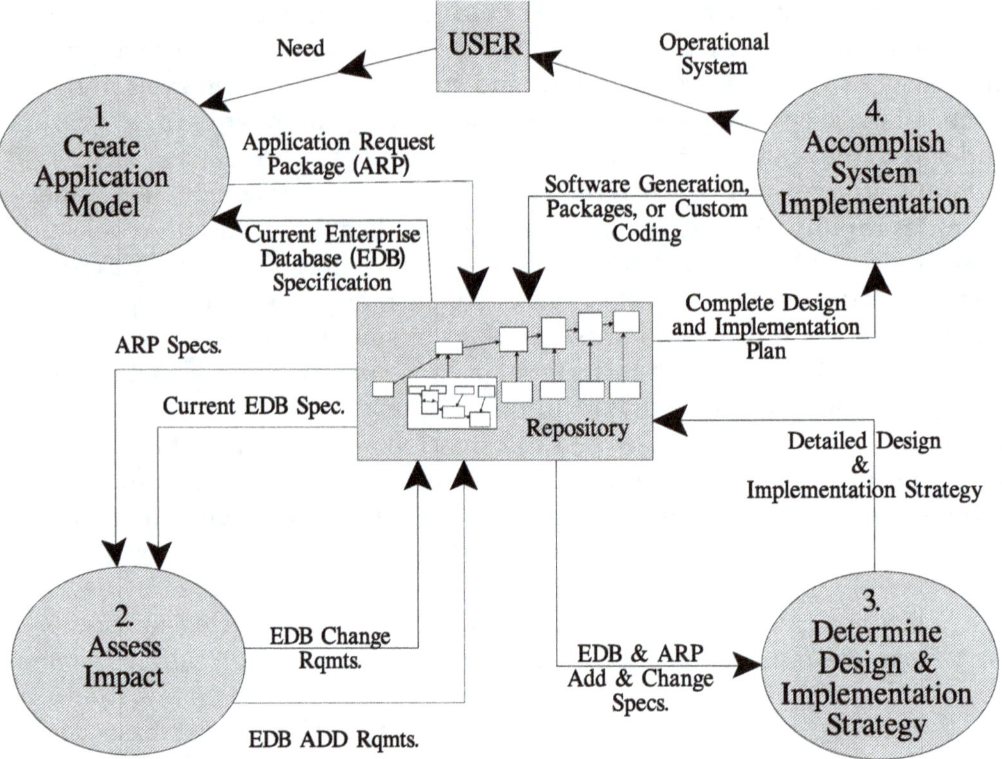

Figure 10. Continuous flow environment.

- Create application model.
- Assess impact.
- Determine design and implementation strategy.
- Accomplish system implementation.

Specification and impact analysis is represented through the left two processes. Implementation design and accomplishment is represented by the right two processes. Two key characteristics should be immediately apparent. First, unlike the waterfall or spiral approach, the processes that are the ellipses 1) Create through 4) Accomplish do not flow one to the other. They are disjoint. In fact, they may be done by different teams, on different time schedules, and involve different quantities of products under management. In short, these four processes are independent one from the other. Their only interdependence is through the Metabase.

The second characteristic flows from the first. Because these four processes are independent one from the other, the enterprise evolves through releases across collections of databases and/or business information systems rather than through the wholesale replacement of specific databases and/or business information systems.

If the enterprise evolves through whole databases and/or business information systems, the four processes would be connected either in a waterfall or a spiral approach, and the enterprise would be evolving through major upgrades to encapsulated functionality within specific functional areas.

In contrast, the release approach causes coordinated sets of changes to multiple business functional areas to be placed into production. This causes simultaneous, enterprise-wide capability upgrades across multiple business functional areas.

Through this continuous-flow process, several unique features are present:

- All four processes are concurrently executing.

- Changes to enterprise databases and/or business information systems occur in unison, periodically, and in a very controlled manner.

- The Metabase always contains all the enterprise databases and/or business information systems specifications: current or planned. Simply put, if an enterprise resource semantic is not within the Metabase, it is not considered to be enterprise policy.

- All changes are planned, scheduled, measured, and are subject to auditing, accounting, and traceability.

- All documentation of all types is generated from the Metabase.

As an aside, the release management environment must be managed through a project management system that can know of the Metabase and also manage multiple databases and business information systems in a concurrent and coordinated manner. Such a project management system is described in Chapter 5.

The final "essential" relates to work management. That is through the uses of project, deliverable, and task templates. Since every project has varying quantities of deliverables, differently skilled employees and different work environment factors, the base staff and time estimates originally generated have to be modified to reflect the unique work environment factors. The final project plan is able to be explained to management because it is a combination of standard project, deliverable, and task templates that are resource-modified by the determined quantities of deliverables, the available employees, and different work environment factors that affect the base estimates.

2.8 Metrics and Work Environment Multipliers.

All work should be accomplished through highly engineered projects. When projects are so engineered, repetitive patterns surface. This enables the creation of standardized and highly engineered deliverable templates and task templates. The Metabase, along with business information system generators like Clarion, greatly enhances the ability to manufacture designs and software because unnecessary and non-standard-conforming designs and resulting custom-developed computer software code are engineered out of the entire process.

Methodology and metrics can be standardized. These, coupled with the Metabase and business information system generators like Clarion, can result in a software manufacturing environment. What differentiates one actual project from another is the quantity of deliverables produced, the quality of the staff assigned, and the environment factors that affect knowledge worker productivity.

Work environment factors govern the additional quantity of hours that must be assigned to a task to compensate for abnormal work environments. The work environment factor categories include:

- Reviews conducted by the client.
- Equipment available for an analyst/programmer.
- Equipment outages.
- Extent of user contact.

Each factor can have a numeric value that is employed as a multiplier of the normal hours for a task. Given that the standard for "Equipment available for an analyst/programmer" is a work station connected with a shared Metabase environment, the metric is be 1.0. If there are fewer resources than that, that is, only stand-alone PCs with Metabase, or only PCs, or no equipment for the analyst or programmer, the multipliers would be 1.10, 1.25, and 1.30 respectively. A deliverable that used to take 10 staff hours under a 1.0 work environment factor now takes 13 staff hours under the 1.3 work environment factor.

The work environment factors for each category are determined for each work task. Their multiplicative summation is then used to determine the final work environment factor that is employed to determine the final factored hours. Table 14, for example lists a set of factors for a particular task and then the multiplicative summation. The ramifications of these factors can be "painful."

In this particular example, the normal hours for this particular task must be doubled because of these multipliers. If this is applied to the project as a whole, then a project "normally" projected to cost $2 million would cost almost $4 million. While management might indicate that they don't have the funds necessary for "costly" infrastructure such as Metabase and business information system generators, it is doubtful that any such suite of software would cost $2 million. Thus, these "assists" are cost effective indeed.

In addition to work environment factors, there also are staff experience and skill level multipliers. These are determined by skill type and performance level within skill. Once the Factored Task hours are computed, a staff person can be assigned in terms of the skill level possessed by the person. This staff skill level multiplier becomes the final multiplier of the factored hours to give the real hours that are to be provided to the project's customers.

The value of this approach is that the project's customer can see the direct effects due to the working conditions and/or the skill levels of the assigned staff. A more detailed presentation of estimate generation is provided in Chapter 5, Whitemarsh Project Management.

Factor Name	Factor Value	Factor Description
Reviews conducted by the client	1.10	Reviews are conducted but by inexperienced reviewers
Equipment available for an analyst or programmer	1.25	A PC with no CASE or Metabase environment
Equipment outages	1.16	For each hour below the average of six that the equipment is unavailable
Extent of user contact	1.20	If users are available but only within four business days of request
Multiplicative Summation	1.914	1.10 * 1.25 * 1.16 * 1.20

Table 14. Example of a set of work environment factors for a specific project task.

2.9 Summary

The intent of the material in this chapter is to present the essential environmental factors that affect information technology success, and state why having such an environment returns many times its cost in savings. These factors include:

- The Knowledge Worker Framework that identifies the different major classes of artifacts needed to support enterprise, database, and business information systems development.

- The enumeration of the types and kinds of information technology errors, and the critical sources of these failure reasons. The most surprising part of the allocation of failure reasons is that 95% of all reasons for business information systems failure are outside of information technology.

- Data-driven methodologies are specially designed to advance the quality of the very requirements that must be present for successful business information systems and databases.

- Database Object Classes greatly enable the encapsulation of commonly defined and employed data and processes.

- The different database architecture classes and the different data model generalization levels that allow enterprise-wide data to be managed.

- Business information system generators that accomplish prototyping are a key accelerator to business information system development.

- Metabase environments that increase productivity and standardization.

- A release-environment that reorients from a stove-pipe project-based mentality so that capabilities across multiple business information systems to be accomplished in a coordinated fashion.

- The key metrics and work environment factors that dramatically affect both the quality and the timeliness of database and business information system accomplishment.

The next chapter focuses on the 9-steps of the methodology. This includes the creation of a comprehensive and valid prototype that can be provided to an information technology implementation team so that there only needs to be one round of development. Provided also, are the discovered specifications stored in the Metabase. Thereafter, the business information system is immediately deployed and to then undergo only minor rounds of modifications throughout its life.

2.10 Questions and Exercises

1. Rank the eight "essentials" from most to least important. Is that a fair request? Are these really able to be ranked or are they too different from each other?

2. Do you have all eight of the "essentials" in your organization? How much did each cost in terms of procurement, training, and support? Was there a return on investment (ROI)? What was the ROI in terms of money, time, and business opportunities?

3. Which of the eight "essentials" is missing from your organization? What has its absence cost in terms of money, time, and lost opportunities? How did you determine the costs?

4. How do the eight "essentials" interact with each other. Do you get benefit from having bought them in a special order? For example, if you have one then you get more benefit from the next rather than the other way around?

5. Does your organization have a "new toys" lab where controlled experiments are conducted to determine real value prior to any enterprise-wide implementation?

6. Do you have something like the Knowledge Worker Framework? What has been its value? Does it have a positive ROI in terms of time, resources, and money?

7. Do you agree or disagree with the discovered GAO reasons for business information system failure? What has been your actual experience as to the reasons?

8. How does your organization accomplish "change management?" That is, the "50%" changes in the business function and business organization columns? Is "change management" incorporated into your methodology right from the get-go, or does it always seem to be an unwelcome surprise?

9. Have you attempted both data-driven and process-driven methodologies? Compare and contrast the two approaches. What has been your conclusions? Can one exclusively exist without the other or must there be a hybrid approach?

10. Have you observed that the quantity of work products associated with the process-driven approach exceeds the quantity of work products from a data-driven approach? What are some of the reasons for that?

11. Given this books definition of missions and functions, are database designs that are founded on mission-based policies inherently more stable than database designs that are based on a function-based approach? Why is that so? Aren't functions essentially processes? If database designs are based on functions, and if the functions change shouldn't also the databases change?

12. Can you see the existence of database object classes within your enterprise? Have you designed databases and business information system around what ends up being database object classes? Would a formal definition of database object classes be of value? Why?

13. Do you have database architecture classes identified within your enterprise? How have ERPs impacted database architectures within your organization? How do these database architectures interact? Do you agree with the Attachment #2 definitions of the database architecture classes?

14. Do you have a TDSA? How has it been implemented? Pull or Push? Does a TDSA enable standardization on granularity, precision, temporal aspects, and value domains? Is that of value? Why?

15. Do you have a business information system generator like Clarion? If so, what has been its value? Does your business information system generator automatically create its own metadata that can be modified to change the behavior and processes of the business information system? Can you integrate the business information systems that are generated through other business information system generators

created differently? How? Can you jump start your business information system generator with inputs from the Metabase?

16. Do you use your business information system generators as the mechanism for creating and evolving prototypes?

17. Do you have a Metabase-like environment? Is it on the critical path of projects? Can it be? Should it be? If it can, why isn't it? Does the metadata across all the Metabase users integrate so that each set of metadata reinforces the others?

18. Does your organization have a release-like development environment? How does it compare with the Waterfall or Spiral environments? If you don't have a release environment, how do you coordinate changes across multiple systems?

19. Have you captured metrics such that you can use them for project estimating and management? If yes, what's the value. If no, why not?

3

Nine Step Approach to Business Information Systems Development

This chapter presents the nine-step approach using screen-shots from the Metabase and the Clarion environment. The example data is taken from the Movies example provided with the Metabase system download from the Whitemarsh website. The Movie Rental Corporation is a "nom de plume" for the largest movie rental business in the United States. The requirements development organization is responsible for all the steps. The business information systems development organization is only required starting in Step 8, which focuses on business information system implementation.

The main objective is to enable functional users to advance their awareness of their requirements and to evolve this awareness through prototyping until it is ready to implement: one time and correctly.

The overall objective of the 9-step approach is to accomplish the correct implementation of a database and/or business information system requirement the first time. That can only occur if the "requirements" are both fully laid out, and accurately reflect the true nature of the problem. There are a number of unique benefits from this 9-step approach including building the required metadata that supports accelerating the development of other business information systems, and the creation and almost automatic evolution of enterprise architectures and business information system plans that are so critical to enterprise survival.

What is so common about this 9-step approach is that almost every other science and engineering-based discipline has, over a long quantity of years employed a variant of it, that is, formulate a hypothesis, create alternatives, test them, select one, and formulate a go-forward plan. Only recently have the infrastructures tools that support this approach within Information Technology become commonly available. All the reasons for not being able to cut the cost and time for business information system development with an enterprise-wide orientation are now gone.

The nine steps that address the problems cited in the Standish and GAO information technology studies are:

- Develop missions.
- Design the database.
- Generate the prototype.
- Evolve the specification through prototyping.
- Create the request for proposal.
- Evaluate the vendor responses.
- Award the contract.
- Manage the contractor.
- Test conformance to prototype.

A feature of this approach is that the contractor or organization that accomplishes the production implementation does not get something to actually implement until step eight. This stands in stark contrast with the scenario in the Preface where the contractor was handed the entire effort at the very beginning. The contractors in that situation were charged with accomplishing the entire problem domain, which in almost all cases is impossible.

3.1 Step 1: Develop Missions

A common lament from information technology professionals is that whenever new or changed requirements surface during the business information systems implementation phases, slippages, cost overruns and significant rework are almost always the result. Users counter that new or changed requirements arise because they didn't fully understand the "problem" that was being solved.

Given that requirements "naturally" change and are also significantly affected by accelerating technologies, the ability to posit an accurate and long-term set of requirements at the beginning is close to impossible, and any business information system developed on the basis of unstable requirements is doomed from the outset.

An alternative to attempting to build a business information system on an unstable platform of requirements is to build from a platform of stable enterprise missions. Mission descriptions are characterizations of the end result to be achieved independent of technology, "who," and "how." Well done, mission description documents are timeless, technology free, and apolitical. Figure 11 provides a mission description for Human Resources.

At first, this looks like a functional description. Missions are not functions however, because missions do not contain any descriptions of "how" anything is done. Nor do missions state "who" accomplishes the human resource's mission. Finally, there are no descriptions of what technology is employed to accomplish the results.

Mission Example: Human Capital Management (HR)

The Movie Rentals Corporation maintains a highly motivated staff of dynamic employees in all areas of our company from the Retail Store to Region/District operations management, to Distribution Center management, and various other corporate opportunities.

The Corporation places a high value on providing equal employment opportunity and maintaining a diverse workforce. The Corporation works hard to comply with all applicable laws prohibiting discrimination and strives to make the workforce reflect the rich diversity of our society and our customers.

The Corporation recruits and hires without regard to race, color, sex, religion, national origin, ethnicity, age, marital status, sexual orientation, disability, veteran status or any other basis prohibited by law. The Corporation strives to administer all personnel actions such as hiring, compensation, promotions, benefits, transfers, layoffs, company-sponsored training, education, tuition assistance, terminations, social and recreational programs in a consistent manner.

Figure 11. Human resources mission hierarchy.

In practice, missions are often constructed that look like functions. That is, mission descriptions that contain who, how, and technical details. When this happens, reviews will go badly, arguments related to style will ensue, and the overall results will be unsatisfactory. If these functions are merely stripped of their "who", "how," and "technology" artifacts, the reviews go remarkably well. To help understand the differences between missions and functions, Table 15 provides a set of critical comparisons.

Contrast between Missions and Functions	
Mission descriptions are descriptions of the characteristics of the end result. Mission descriptions are noun-based sentences.	Functions are descriptions of how to accomplish an end result. Functional descriptions are verb-based sentences.
Mission descriptions are apolitical. They are devoid of who, how, and technology. There should only be ONE mission description for a mission.	Function hierarchies are commonly affected by organizations and styles. There could be any number of equivalent functional statements about a given function.
Databases and business information systems are based on missions.	"Human" activities and organizations are based on business functions.
You fundamentally change your business when you re-engineer Missions.	You change and/or optimize you business when you re-engineer functions.
Mission descriptions are strategic and long range	Functions are tactical to operational, and medium to short range, and are organizationally sensitive

Table 15. Critical difference between missions and functions.

Missions are related to organizations. Every organization should have at least one mission responsibility. Else, why have the organization? Ideally, missions are evenly distributed across organizations. Whenever there's an organization responsible for many, many missions, then an analysis error is likely to have occurred or else the organization is not properly deployed across the enterprise. Functions are then allocated to the mission-organization pairs. Thus, missions and functions are indirectly related through many-to-many relationships. That means there may be many different functions that accomplish the same mission-organization and many mission-organizations that are addressed by the same function. The different functions may be essentially the same except for style.

It is important to note from the Knowledge Worker Framework, set out in Table 2, that functions are entirely in the "Man" column set, while missions are neither in the "machine" nor the "man" column set. Missions belong to the enterprise and change only when there are fundamental changes in the enterprise.

Re-engineering a collection of organizations is not a mission change. Re-engineering or optimizing a collection of functionally based activities is not a mission change. If a manufacturing and distribution enterprise decides to go into retailing of its and other product brands, that is a mission change. Mission hierarchies are commonly brought down only several levels in most areas. Finally, missions are accomplished first because they set the boundaries of the enterprise.

In contrast, organizations frequently change year to year and manager to manager. Functions change to reflect new or changed business conditions or to reflect changes in management. Business information systems are thus more stable when they are founded on long lasting enterprise missions than when they are built on ever-changing organizations or functions.

Figure 12 presents the Metabase support for Missions. Missions, Organizations, and Functions are hierarchical. Missions and Organizations are first interrelated through many-to-many relationships (Mission-Organizations). This was done so that the "human" organization could address the accomplishment of missions through its own functional style.

The Metabase's module that contains missions is called MOFPA (Mission, Organization, Function, Position, and Assignments). From its name, it also contains organizations, functions, and positions. This module also contains database domains and all the assignment processes to interrelate all this critical enterprise architecture related data.

All the arrows on Figure 12 and other meta model figures represent one-to-many relationships. For example, Organization has zero, one or more contained Organizations, and Organizations have zero, one or more Mission-Organizations.

Figure 13 presents the MOFPA main window. The four-button cluster to the left controls the contents of the hierarchy display. The Print Tree button causes a hierarchy report to be presented. The Metabase system also supports ODBC-based report writers such as Crystal Reports. 100 or so report templates can be downloaded from the Whitemarsh website. The button cluster to the right controls the insertions, changes or deletions of mission.

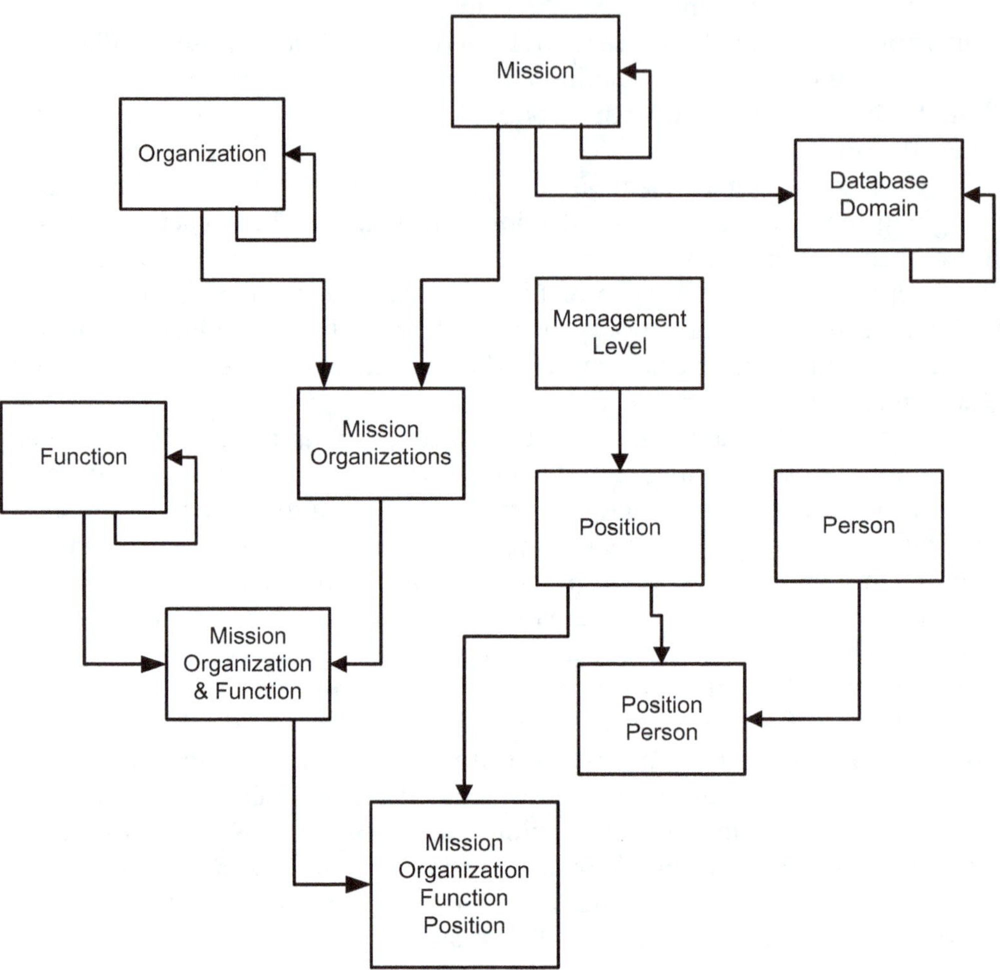

Figure 12. Metabase support for mission, organizations, functions, and positions.

Similar browses exist for Organizations and Functions. Positions are loaded within the context of their management levels. Database domains are addressed in Section 3.2. Finally, there are assignments. An assignment allows missions to be related to organizations, and mission-organizations to be related to specific functions. Each intersection record that results from an assignment can have its own local name and description. Thus, there may be generic functions such as planning, execution, and review, that within the

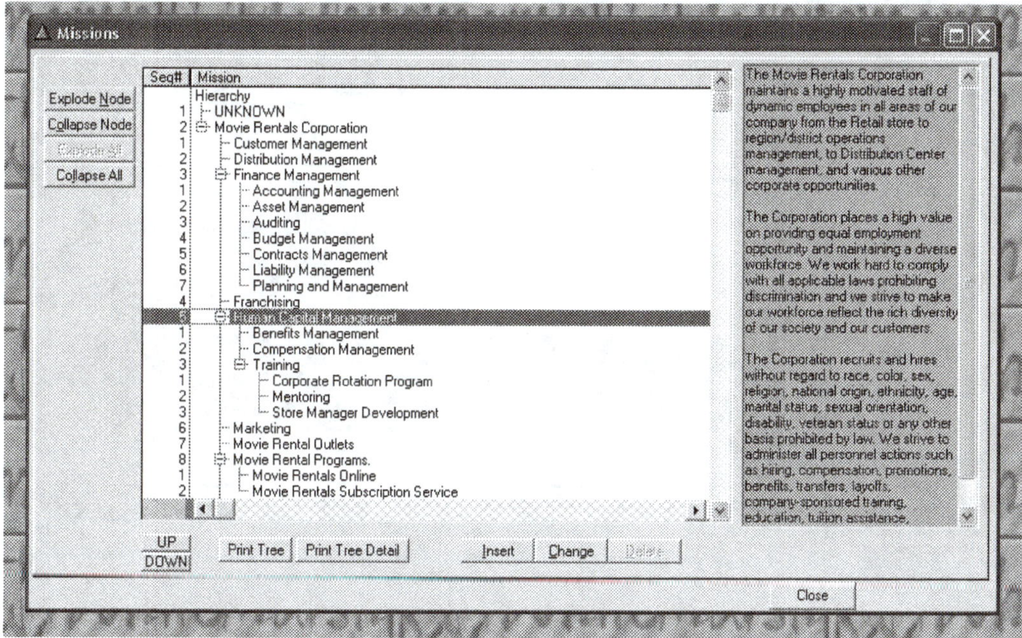

Figure 13. Metabase mission hierarchy screen.

context of a specific mission and organization take on a specialized name and description.

A key component of any Metabase application is reports. The Metabase is just a SQL-engine-based database-centric business information system. Thus, reporting from the Metabase is simple for these two reasons:

- The Metabase system's database schema is explicit and is thus obvious in terms of tables, their columns, and the relationships among all the Metabase tables.

- Report Writers like Crystal Reports can easily be interfaced to produce any number of textual, tabular, and graphical reports. Users with even the cheapest version of Crystal Reports can quickly become expert report developers.

Assignments are created through the process of tagging. Figure 14 presents a tagging window for assigning organizations to particular missions. The upper

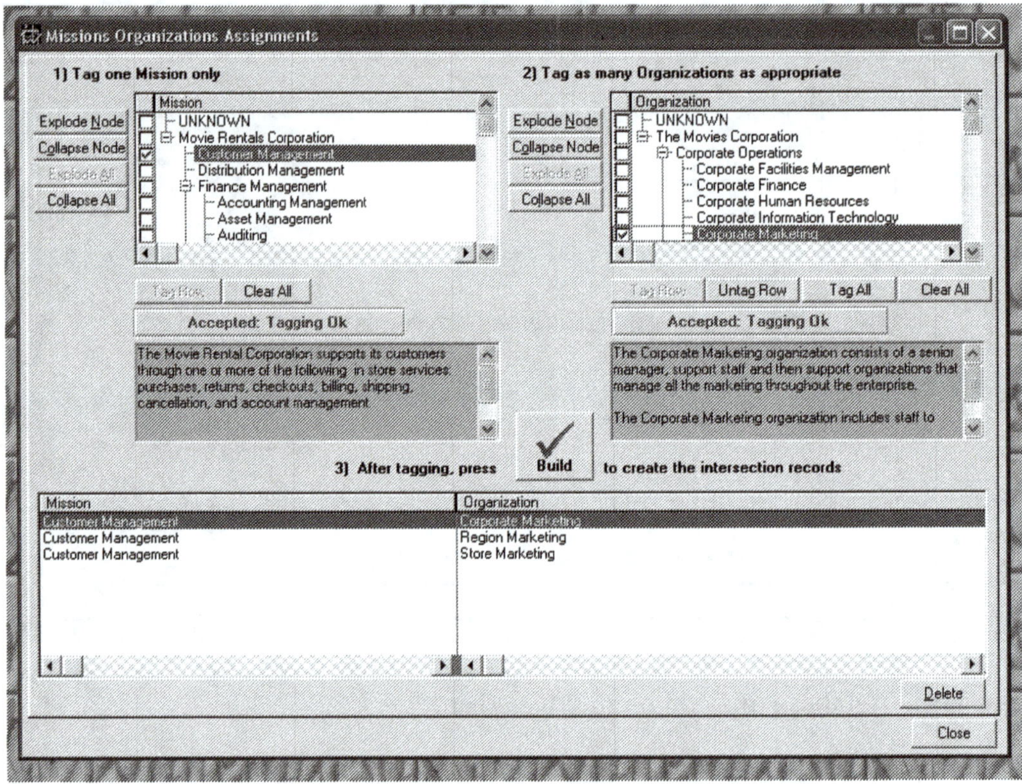

Figure 14. Metabase mission organization assignment.

left browse contains the mission hierarchy. The upper right browse contains the organization hierarchy. The bottom browse contains the result of intersecting one mission with one or more organizations. To create the intersection record, a single mission is tagged. Then, one or more organizations are tagged. Finally the Build button is pressed. The intersection records are then built and displayed in the bottom browse. In this example, the mission, Customer Management, has been allocated to the Corporate Marketing department.

The Metabase data represented by missions, organizations, and functions represent the contextual environment of the enterprise. It is within this environment that databases and business information systems exist.

3.2 Step 2: Design Database

After mission development, the database's design is the natural next step. What becomes the basis for a database's design is its assigned missions. Collectively, the totality of the data represented by the enterprise's databases should match the overall scope of the enterprise's missions.

Data captured through databases via the supporting business information systems become the proof that missions are accomplished. As Knowledge Workers execute policy through the procedures incorporated in the data capture processes of the business information systems, the captured data become the evidence of the policy's execution. In a way then, *Data is executed policy.*

A database's design is the overall schematic of the data inferred from the assigned subset of missions. The policy domain inferred by the missions must square with the domain of the database. If a policy's execution is represented through data, but there is no underlying authorizing mission, something is wrong. A quality database design properly reflects the enterprise policy domain.

The GAO studies from Chapter 1 and Table 5 show that most information technology projects fail not because organizations chose the wrong technology or are not fast or flashy enough, but because they do not engage in the activities that result in proper mission descriptions and policy determinations. These are essential to form the foundations for quality database design.

Database designs, which are the data-based schematics of policy domains, must be accomplished by policy experts, not data processing experts. Essentially, quality data modelers are really policy modelers. Abrogating database design responsibilities to information technology professionals is a major cause of project failures.

A quality database design methodology that is fast, efficient and above all engineered to properly reflect the policy domains of the enterprises, is accomplished through these steps:

- Discover database domains.
- Create entity relationship diagrams from the database domains.
- Determine Database Object Classes.
- Build the Data Element Model.
- Build the Specified Data Model.

- Build the Implemented Data Model.
- Build the Operational Data Model.

If this effort is to be "one-off" without any attention to enterprise applicability and/or metadata reuse, then the only steps that need to be performed are:

- Build entity relationship diagrams.
- Build the Specified Data Model.
- Build the Implemented Data Model.
- Build the Operational Data Model.

However, since this book is all about creating an environment of data interoperability across the enterprise and the ability to re-use metadata to get a very high re-use return on expended efforts, the extra steps enumerated in the first list versus the second list have the following values:

- By discovering database domains from within missions, the database designer is setting the subsequent database steps within one or more mission-centric domains of the enterprise. This causes focus and provides boundaries to a data modeling effort.

- By creating entity-relationship diagrams from the database domains, the database designer is forced to again set the work within the context of the boundaries of the missions As projects occur, fewer new artifacts will be created because they will already have been discovered, stored in the Metabase and are available for reuse.

- By discovering Database Object Classes from within the database domains, the database designer is taking a holistic approach that will ensure complete data structure, process and state transformation specifications rather than just data structure creation.

- By discovering enterprise-wide data elements, the database designer is establishing an inventory of enterprise-wide business facts that will be employed over and over again during the specification of databases throughout the enterprise.

- By creating the database design to accomplish the Specified, Implemented and Operational Data Models in their proper form and sequence, the overall suite of data models will take on enterprise characteristics that enable maximal integration, reuse, and semantic harmonization.

While prototype applications can be built directly from the Implemented Data Model without the detailed precision necessary for a full production database, this book illustrates the use of a full set of artifacts from the first list above to show comprehensive, enterprise-based development. An immediate objection to this approach is that it will take longer and cost more. Not so, because experience has shown that omitting these "extra" steps causes more work later in the project, which always costs more, delivers less, and increases the risk of failure.

Thus, the longer list ultimately represents less work, even on the first project. Remember also that the goal here is to evolve data and process requirements via iterative cycles of designing and prototyping. When this is done, subsequent projects can make use of the enterprise-wide artifacts already created. That increases productivity and quality, and also lowers risk and cost.

Database domains are noun-intensive detailed descriptions of the data implied by the "leaves" of the mission descriptions. Figure 15 presents the database domain for Movie Outlet. Mission hierarchies are in the top browse. Database domains, selected by highlighting a mission are shown in the bottom browse. This was drawn directly from the subordinate mission description for Movie Outlet.

In Figure 15, Movie Rental Outlets is a leaf because it is not further subdivided. If there are three to five levels in the mission hierarchy, then the quantity of database domain levels is few. Conversely, if the mission hierarchy is shallow, there often are multiple database domain levels.

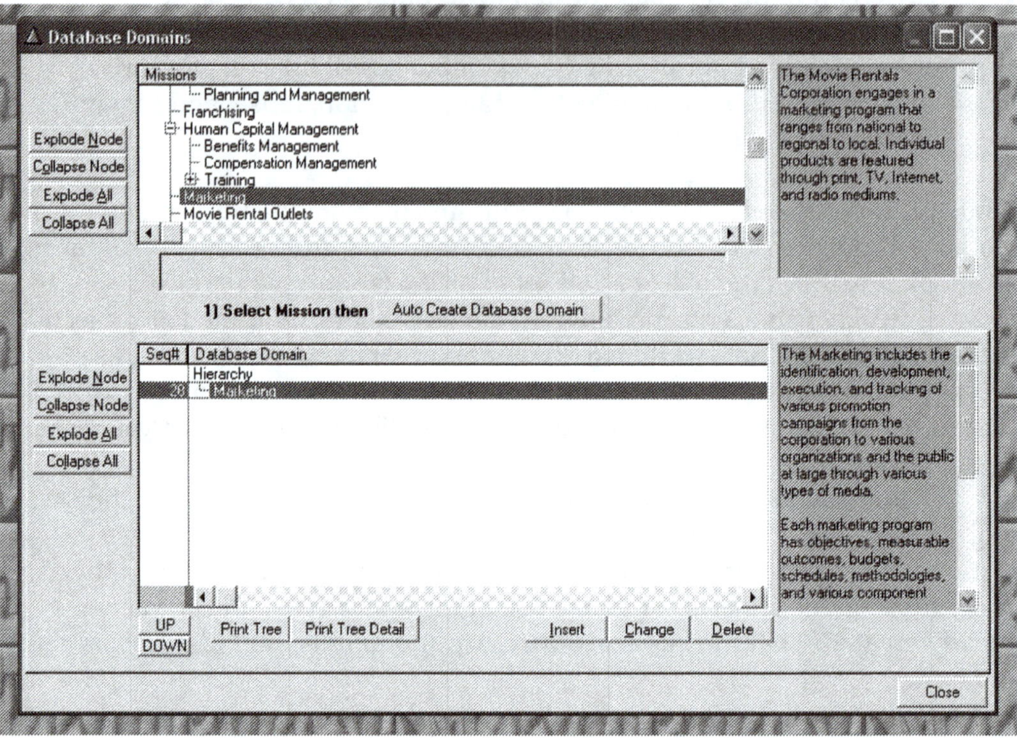

Figure 15. Movie rental outlets database domain.

Once a database domain is created, it is examined to determine the entities represented by the nouns. Figure 16 presents a data model diagram (often also called an entity-relationship diagram) that was created from the Movie Outlet database domain.[14] Note that if this diagram were just an entity-relationship diagram, the attributes not be shown. This data model diagram

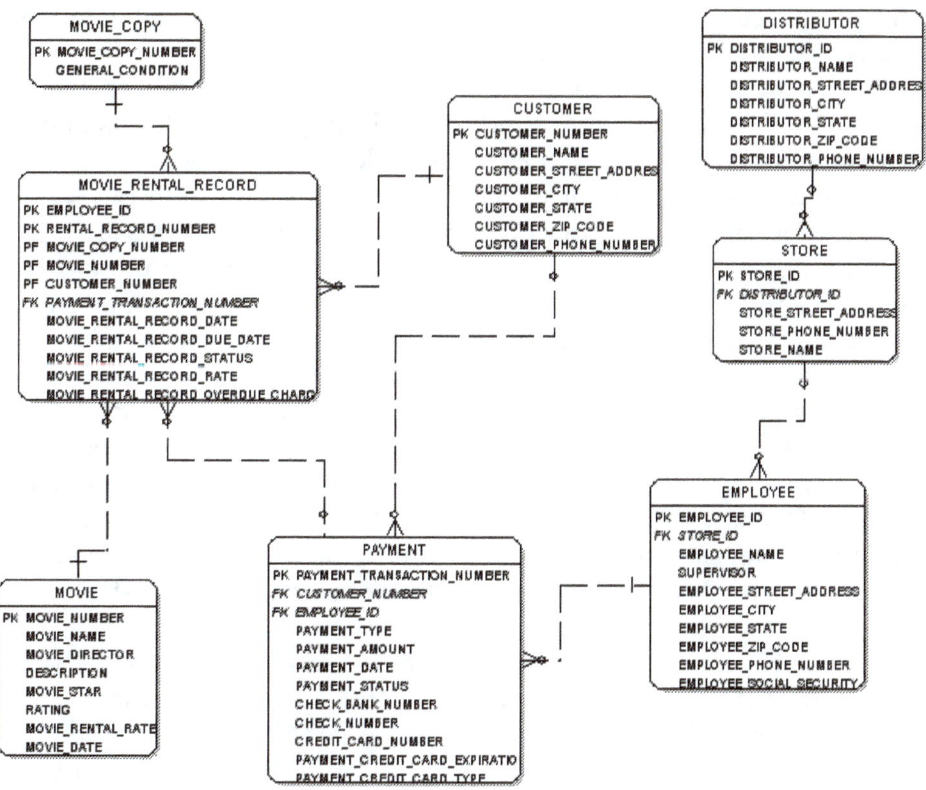

Figure 16. Entity-relationship diagram model for movie rental outlets.

<hr>

[14] This diagram was created by Dezige from DataNamic (www.datanamic.com). The metadata for this model was exported from the Metabase and was imported directly into Dezige. Entity-relationship modeler systems such as Dezige cost less than $250 (USD) and are as powerful as those costing between $5-10,000.

represents just a subset of the data models that would be ultimately represented in a complete database design for movie outlets.

For the purposes of prototyping, database applications built at the database domain level are ideal as they are focused enough to cause the refinement of requirements. Again, it is important to remember that the purpose of the prototype is to assist in the refinement of the combined set of data and process requirements, not the development of the actual database-centric business information system.

If there are 27 mission leaves, there are 27 top-level database domains. A leaf is a node that is not further subdivided. If there are two levels to the database domains with three database domain leafs on each level, there are 81 database domain leaves. That means that there are 81 "mini" entity-relationship diagrams. These "mini" entity- relationship diagrams are quick to create because they are highly partitioned and focused. It is common to require only 10 to 15 minutes to create each of these database domain leaf entity relationship diagrams. 81 entity-relationship diagrams thus takeS less than four staff days.

Entities commonly repeat across database domains and entity relationship diagrams. That indicates shared data. Any given entity is likely to repeat on average, four times. Thus, if all the entity relationship diagrams have about 2800 entities, there are probably only about 700 unique entities. Given that the database domains are placed into the Metabase and the entities are also stored in the Metabase, the redundancy becomes immediately apparent.

Whenever an entity is discovered with the same name, it must be examined to determine if it really is the same. If not, the staff member who entered the first entity must be consulted to resolve the differences. They either must make two entities, or to modify the definition of the existing entity. For example, Student takes Courses. University offers Courses. Is Courses the same entity for both the student and the university? That is, the same definition, granularity, precision, and temporal characteristics? If yes, then it's the same entity. Otherwise, like in this case, the entities are different and one or both have to be renamed and more precisely defined.

Once the entities are identified, they are entered into the Metabase. Figure 17 shows the meta-entity model of the Metabase that supports the entry and maintenance of the Metabase's Specified Data Model. Since this is a data model of a Metabase, the entities of this class of data model are commonly called meta-entities. The attributes in meta-models are often called

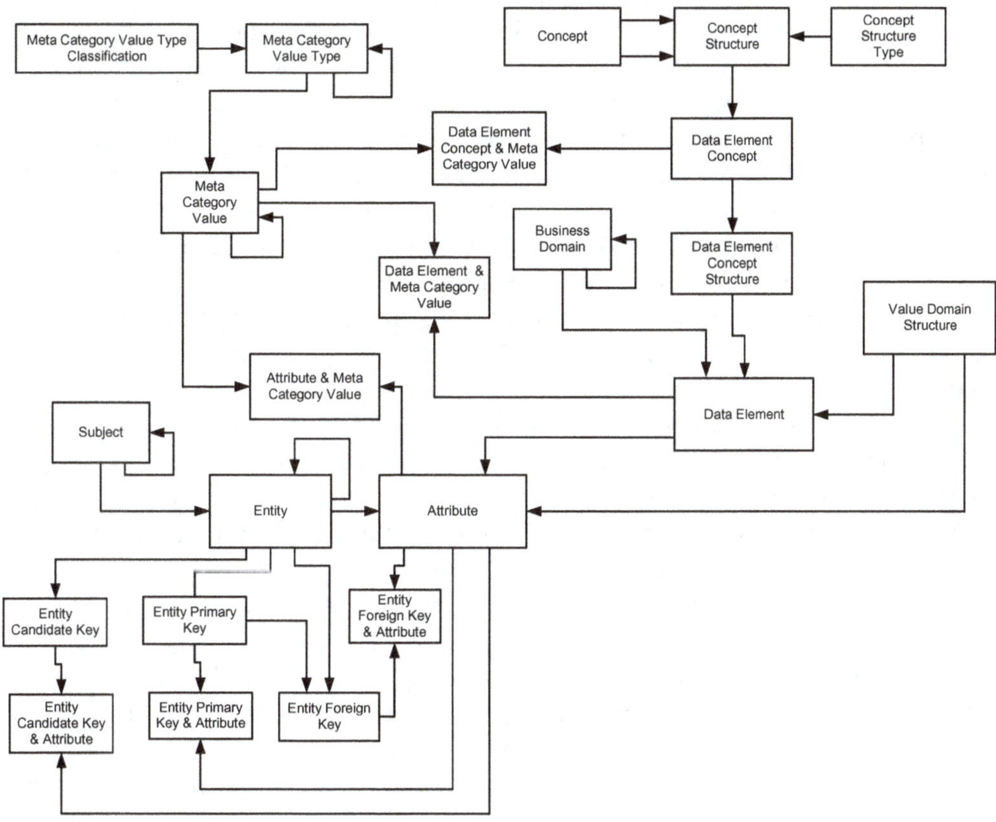

Figure 17. Meta model for the specified data model.

meta-attributes. In reality, the constructs of this data model is no different than what is shown in Figure 16 except that it's one level of abstraction higher.

Each entity from Figure 16 becomes a row of data (i.e., metadata) in the meta-entity, Entity, that is shown in Figure 17. Similarly, each attribute from each entity in Figure 16 becomes a row of data in the meta-entity, Attribute, that is shown in Figure 17.

Each relationship shown in Figure 16 becomes a set of rows of data within the meta entity, Entity-Foreign Key, and Entity-Foreign-Key-Attribute shown in Figure 17.

Each primary key from Figure 16 becomes a set of rows of data within the primary key and primary key attribute meta-entities shown in Figure 17.

The set of entities from Figure 16, for example, payment, employee, and movie along with their attributes and relationships form an entity-relationship model. The data represented on the Figure 16 entity-relationship model is metadata, and metadata is what is stored in a Metabase. In contrast, a meta-entity model is a level of abstraction above an entity-relationship model. In meta models, the entities are, as shown in Figure 17, Entity, Attribute, Relationship (e.g., Primary Key, and Foreign Key).

The non-redundant set of entities (i.e., movie, employee, and payment) from Figure 16 are stored in the repository and are grouped underneath specific Subjects.

Subject areas can be hierarchical and are slightly different from database domains as database domains are more closely related to applications which necessarily involve data from multiple subject areas. Figure 18 also shows the meta entities for data elements[15] which, in turn, act as semantic templates for attributes of entities. Data elements as this term is defined in the ISO Standard 11179, Data Element metadata, are shown as semantic templates for columns of tables.

Figure 18 shows that data elements are grouped into business domains, which also may be hierarchical. Data elements are most often discovered during the process of database design.

A data element's semantics are inherited by the attributes of an entity. For example, if there was a data element, Area Code, that would be "301" for part of Maryland, that data element's semantics would include its name, definition, abbreviations, and data type. If there were attributes such as StudentTelephoneNumberAreaCode, or CustomerHomeOfficeAreaCode, or CellPhoneNumberAreaCode, key semantics from the source data element, Area Code would be automatically inherited. That enables the semantics of data elements to be employed multiple times across a set of entities. As shown in this particular example, a data element's name may be different from its deployed reprsentation, as an attribute, within an entity. That is because a data element is "generalized" within a business domain's context as opposed to being within an entity's context. There is much more to data elements than

---

[15]. The actual data model for Data Elements is much more complex than what is shown in Figure 18. For a complete description, consult the Metabase user guide for Data Elements.

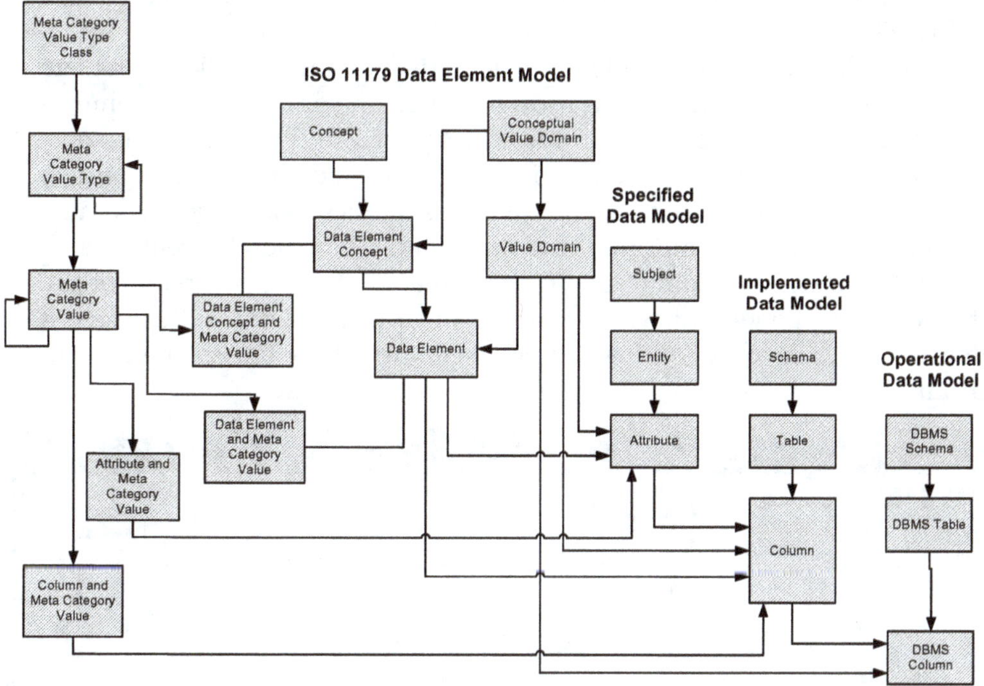

Figure 18. Meta-model for the data elements through to DBMS columns.

is presented in this book. Readers are encouraged to obtain additional material from the Whitemarsh website.

Entities are interrelated through primary and foreign keys. It is bad practice to have surrogate keys as substitutes for the naturally existing data attributes as that would defeat one of the main purposes of the effort -- requirements iteration. With natural primary keys, any time an attribute is added or deleted that fundamentally changes granularity, surrogate keys hide that effect. In this situation, hiding is not good as it masks the true business nature of the entity.

Within the Metabase, attributes within entities are created through tagging. Figure 19 presents the tagging window that is activated through the Metabase's Specified Data Model's Create Attribute menu option. First, an entity is tagged in the middle left browse. Then, one or more data elements are tagged in the middle right browse. Finally the Build button is pressed. Once pressed, the newly created attributes are created and appear in the bottom browse. When this happens, all the semantics associated with the tagged data element are automatically inherited by the newly created attribute. Two steps remain to finalize the created attributes. First, in addition to the Metabase generated attribute name, an additional name, the user-set name, can be created. Second, additional semantics may be assigned to the attribute.

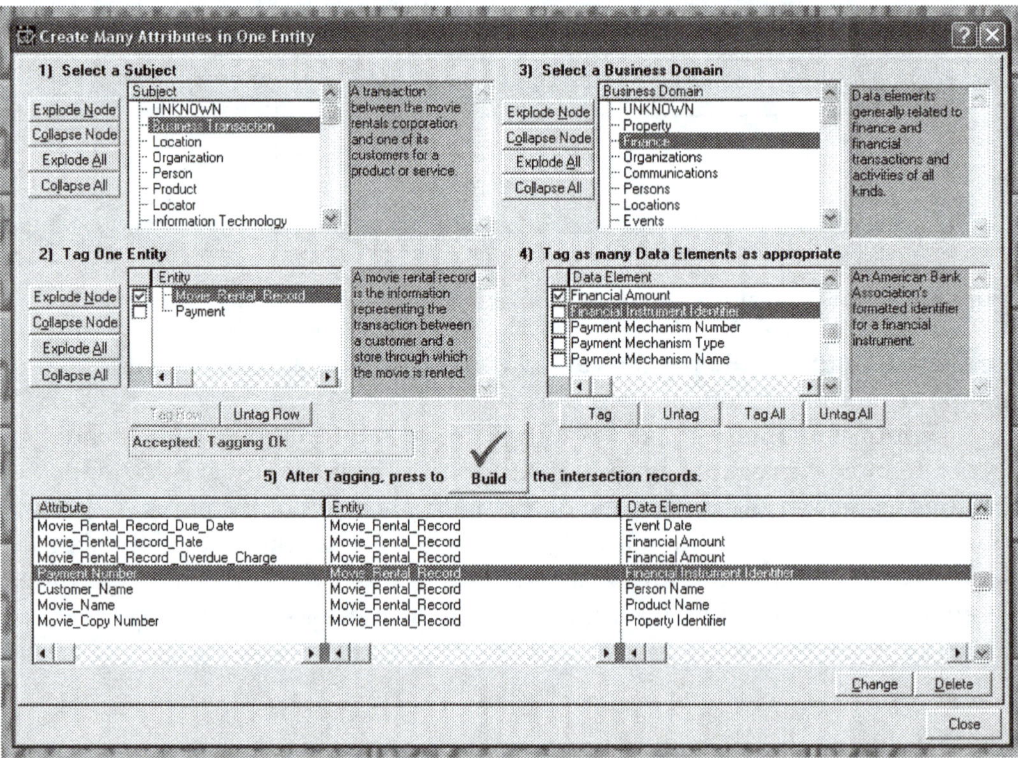

Figure 19. Tagging window for creating attributes.

In this particular example, the various Movie Outlet entities have been grouped into subjects. In this case it's Business Transaction. The entity, Movie Rental Record, contains a collection of attributes as shown in the bottom browse of Figure 19. To create an attribute, the subject is selected and the entity is tagged, then a business domain is selected, and finally, a data element is tagged. The Build button is then pressed and the attribute is created. In this particular example, this was done twice as the data element, Financial Amount, was used to create the semantics for the two attributes: Movie Rental Record Overdue Charge, and Movie Rental Record Rate.

When, for example, a telephone number data element is associated multiple times within an entity, the appearance of duplicate attributes results.

One may be for the home phone, another for the office, a third for a cellular, and a final one for a fax machine. In each case, the only real difference is the localized name and use of the telephone data element. In this case, the only change needed is the modification of the attributes' local name.

Figure 20 shows the window for modifying the metadata associated with an entity's attribute. The attribute, Movie Rental Record Due Date, is highlighted and the Change button is pressed. The change window is then presented as shown in Figure 21. The window shows the data element source, the containing entity, the currently assigned value domain, its common business name, abbreviations, and the Metabase's manufactured name and the user's supplied name. Finally the window shows the local definition.

The next and final step in finalizing attributes is the creation of any additional semantics. When additional semantics are added to an existing attribute, they represent a subset of those already allocated to the data element. If a data element's semantics include, for example, the geographic semantic, North America, then the attribute's semantics, if it included the geographic semantic must be something like "United States," or "Canada," or something that represents a geographic subset to North America. Figure 22 presents the tagging window for allocating semantics to an attribute. First the attribute is tagged, then one or more semantics are tagged. When the Build button is pressed, the intersection records that relate the attribute to the selected semantics are created. Before each one is created, the associated semantics are checked. If any allocated semantic is not a subset semantic, an error message is presented and the intersection record is not built.

In this allocation of semantics, the accuracy semantic, "Final," was added to the attribute, Movie Rental Record Overdue Charge. So too was the semantic, "Price," which exists within the domain, "money." If the attribute is

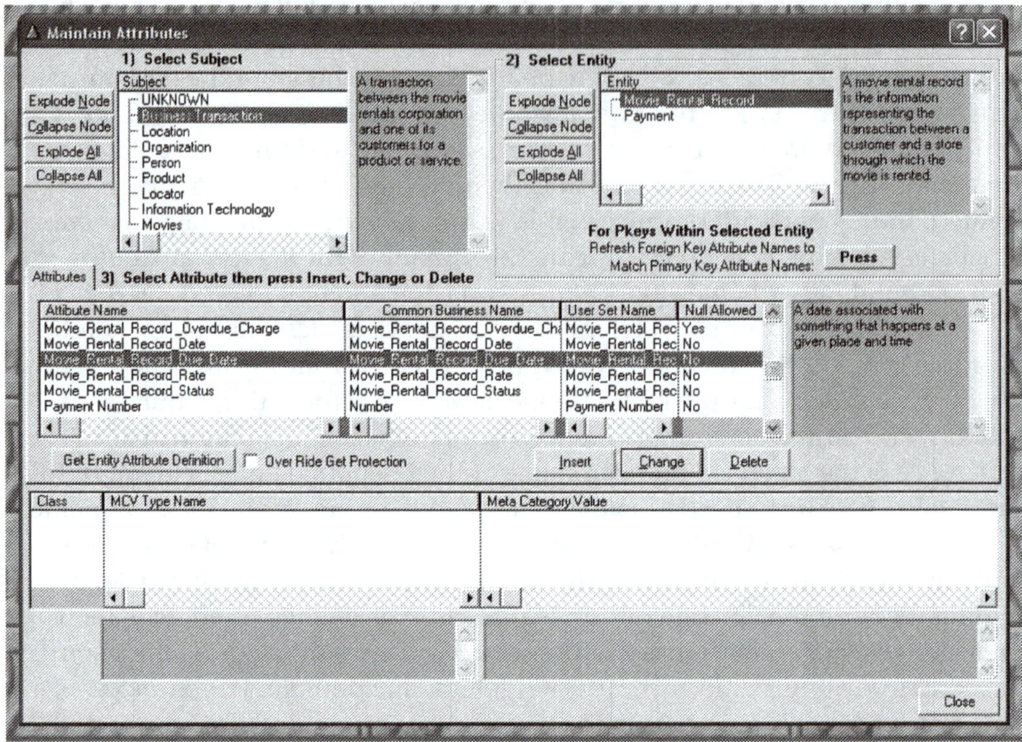

Figure 20. Changing an attribute.

updated again via Figure 21, and the "Reset" button on that window is pressed, the two additional semantics are automatically added to the attribute's name. A complete description of how this is accomplished is in the Metabase user guide, Specified Data Model, which is available from the Whitemarsh website.

If the set of semantics associated with a data element is the complete and necessary set for the attribute, then no additional attribute semantics need to be associated. In fact, efforts to assign exactly the same semantic will be rejected as the semantic will not be seen as a subordinate semantic. In actuality, the attribute's name is just one of the attribute's semantics. The full set of semantics for the attribute are first, those associated with the data element, plus those which represent further refinements or restrictions that are directly assigned to the attribute.

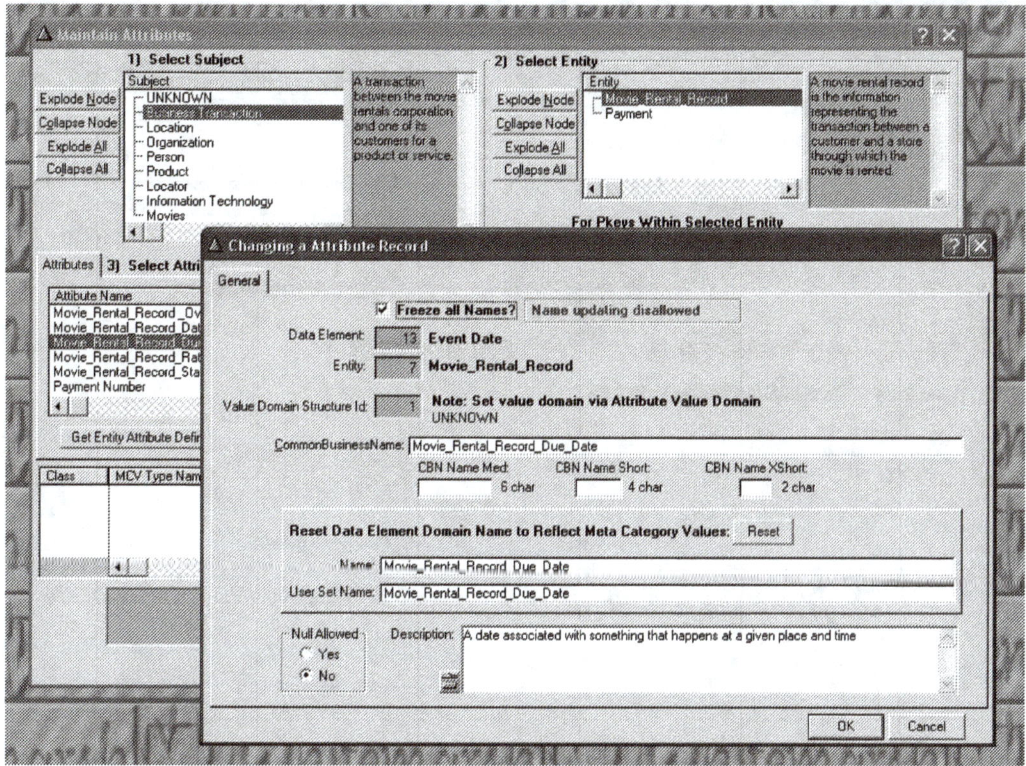

Figure 21. Update screen for changing an attribute.

A review of the metadata model in Figure 17 shows that the semantics associated with an attribute are organized from Concept to Data Element Concept to Data Element to Attribute. Each is to be a semantic subset of the previous. Similarly, the value domains for each also must represent a set of nested value domains. These hierarchies are described in Whitemarsh materials dealing with data modeling and with the data modeling module of the Metabase.

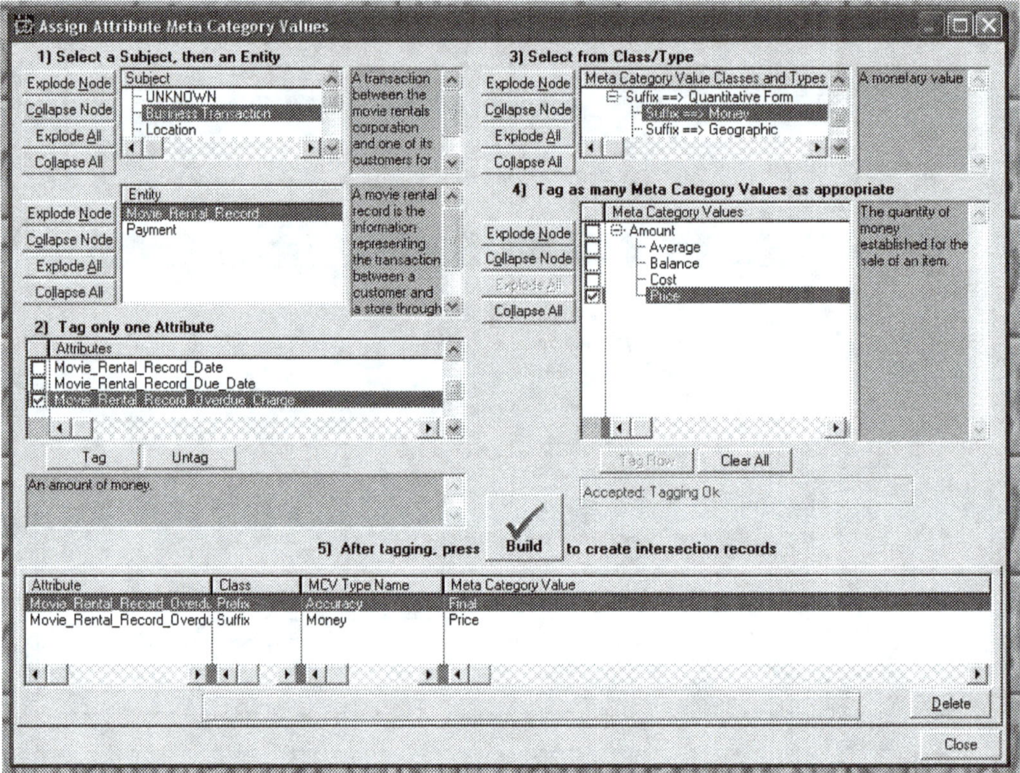

Figure 22. Adding semantics to an attribute.

The benefits derived from these hierarchies include:

- Saving human effort in the creation of attributes within the Specified Data Model, columns within the Implemented Data Model, and DBMS columns within the Operational Data Model.

- Enabling enterprise-wide semantics across databases of different data architecture classes.

- Minimizing unintended semantic errors and maximizing data standardization quality.

In support of these hierarchies, Figure 23 presents the five different data model generalization levels within the Metabase. They are:

- Data Elements.
- Specified Data Model.
- Implemented Data Model.
- Operational Data Model.
- View Data Model.

The data models exist in an implicit hierarchy. First there are the semantic hierarchies and context independent business fact templates that form data elements. Second, there are the functional Specified Data Models, that is, data models of concepts that serve as templates, which inherit data element semantics for the attributes of the entities. Third, there are the Implemented

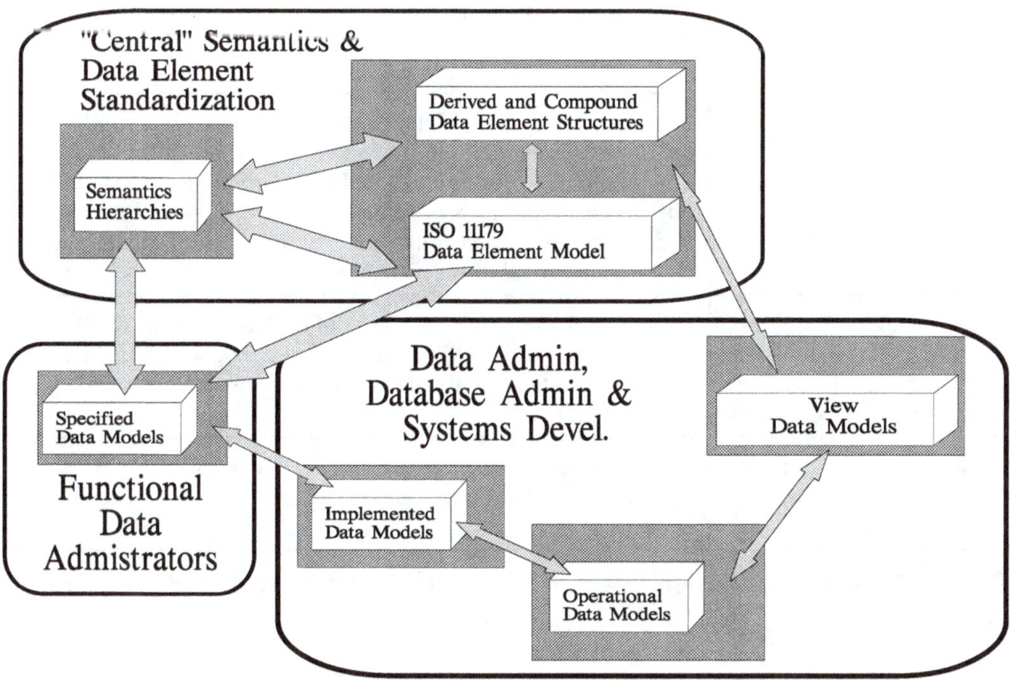

Figure 23. Metadata models for data modeling.

Data Models that inherit semantics from one or more Specified Data Models. Fourth, there are the Operational Data Models that inherit their semantics from one or more Implemented Data Models. Finally, there are the View Data Models that convey both the semantics and data values represented by the Operational Data Model from the databases to the business information system programs. Mappings are preserved among all these models so that where-used and version reports can be produced. A brief definition of each data model class is provided in Table 16.

Data Model Type	Brief Description
Data Elements	Data elements are semantic templates for attributes and columns. Included are semantic hierarchies that enable data standardization across the enterprise
Specified	Specified Data Models consist of subject areas, entities and attributes that are technology independent. Entities are interconnected by primary and foreign keys. These are data models of concepts.
Implemented	Implemented Data Models consist of schemas, tables and columns that are technology dependent but are DBMS independent. For example, ANSI SQL, or Spread sheets, etc., but not Oracle or Sybase. Tables are interconnected by primary and foreign keys. Columns and attributes are interrelated by many-to-many relationships.
Operational	Operational Data Models consist of DBMS Schemas, DBMS tables, DBMS and DBMS columns that are both vendor and location specific. DBMS tables are interconnected by primary and foreign keys.
View	View models are SQL views that connect specific DBMS columns from operational databases to business information systems .

Table 16. Names and brief descriptions of the data model classes supported by the Metabase.

The Metabase supports the importing of existing SQL schemas directly into the Operational Data Models so that enterprise-wide semantics can be gradually achieved. Enterprise-wide semantics are achieved if the participating organizations ensure that their Operational Data Models are mapped to common Implemented Data Models. It is the common Implemented Data Model that represents the enterprise-wide semantics across databases.

The relationship between the Implemented Data Model and the Operational Data Model, as supported by the Metabase, is many-to-many. While it is commonly thought that a given Implemented Data Model maps only to one or more Operational Data Models, reality informs otherwise. The data warehouse data architecture is a case in point. A data warehouse's data commonly comes from multiple databases. Hence, if there is an Operational Data Model for the data warehouse, there must be multiple Implemented Data Models from which it is mapped. In short, common practice supports one-to-many, and reality additionally supports many-to-one. Hence, many-to-many.

Data models appropriate to be imported into the Operational Data Model are those bound to a particular DBMS and that represent the data models of one or more operational business information systems. If other data modeling efforts have occurred in the enterprise, for example, a Specified Data Model effort, that is, a model of concepts, or an Implemented Data Model, that is a logical data model that is not bound to any particular DBMS, these models can be directly imported into the Metabase's Specified and Implemented data models.

Data elements exist as semantic templates for attributes in the Specified Data Model and also for columns in the Implemented Data Model. This is to allow a column to represent a semantic subset of an attribute. If there already is a cache of enterprise-wide data elements, the Metabase can import these too.

Data elements may also be component parts of derived and compound data elements. The semantics for data elements are drawn from the semantics of data element concepts and value domains. Data element concepts are drawn from concepts and conceptual value domains. Value domains are drawn from conceptual value domains. Data elements act as semantic templates for both attributes and columns because a column may have a slightly different set of semantics than the attribute from which is it is drawn.

Included in the semantics associated with data elements, attributes, columns, and DBMS columns are value domains. These assigned value domains are arranged hierarchically so there is an increasing specificity or narrowing of the assigned value domains starting with the data element concept all the way down to the DBMS column. If the value domains are fully known at the data element concept level, assigning at that level is all that is necessary because the Metabase supports automatic inheritance.

Figure 23 also shows the distribution of data modeling work. This enables a comprehensive and enterprise-wide effort to standardize data semantics. It is clearly shown in Figure 23 that the ISO 11179 Data Element Model and the Specified Data Models are the province of data administration and functional data administrators. This fits squarely with the concept of this book for the iterative creation of requirements through prototyping.

The next step in the creation of a database design is the creation of the Implemented Data Model. Created by this time are the Data Elements and the Specified Data Model. The set of entities within the Specified Data Model can exist within one or more subjects. Specified data models are data models of concepts set within subjects, not data models of databases. Since database data models seldom embrace just one subject, an Implemented Data Model database almost always draws from entities within multiple subjects.

To create an Implemented Data Model, that is, to create a single schema and a collection of schema-bound tables, start the Metabase module, Implemented Data Model. Then, employ the Metabase process, Import Subject-Entity Set, if all the entities within a subject are needed for a portion of the Implemented Data Model. If only a subset of a subject's entities is needed, or if just a few of an entity's attributes are needed, other subset import processes can be invoked. If, as is normally the case, multiple subject-based entity sets are needed, then import these subject-entity sets one after another.

After importing, add new relationships between the imported entities, which are now tables, as may be appropriate. At this point, not only will an Implemented Data Model schema exist but relationships between these newly created tables and their source entities will exist in the form of relationships between the attributes of the entities and the columns of tables.

The Metabase allows entities and attributes from subjects to be imported multiple times and given different local names. An example of this is an attribute cluster for a person's name. A name might consist of: title, first name, middle initial, last name and other name parts. If a person's name is to appear multiple times in an Implemented Data Model, say for customer, contract representative, officer, and the like, these would all be different and multiple uses of the same person-name data model template. Again, all this supports the define-once, use many-times approach.

The last step in the database design process is to create the Operational Data Model. For prototypes, this is just a clone of the Implemented Data

Model. So, activate the Metabase's Operational Data Model module and import the entire Implemented Data Model schema. It is from the foundation of the Operational Data Model that the prototype is generated. These steps are not shown here as they are illustrated in the Metabase user guides.

The resultant database design within the process of requirements iteration is a set of tables, columns, and relationships are fed to a business information system generator. Each table should contain only the minimum essential set of columns to support the demonstration of the prototype. Every table should have one last column of the form, *Other <table name> Columns.* This provides the forum for soliciting the names of attributes that may be missing.

While absolute and total adherence to all the data modeling guidelines above ultimately improves productivity and quality, lowers risk and saves money, such absolute and total efforts performed during requirements iteration may be counterproductive. It is important to remember that the goal is to create a set of entities and the minimum essential attributes to proceed to the prototype generation step. That is why, for example, every table should only have those columns necessary to convey its real and essential purpose, not its absolutely detailed and complete purpose.

Figure 24 presents nested Metabase browse lists that contain the DBMS schema, DBMS tables, DBMS columns, and relationships (not shown). Collectively, these browse represent the data model that forms the basis for the prototyped business information system. This model is at the Operational Data Model level having been created from tables and columns at the Implemented Data Model level, which, in turn, was created from entities, attributes and relationships at the Specified Data Model level.

3.3 Step 3: Generate Prototype

Business information system generators, a class of computer software, take in database design specifications and produce working business information software systems. Generators have been growing in sophistication and capability over the past 20 years. Business information system generator environments, such as Clarion (www.SoftVelocity.com) produce first-cut working business information systems from database designs in one-hour or less.

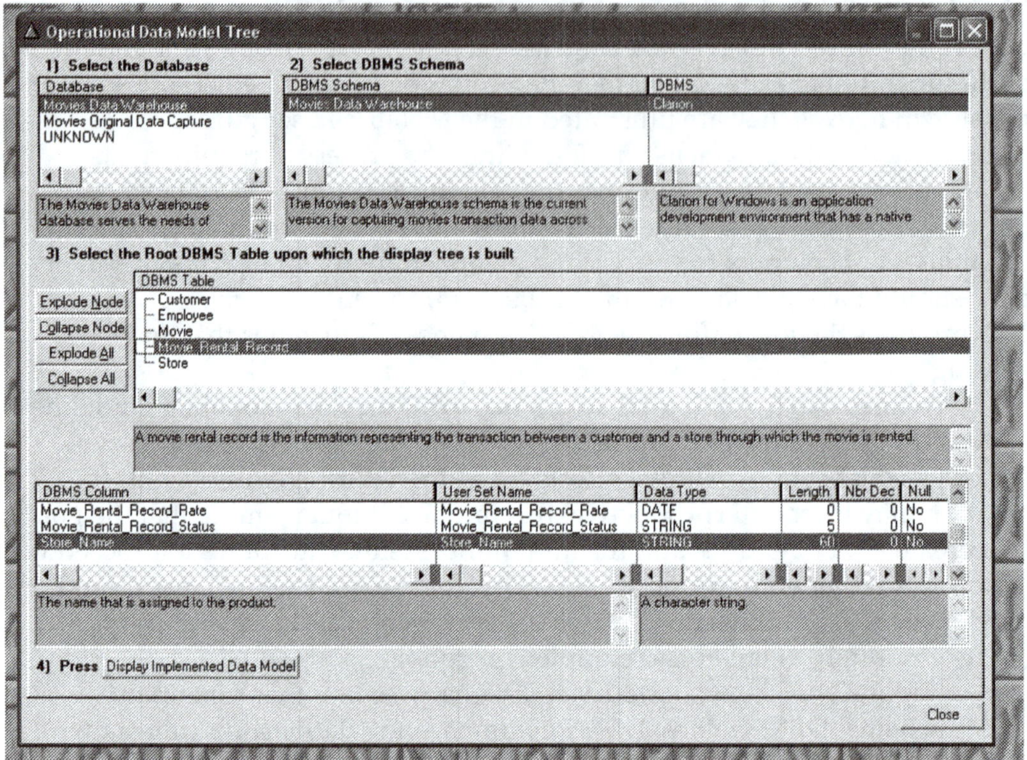

Figure 24. DBMS schema, DBMS tables, DBMS columns, and relationships.

In contrast, hand-coded business information systems take upwards to two staff weeks per module. Thus, for a 50-table database that requires 150 modules, a hand-coded first-cut working business information system requires about 300 staff weeks, or six staff years. As a prototype, that's unacceptable. The equivalent business information system in Clarion takes less than one staff week. For a prototype that's acceptable.

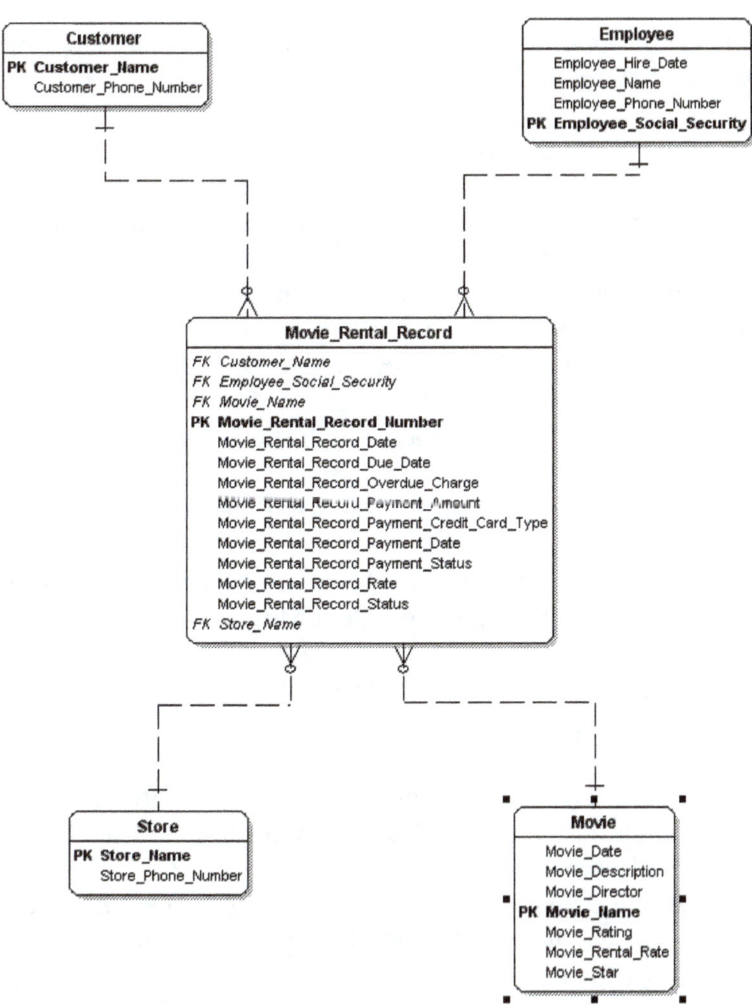

Figure 25. Movies data warehouse table relationship diagram.

The general two-step process for code generation with Clarion is:

- Create Clarion tables, columns, and relationships from existing tables, columns, and relationships.

- Generate the business information system.

Figure 25 presents a simple five table database used to illustrate the code generation process. In this small application, the Movie, Store, Customer, and Employee tables are "parents" to the Movie Rental Record table.

This very simple store-based data warehouse was created from the existing Movies metadata already in the Specified Data Model of the Metabase. The design creation process for the Movies data warehouse took about 20 minutes. The process consisted of the following steps:

- Create the movies schema within the Implemented Data Model.

- Import the Movie, Customer, Employee, Store, and Movie Rental Record entities from the Specified Data Model.

- Create relationships between Movie, Customer, Employee, Store, and the Movie Rental Record.

The value of using the Metabase for these actions is illustrated in Figure 26. It shows the reuse of metadata from the Data Element through the Operational Data Models.

In Figure 26, the data element, Person Name is reused in a number of different forms such as Customer Name in the Specified Data Model. Customer name is used three different times in the Implemented Data Model. One time is for one schema and the other two times is within different tables in a second schema. The selected Implemented Data Model column is employed twice in the Operational Data Model. This is another example of define-once, use many times.

Figure 27 presents the paradigm for application generation that exits with Clarion. On the left side are the abstraction levels employed in the Metabase. The application specification is divided into a data model and a process model. As appropriate they are merged into a Database Object

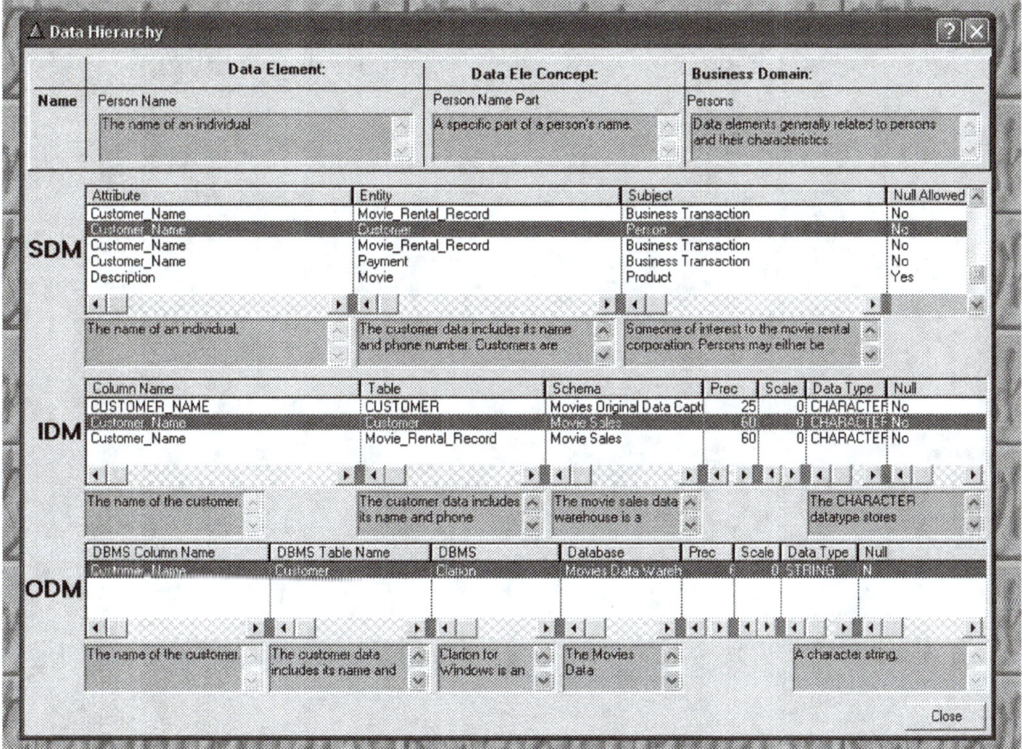

Figure 26. Reuse of metadata across data element through operational data models.

abstraction. These are bound to a DBMS and are imported into the business information system generator. On the right side of the figure are the various levels of abstraction of the Clarion business information system generator environment. In Clarion, there are three distinct types. In this figure, the techniques, technology, and look & feel types are shown. The look and feel template types provide facilities for windows, buttons and icons of various shapes and sizes.

The technique abstractions provide browses, menus, forms, and, as shown in the Metabase, the ability to do hierarchies, bills-of-materials (i.e., networks), tagging, column-header-based sorting, Internet access, multiple-database linking and federation, email, and the like.

Finally, the technology abstractions provide for ability to actually generate code, compile, link edit, and the other critical features that enable

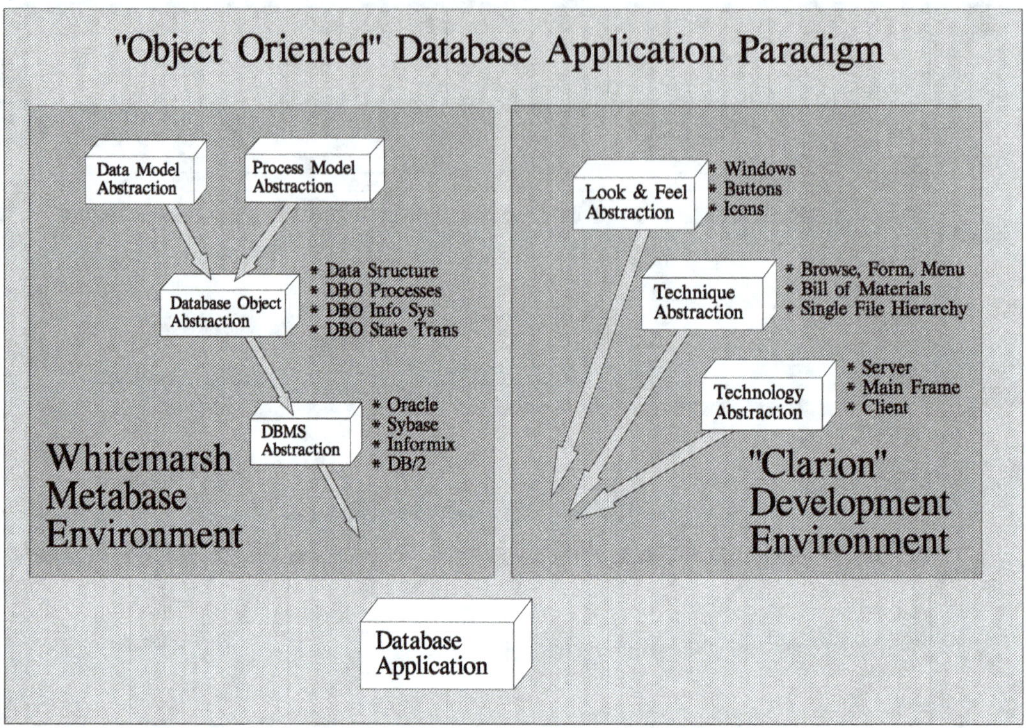

Figure 27. Object oriented application generation paradigm.

proper business information system construction and execution. Within each of the Clarion abstraction levels, there are multiple subordinate levels. Selections from each are combined with the application metadata to complete the input for the generation process.

Step 3.1: Create Clarion Dictionary

Figure 28 presents the result of defining tables, columns, and relationships within Clarion. These Clarion-based data model artifacts were created by a Metabase function that creates Clarion DDL, which, in turn, is imported into Clarion.

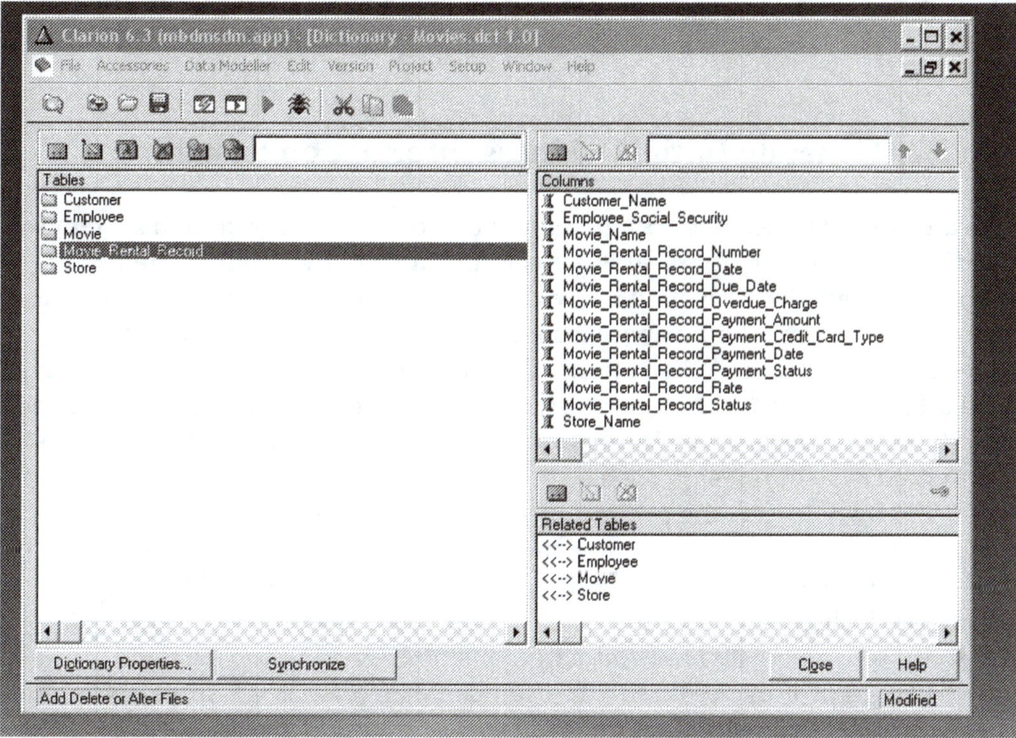

Figure 28. Movies data warehouse of tables, columns and relationships.

If Clarion is not being used as the business information system generator, just export the data model as SQL DDL and import it into a different business information system generator.

The tables are listed on the left side. The columns for the selected table are on the right side top browse. The relationships between the Movie Rental Record and the other tables are shows on the right side, bottom browse. In this example, the "many" table, Movie Rental Record, is the one highlighted in the left browse. The "one" tables are Customer, Employee, Movie, and Store in the related table browse. The "<<" and the ">" icons in the Related Table indicate the "many" and the "one" tables, respectively.

Relationships in Clarion are either one-to-one, or one-to-many. When a one-to-one relationship is specified, the set of columns that comprise the foreign key in the "many" table must be given the Unique value attribute so that duplicate values are automatically prohibited by Clarion (or the SQL backend DBMS).

Step 3.2: Generate Initial Business Information System

The value of the first-cut working version of a business information system is that it provides a first "look" at what is inferred from the "requirements." If each subsequent "look" is only a few days away, then, prior to committing to the first real version of a business information system, a prototype can proceed through five to 15 iterations. The value is dramatic. First, because it is a real attack on the cost of initial business information system production, and second, because there is an elimination of many causes of the major business information system revision cycles.

Figure 3 depicts the process of specification evolution through prototyping. The scale, also in time, but now in weeks, is greatly reduced from that displayed in Figure 2 because of business information system generation. If the resultant prototype is considered acceptable, it is turned over to those who create the production business information system..

Once a prototype is created, it can be taken on a "road-show" wherein critical audiences can see what the business information system actually does. If the "road show"appearances are a day or so apart then minor revisions to the business information system can be put in place and tested with the next audience.

The goal of the prototyping activities is the finalization of business information system requirements. The result of these activities is not only a valid business information system specification, it is also a complete set of metadata that can be employed during implementation and then subsequently evolved during the business information system life cycle. Prototyping also enables the creation of test data used for training, documentation, implemented business information system test cases, and important conformance tests.

There is a great temptation to turn the final iteration of a prototype into a production class business information system and be done with it. There is, however, much more to a production class business information system than just a working set of computer programs. For example, there is the need for multiple types and sizes of hardware, operating systems, database management systems, and so on from different vendors. There are also different approaches to business information system implementation depending on whether the business information systems are to be implemented on a network of micros and servers, or mainframes with multiple LANS, servers, client machines, or through the Internet. Finally there is also the need for formal and informal training, technical support, documentation, and user group meetings.

All these activities are proper for organizations that specialize in the development, installation, maintenance and support of business information systems as their primary business activity rather than a sideline activity as would be in a requirements development organization. While a requirements development organization possesses the core sets of knowledge to specify the essential sets of functions, processes, database designs, training modules, procedures, and the like, the mode of delivery is clearly best reserved for specialized information technology organizations.

For all these reasons, the ultimate purpose of the first four activities (mission development, database design, prototype generation and specification evolution) is to create a completely valid specification of the computer business information system's functionality. The specification will be valid because it will have been generated, iterated, and refined across a wide spectrum of carefully chosen users.

The immediate benefit to this approach is that when business information system organizations actually implement the specification, the costly and time-consuming process of iterating to a correct set of functionality will have already been accomplished.

The actual process of application generation in Clarion consists of:

- Naming the application and identifying the dictionary.
- Indicating the extent of the generation process.
- Indicating the type of look and feel.
- Indicating if existing procedures are to be overwritten.

Figure 29 presents the window that starts the application generation process. In this window, the name of the application is provided (e.g., Movie.app), the associated dictionary that is to guide the application generation (e.g., Movie.dct), the type of result, that is, an executable, the class of templates that are to be employed (e.g., ABC), and finally whether the application wizard is to be employed to automatically generate the procedures. Once this information is entered and the OK button is pressed, the next window, Figure 30 is presented.

Figure 30 and a collection of subsequent windows (not provided as figures), provide various options for window themes, report layouts, subset or all tables in the dictionary, types of controls (e.g., buttons or "VCR" controls), and other customizations. Once these options are either selected and/or defaulted, the application tree generation process starts. Once these options are processed, and the Finish button is pressed, the window in Figure 31, which presents the generated application tree structure is presented.

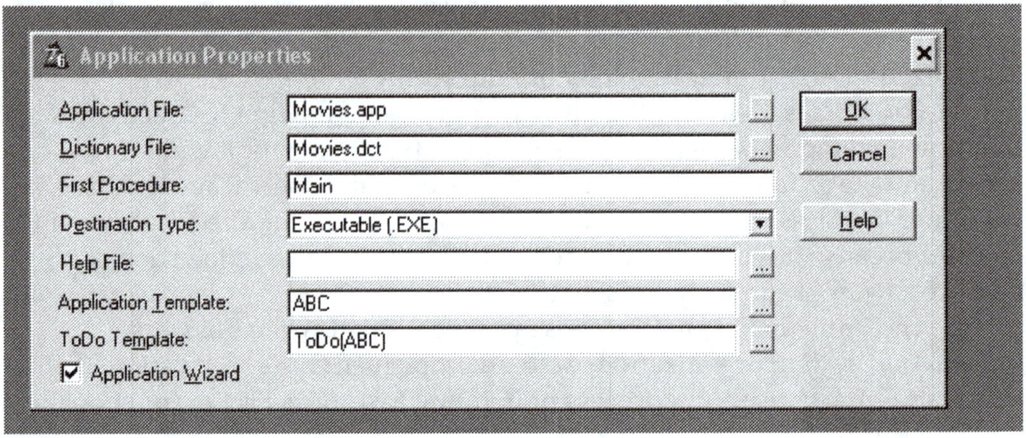

Figure 29. Creating a new application generation.

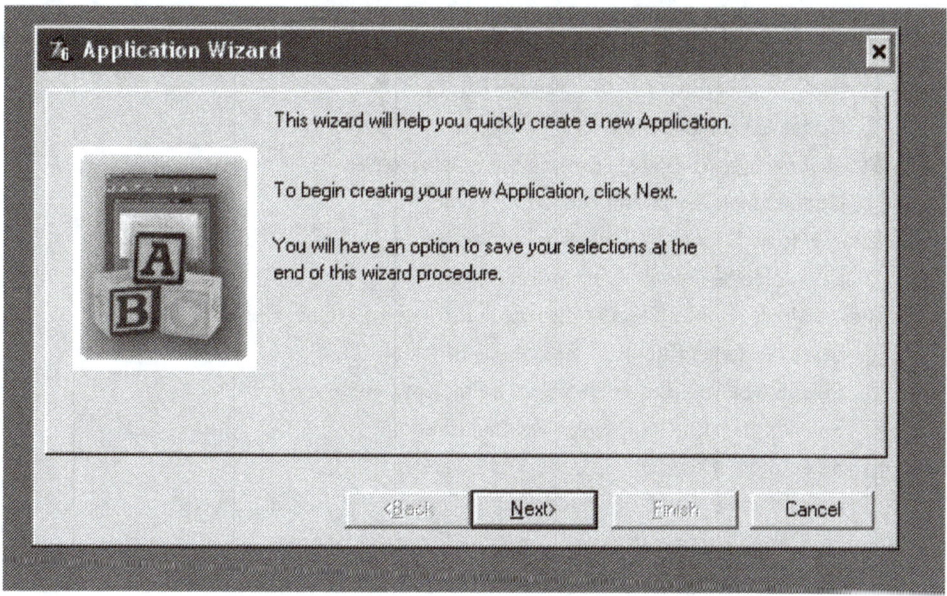

Figure 30. Start process for detailing options for application generation.

Figure 31 shows the application as a hierarchical tree that starts from the "main" frame. There are four Browse modules, and within each there may be some "select" modules. There also may be one or more "update" modules. Organizations view databases through a certain preferred style of work. In this case, the style of work is to populate the Employee, Customer, Movies, and Store tables, and then the Movie Rental Record table.

Since this auto-generated application is really a retail data warehouse (or a data mart), the way data would actually enter this database would be through another business information system that would have extracted data from the "store" business information systems that are illustrated by inference in Figure 16, and load the extracted data through a batch process.

Because of the absolute neutrality that a database design brings to code generation process, a unique situation arises: Too many bug-free modules. At the bottom of the tree there is a listing of the auto-generated reports. The names are truncated so that the figure can be readable. The report names are naturally quite long.

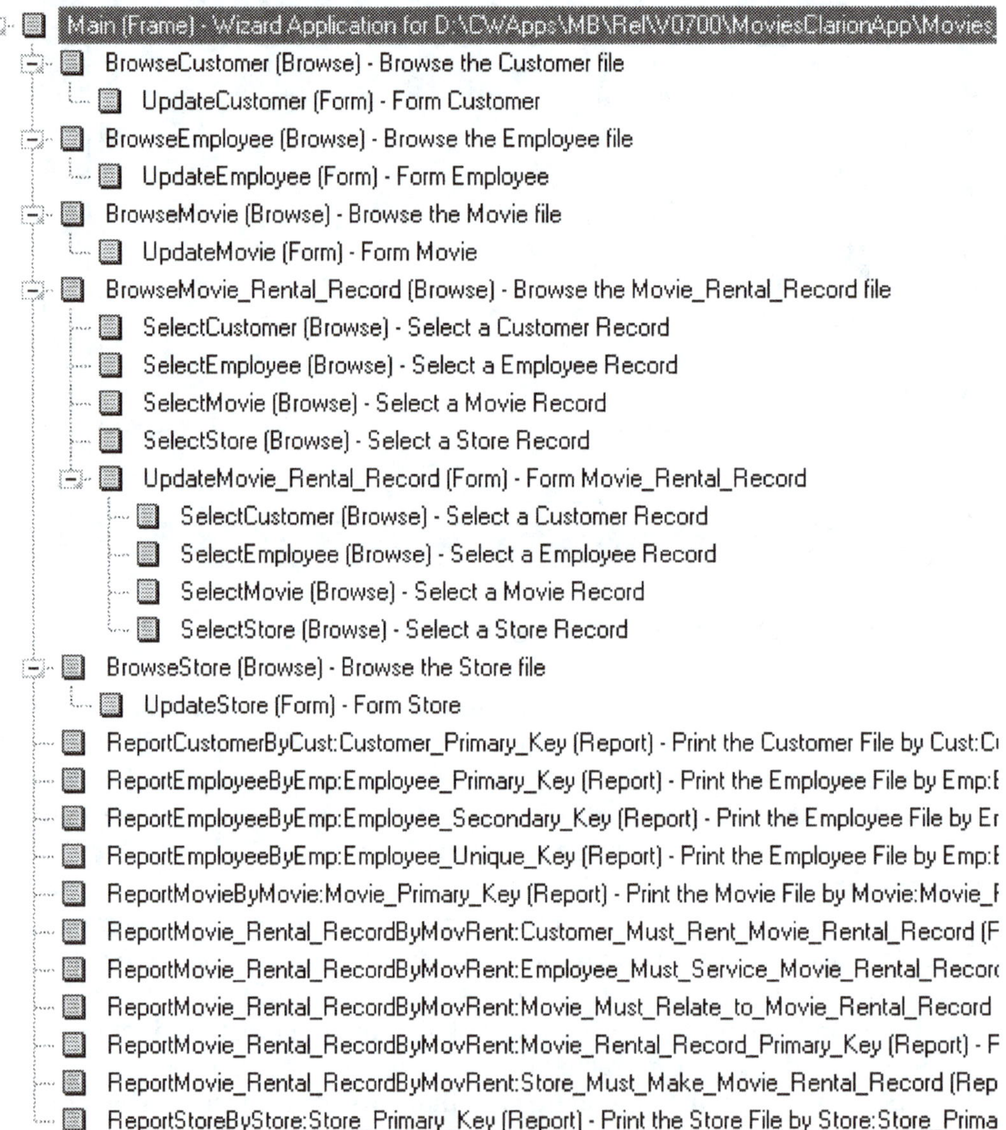

Figure 31. Application tree generated from database table structure.

To create a working application from this application tree, just press the button that causes the actual application code to be generated, compiled, linked, and formed into an executable. This button appears on the top of the Clarion application development window. Once that application is generated, compiled, linked, and starts executing, a window similar to the one in Figure 32 appears. This window is the first window of the actually executing application. It has a traditional Windows frame, and under the menu item Browse, it has a list of all the database-table-based lists.

Figure 33 shows the list of the reports. This list is very mechanical as all the names are derived from the database's design artifacts.

As a consequence of a neutral processing style, each of the five browses, e.g., movies, customer, store, employee, movie rental record, has the browse (list of records), and an update for either entering a new record (Insert button on the browse), modifying an existing record (Change button on the browse), or removing a record (Delete button on the browse).

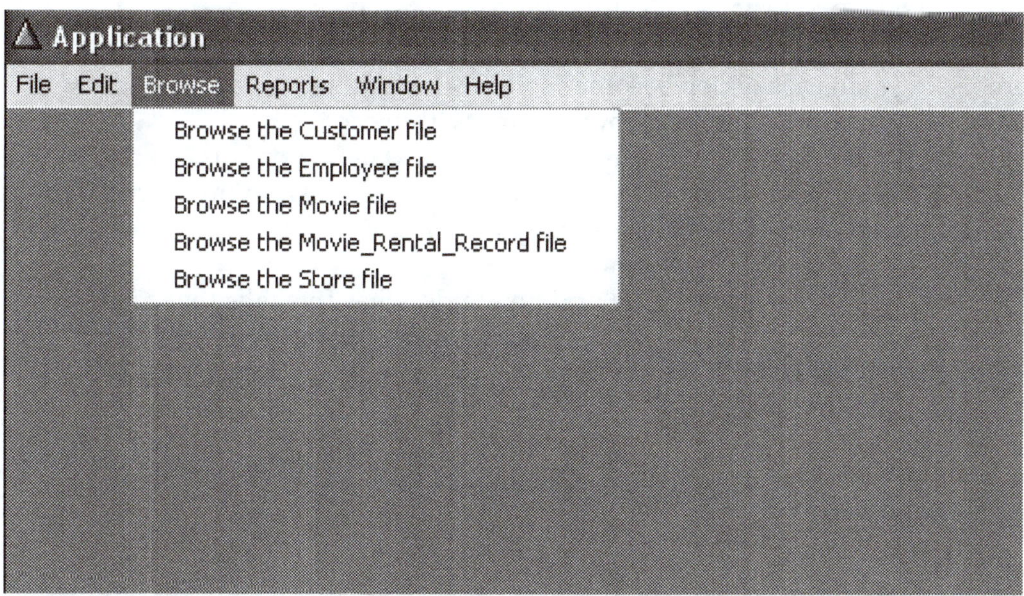

Figure 32. Menu of browses of auto-generated movies data warehouse.

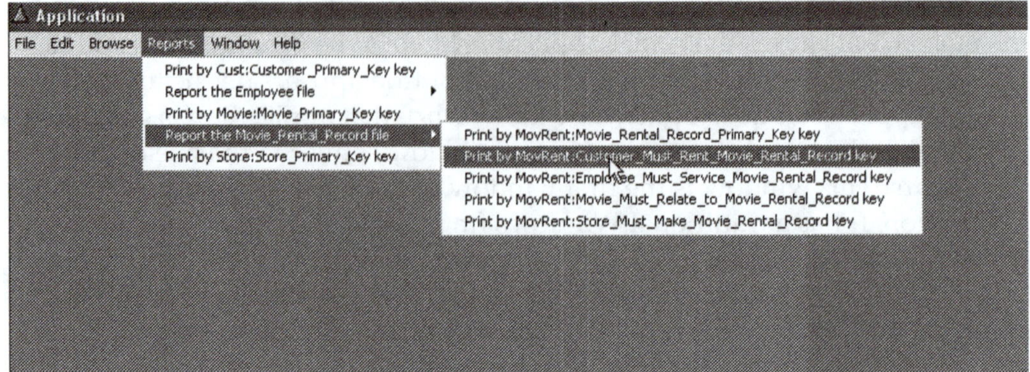

Figure 33. Menu of reports of auto-generated movies data warehouse.

When the application menu bar is created, all the browses appear
below the menu item, Browse. If there are four that may not be too unwieldy,
but when there are 30 or so tables, then a vertical list of 30 browses is
unacceptable. Figure 32 shows the main frame and the Browse menu item
with all the browses in one list. First, there could be better groupings by major
processing scenarios which become high-level menu items, and second, there
could be submenus and then browse items within each.

Another class of "problem" is that the update window is clearly
"basic." Figure 34 presents the generated update window. In this particular
example, several things are immediately obvious:

- The browse "behind" the update window has five tabs that cause the
  Movie Rental Records to be listed by these various orders (e.g., by
  Customer or by Store). Trouble is that the tab label names are not
  obvious named.

- All the column names are all left justified, and the data entry space is
  all fixed.

- Some of the Movie Rental Record data is represented on a second tab
  (e.g., 2) General (cont.))..

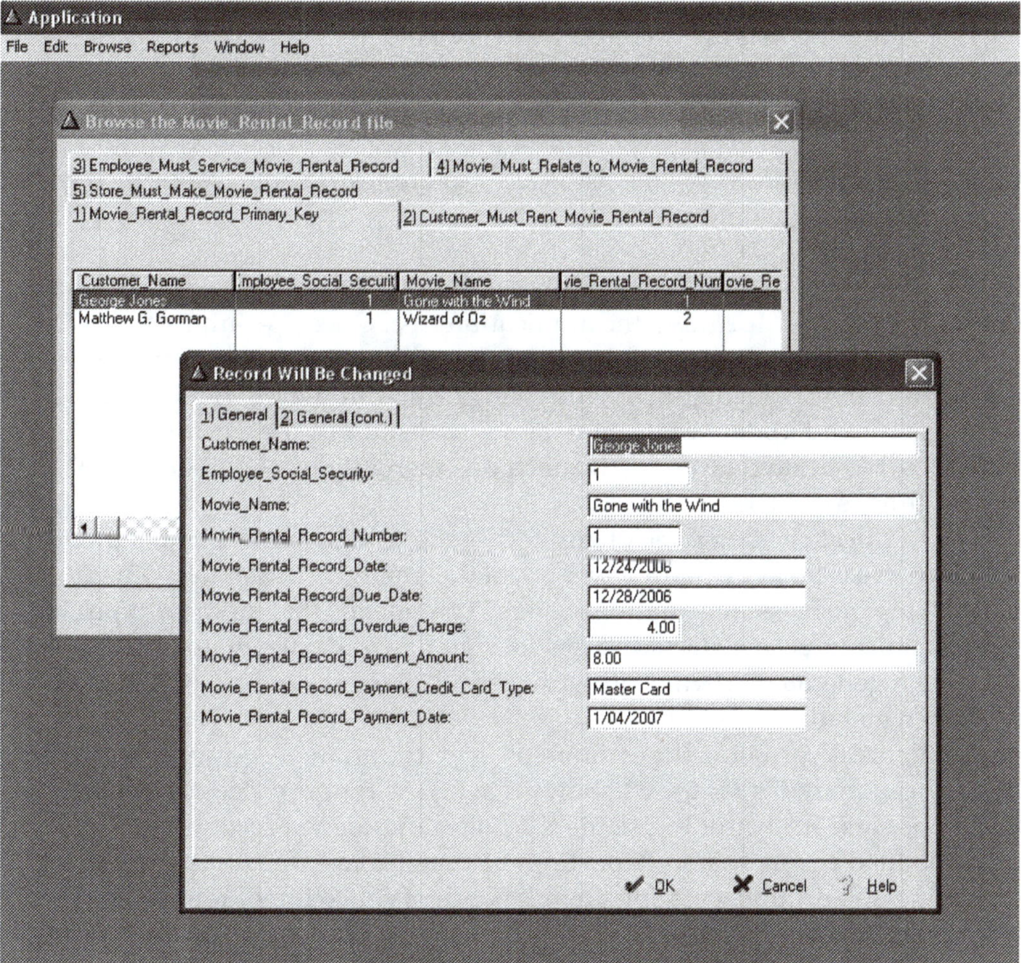

Figure 34. Generated movie rental record browse and update screen.

In summary, while the benefits of generating entire business information systems in a matter of a few minutes cannot be over stated, the automatic generation presents a unique set of side effects. That is,

- Too many modules because of processing style neutrality.

- All browses are stacked under one menu item.

- All browse lists are accessed by every key.

- Headings and labels are "mechanical."

- All reports are very "mechanical" and are restricted to reporting data from a single database table.

To "fix" these five problem classes takes only an hour or so. The process starts with "electronically" pruning the application tree. Once the "unnecessary" modules are deleted, the remaining modules, that is, the main menu, browses, and forms can be "touched-up." One change is to put the Movie Rentals Record select and update as its own menu item and put the Customer, Employee, Movie, and Store as "Dimension" menu items. Another change was to "tune up" the tab headers.

A critical characteristic of any code generating environment is that NONE of these changes should ever affect the ability to ultimately generate the working business information system. That means that all these types of changes must be accomplished at the "design metadata" level. In Clarion, the ability to regenerate is always preserved as all changes are accomplished at the design metadata level.

Figure 35 presents the "trimmed" application tree. A comparison with the application tree in Figure 31 shows that all the report processes were deleted because it's better to use the Clarion stand-alone report writer than the embedded report writer. Reporting the data for just one table would be of little value. In addition, creating an independent collection of report procedures enable reports to be run by anyone who has access to the report writer versus having to have the main application with the application-embedded reports on the user's computer. In this example, the report writer employed is the Clarion report writer. If the underlying database were run by an SQL engine, and if access was through ODBC, then Crystal Reports could be employed.

Another change is typified by the Movie Rental Records browse shown Figure 36. Compared to the top browse from Figure 34, the tab names were all shortened, and the tab that indicated that the records were to be sorted by primary key value was removed. Another change in Figure 36 is that much more of the movie rental record data is shown because each entry is on three lines. A final difference is shown in the update window. The field that was on the " 2) General" tab was moved to the main tab.

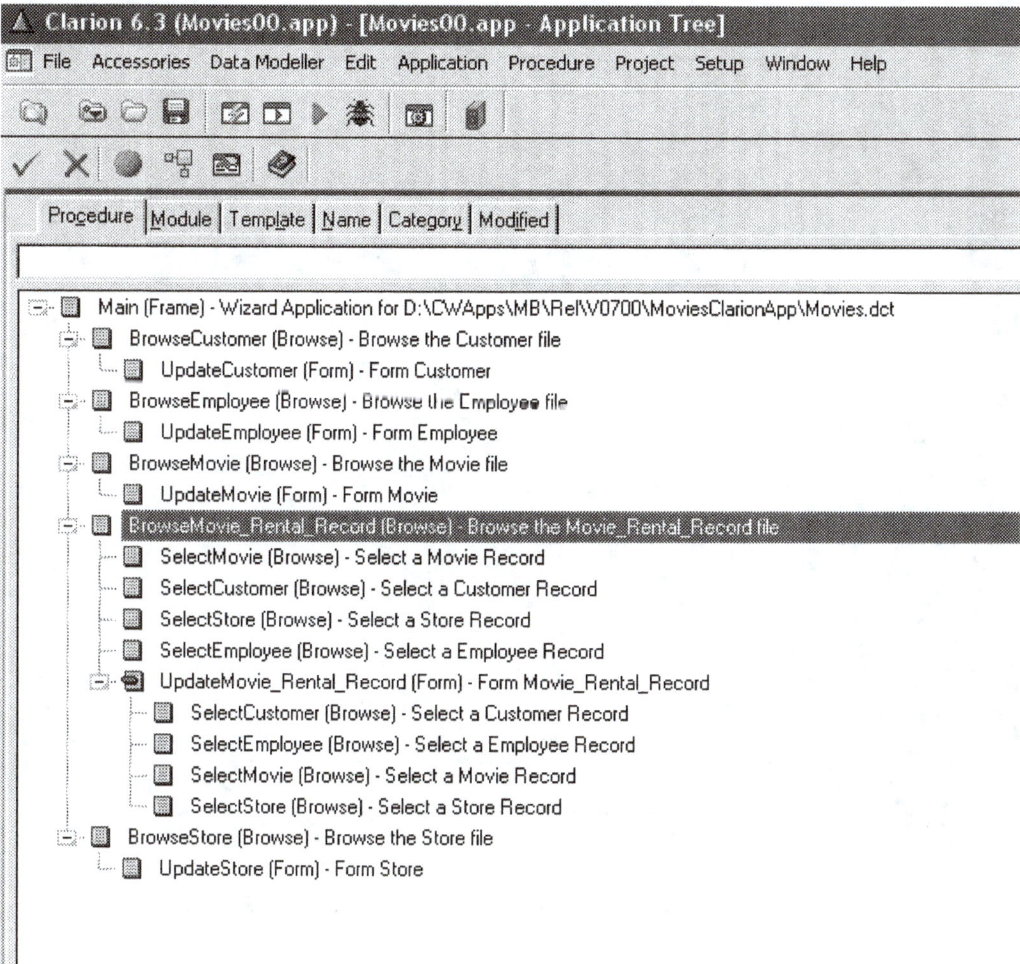

Figure 35. Trimmed application tree.

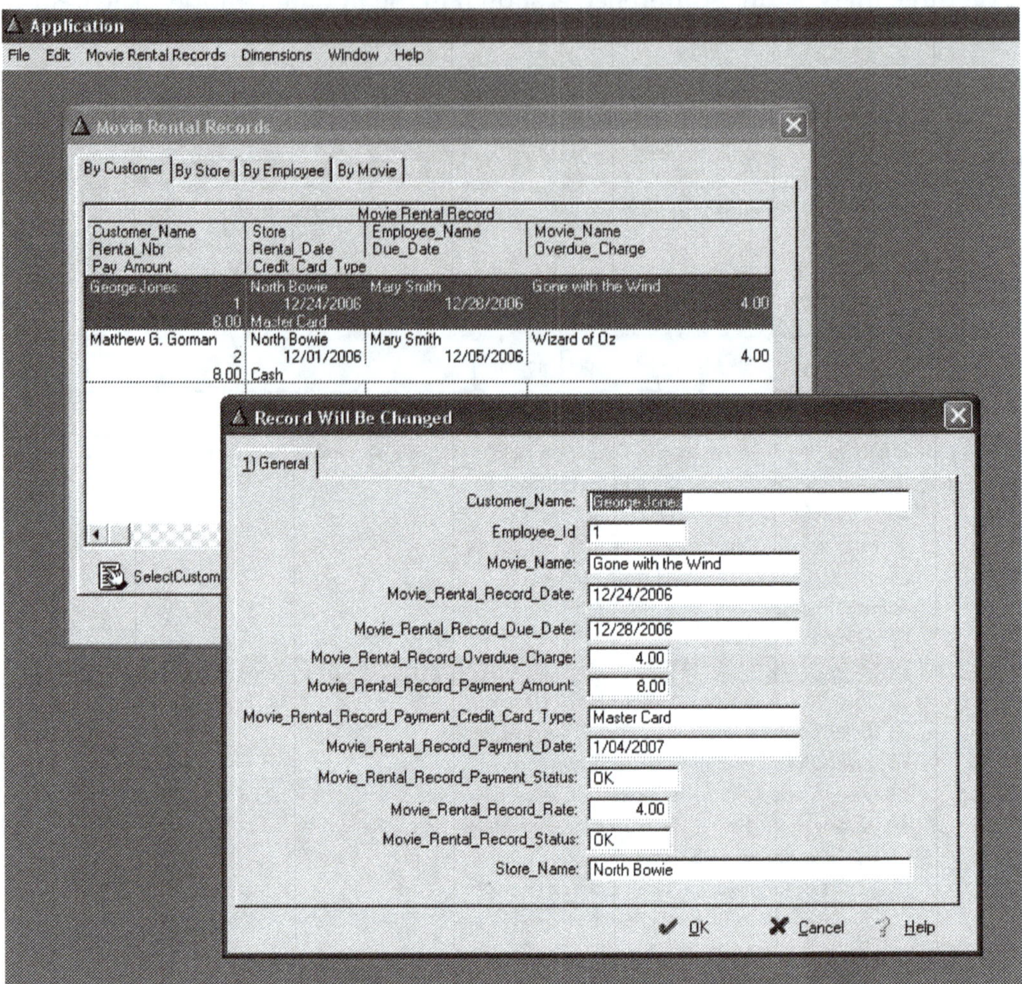

Figure 36. Revised movie rental record browse and update screen.

Figure 37 shows an alternative form of this same window. The tabs are all gone. That's because instead of using tabs to accomplish sorting, a "by column header" sorting template was added. This enables the orders to be accomplished by merely "clicking" the column header.

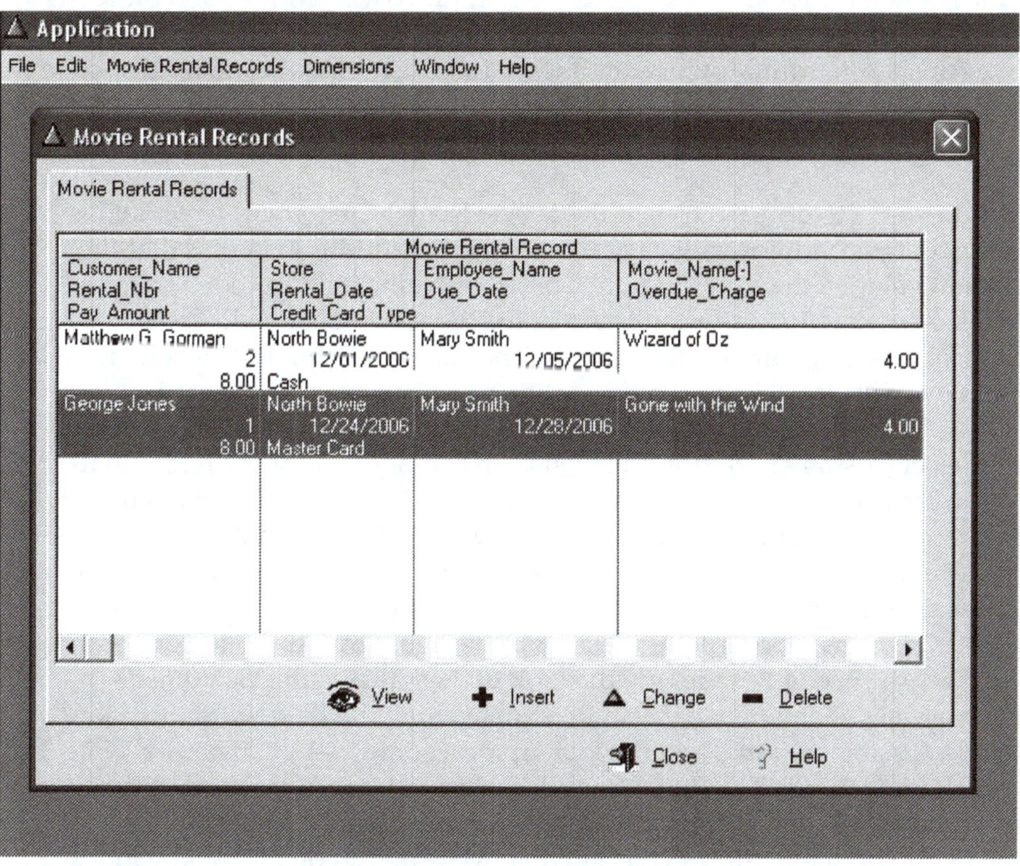

Figure 37. Movie rental records browse with column header sorting.

In Figure 34, look carefully at the Update Movies-Rental-Record procedure. It has a "dash" through its icon. That "dash" icon indicates that an embed (that is, some quantity of custom computer language code) was included in that procedure. In this case the embed was installed to enforce the referential integrity between Movie-Rental-Record records and related dimension table records, that is, Customer, Employee, Movie, and Store. In this particular example, the embedded code is just one line. For a referential integrity check from Movie Rental Record to Customer, the embedded code is:

?MovRent:Customer_Name{Prop:Touched} = True

This line effectively says: When the Movie Rental Customer Name field is touched, the condition must test true. Now, the condition here is that the current value in the Movie Rental Customer Name field cannot be zero or blank. That condition is established in the database schema. If it is either zero or blank, the referential action occurs. That is, the Customer Select window, shown in Figure 38, is presented so that a customer can be selected.

How the application business information system knows to execute the Select Customer window is through the second half of the referential action specification. This is presented in Figure 39. In this figure the update form for Movie Rental Record is presented in back. Note that the Customer Name entry field is selected. Once selected, a <right mouse click> pops up a list of allowed actions that can occur when the field is selected. The one chosen, Actions, pops up the window from Figure 39. At the bottom of that window the needed entries are the look up key, that is the Customer's primary key, that is, Cust: CustomerPrimaryKey, the field within that key, that is, CustomerName, and the look up procedure, SelectCustomer. Note the two checked boxes. The first causes the select to happen if the condition is not met, and the second forces the test again when a value has been placed into the field. The actual line of code cited above is placed on a special window that materializes once the Figure 39 Embeds button is pressed. This special window contains all the embedded code for the procedure.

The bottom window from Figure 38 shows a list of Movie Name choices. This select list is presented as a consequence of the "0" shown in the Movie Name field in the middle window of Figure 38. If the user tabs-through the entry field, for example, Movie Name, without out providing a valid value, then the associated select window is automatically presented.

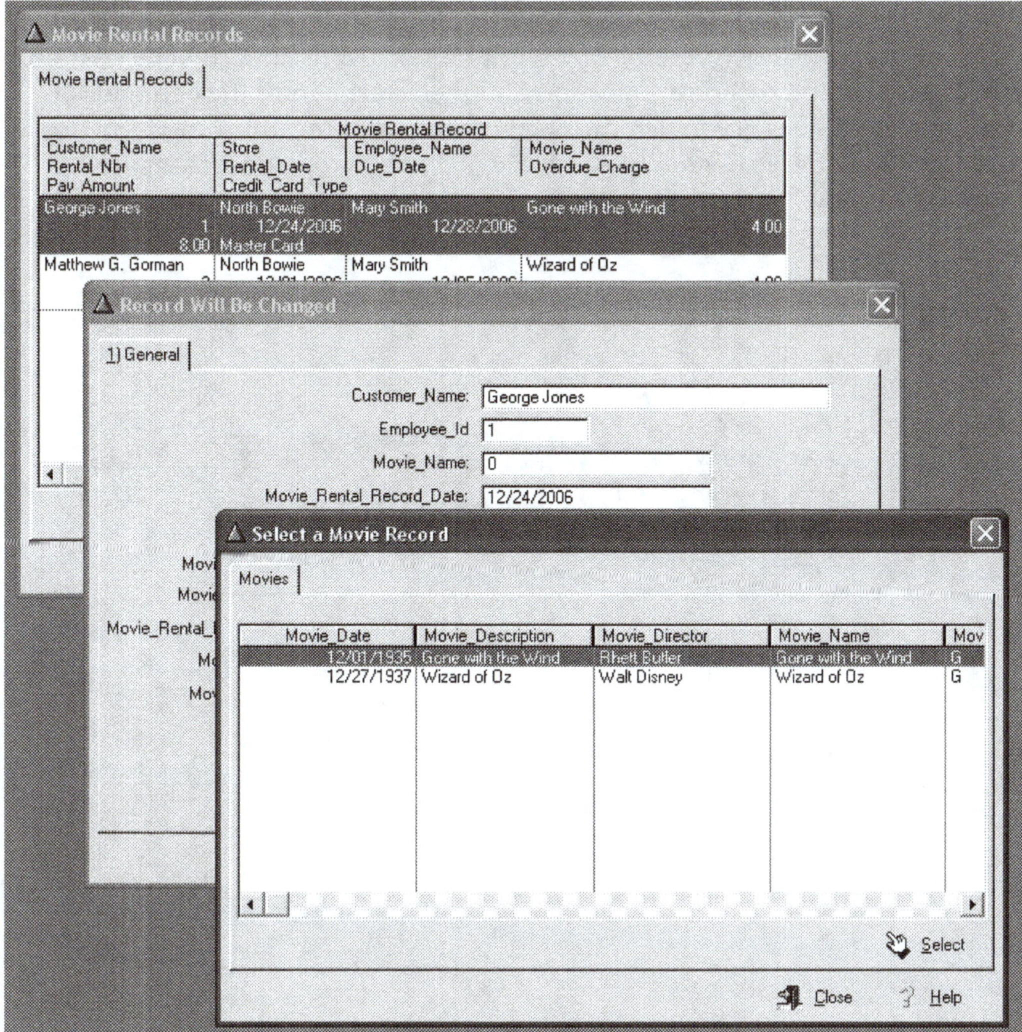

Figure 38. Movie Rental Record update screen with referential integrity select.

Because the process of electronic pruning transforms the application to a preferred style of processing, it is important to acquire an understanding of how the organization prefers to work. But, because the creation of a certain style of work is so inexpensive through business information system generators, organizations can afford to support multiple styles.

It is very tempting to really "pretty-up" the prototype. Resist the temptation because any "pretty-up" work builds in a natural reluctance to trash the whole prototype application and then start over if the behavior of the application does not match the needs of the user. Ideally, the goal of any pretty-up activities is to merely eliminate features that distract from a thorough review.

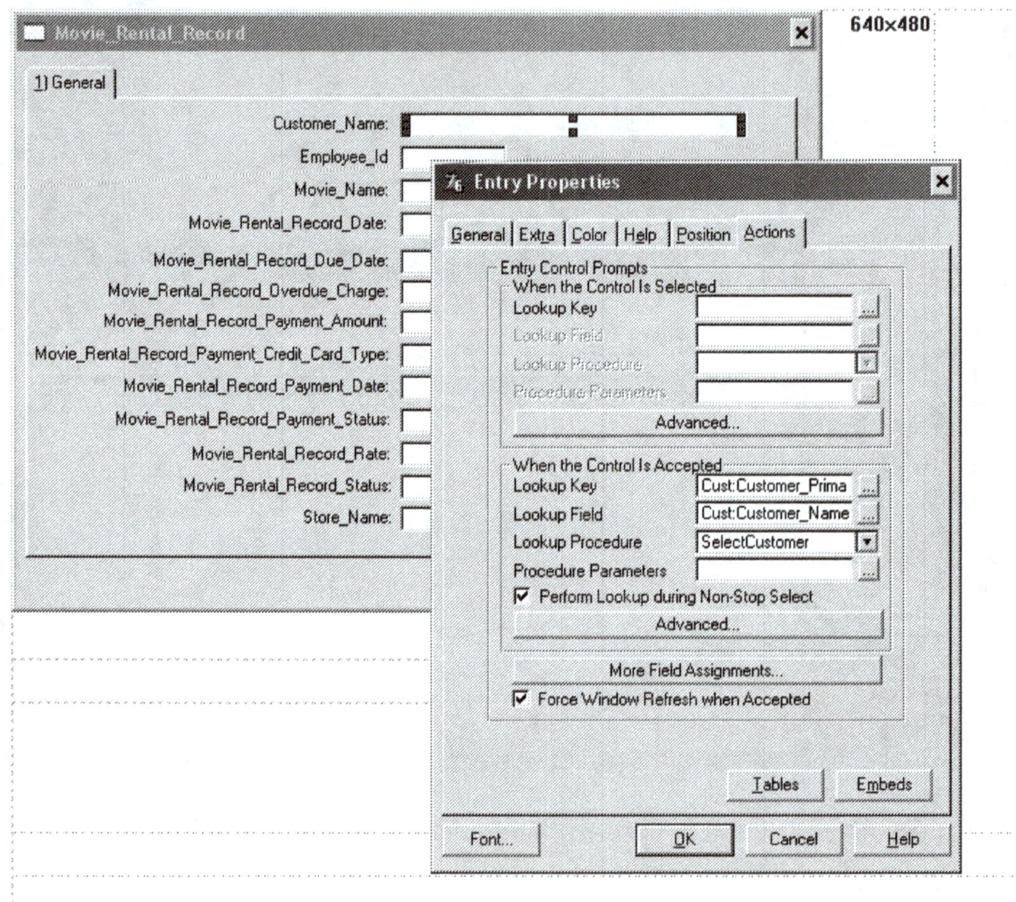

Figure 39. Customer select screen with referential action.

These types of changes should take no more than about one hour per database table to make the result presentable to a set of functional experts, so they can begin their review. For a 20-table application, the total time to create a presentable application should take less than three staff days. This is in contrast to the industry average of about two staff weeks per module for custom created code. For a 20-table application specific database, and three modules per table, the amount of staff time for custom creation would be 120 staff weeks. Three staff days versus 120 staff weeks is quite a contrast.

Whenever there are entire custom calculation routines that must be created, the estimate of one staff hour per table is not valid. In such a case, quality generators such as Clarion enable the creation of the custom created processing logic to be embedded such that the ability to generate the overall application is maintained.

A perverse side effect occurs when a business information system generator is employed for any length of time. There is a tendency to forget how to program. For example, during the development of the Whitemarsh project management system, there was the need to create a number of custom coded modules to create schedules, perform load leveling, and the like. While the programming result, looking back, was quite simple, old techniques and old habits had to be rediscovered.

In the case of Clarion, the time to create a custom module is equivalent to most other 4GLs. That is, about 10-20 times faster than the comparable COBOL program. In a fairly complex calculation process there are about 250 lines of code. The effort takes about two days. Half the time is spent re-learning forgotten techniques. Another lesson that needs to be passed along is that embedded documentation is even more critical because with the significant advance in productivity, the quantity of projects per staff member is likely to grow by 3-5 times with the effect of having staff members spending less and less time on each project.

The final item, mechanical reports, is cured by a reasonable report writer such as the Clarion report writer. The report generation process consists of these four steps:

- Establish report library.
- Import the dictionary.
- Create a report hierarchy.
- Run a report.

This process takes about 15 to 30 minutes for each report. The first step entails establishing the library of report definitions. This process is displayed in Figure 40. At the bottom of the window, the dictionary is identified. During the creation process the critical metadata from the database's dictionary is pulled into the reports' library.

Figure 41 presents the windows that represent the database dictionary synchronization process that occurs whenever the reports' library detects that the current database dictionary is different than is contained in the reports' dictionary definitions.

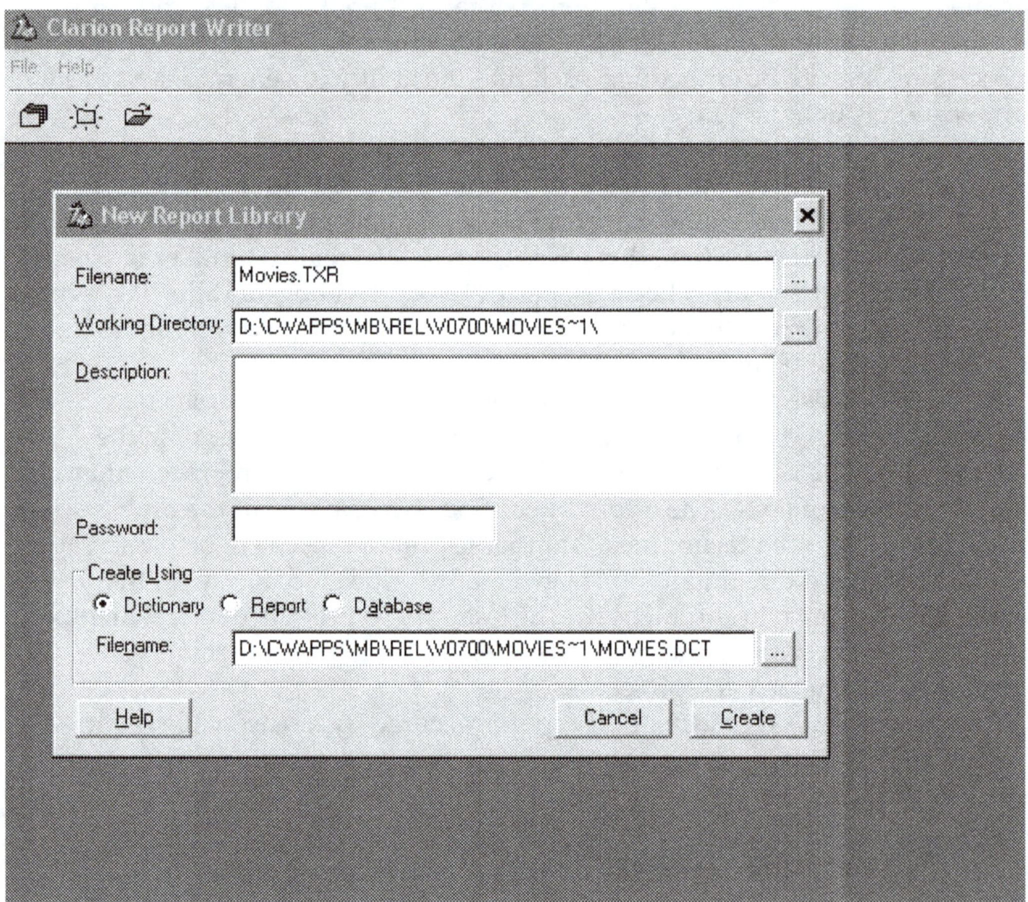

Figure 40. Establishing the reports library.

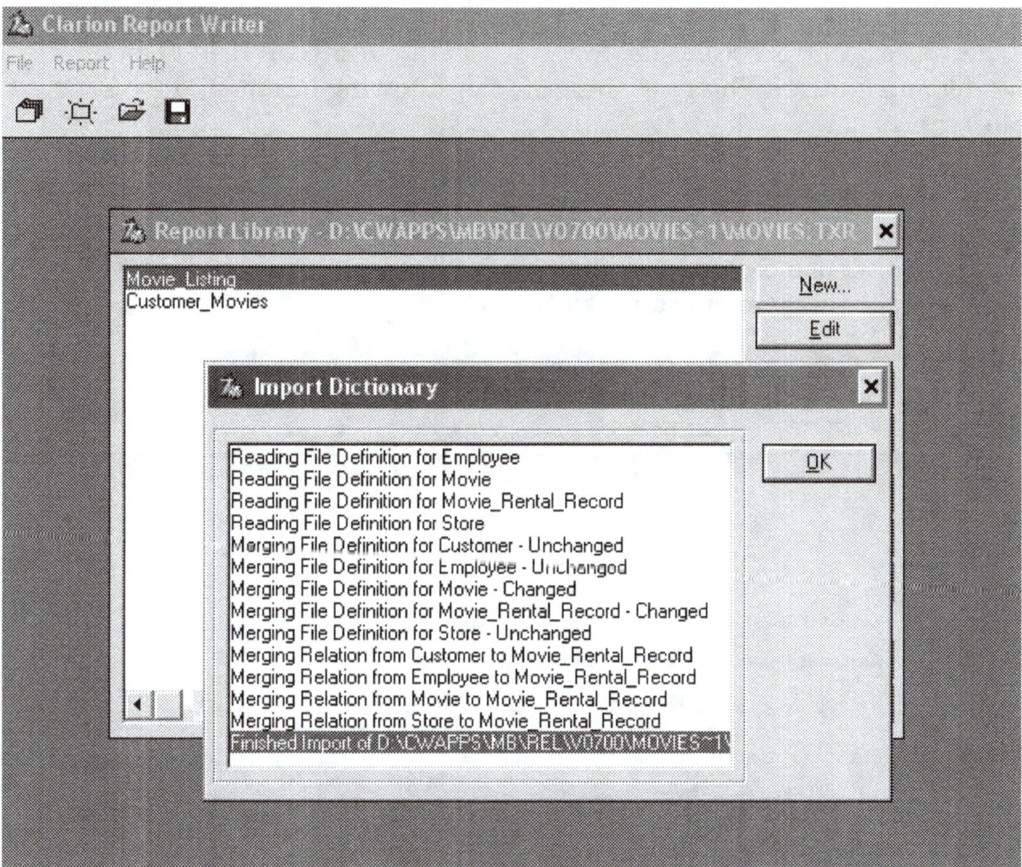

Figure 41. Synchronization between dictionary and report library.

The synchronization is started from within the reports-list window by selecting the File menu item then import then picking the dictionary file then pressing the OK button. This process ensures that the reports' library knows about the dictionary's details.

There are a few steps to instigate the report such as providing its name, selecting its basic format, identifying the fields that are to be contained in the report, and then selecting sort sequence.

Figure 42 presents the sort sequence choices. For fields that are identified as control breaks, the report writer builds a <sort field name> header and footer. In this case, there are the following header and footer blocks:

- Report.
- Page.
- Project name.
- Project assignment start date.

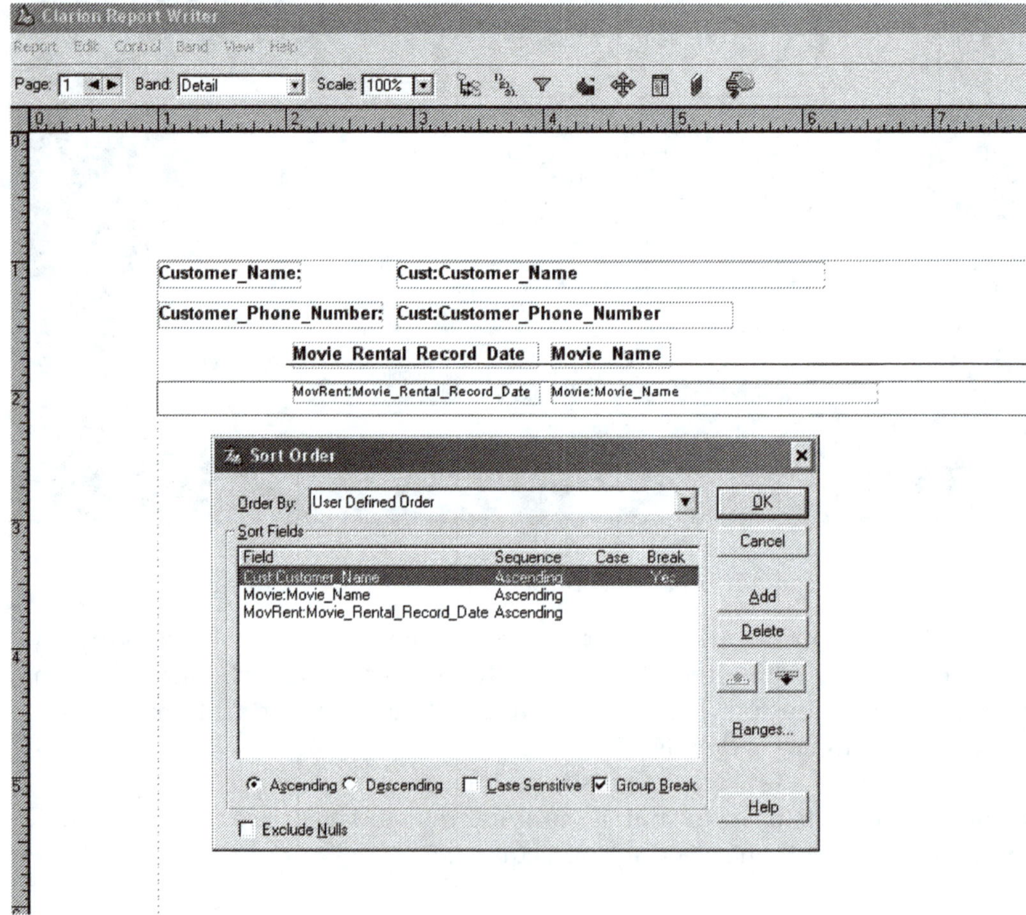

Figure 42. Sort and break fields for a specific report.

For each, the typical report writer functions for summarizing, headers, totals, and the like can be accomplished. Once this is complete, the Finish button is pressed. This starts the report generation process. The result of the process is presented in Figure 43. In this example the report and page header are blank (not shown). The other header, Customer Name is filled in by default. The final block is the Detail block. Within all the blocks the fields can be moved around, and their display characteristics of font type, point size, bold, italics, shading and the like can be modified.

It is easy to forget that the ultimate purpose is to merely create report samples for the purpose of requirements iteration. Figure 44 presents results from running the report.

Once the prototype is made presentable, the first round of presentations to functional experts is in order. The amount of time required to make this first prototype should only be two or so weeks after the database's design is complete. Because the vast majority of the programs are code generated, there is no vested interest. Given that there are 20 tables, and about

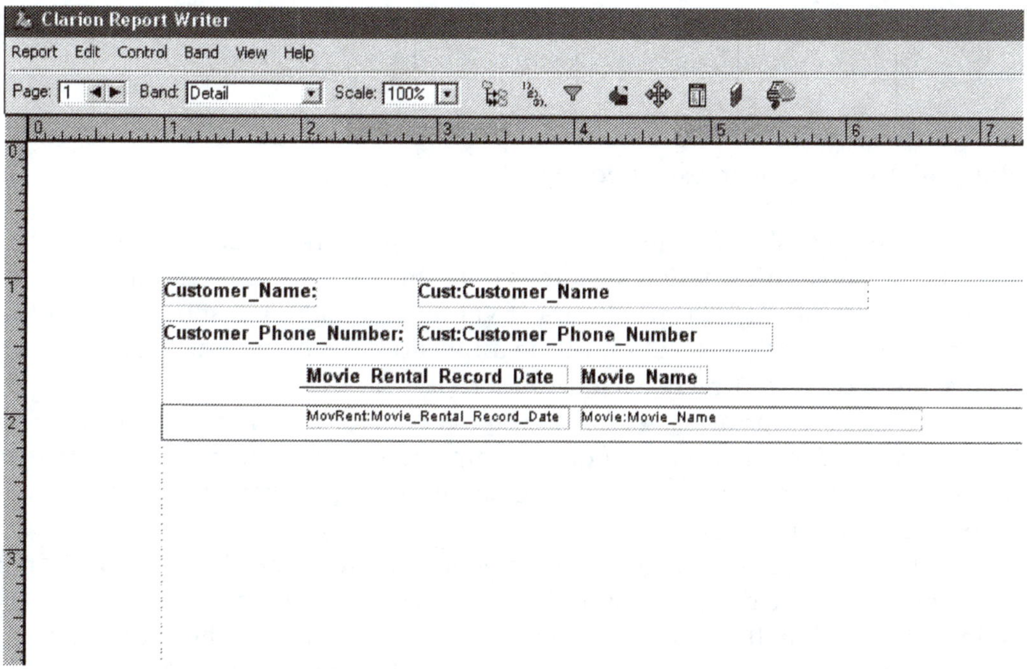

Figure 43. Ready to run report.

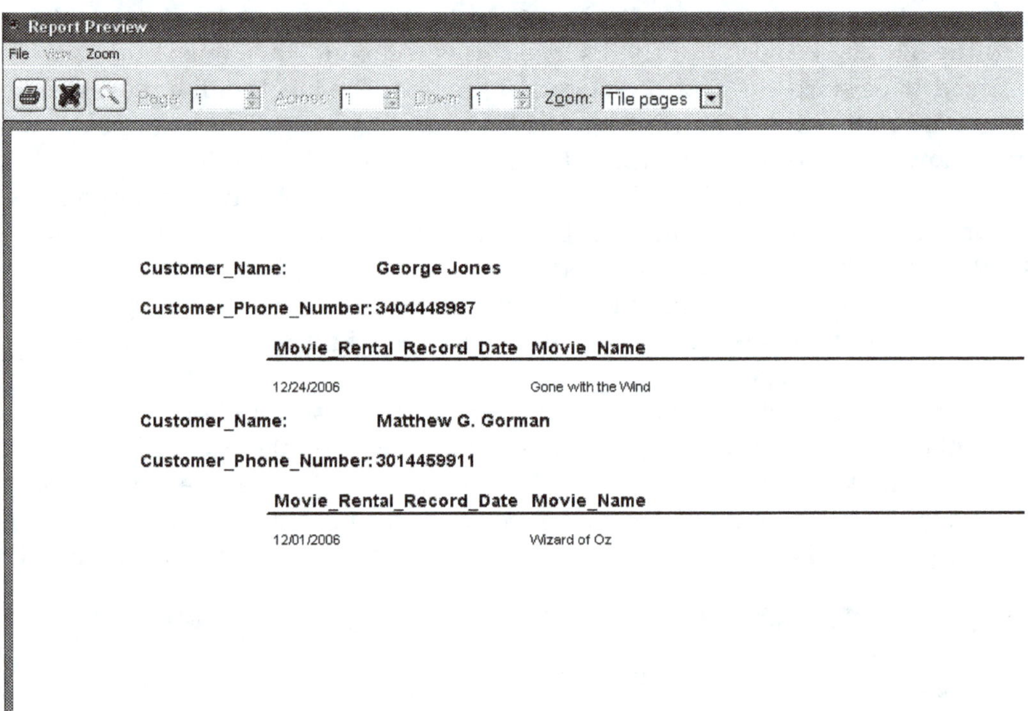

Figure 44. Example of an executed report.

five modules per table, and given that the staff weeks required to create the working business information system is only three weeks, each module represents only about 1.25 staff hours of value. This stands in stark contrast to the normal two staff weeks per module for custom development. That represents about a 75:1 increase in productivity.

A final step prior to "going on the road" is the creation of realistic demonstration data. This type of data is important so that the reviewers can come to the belief that they are viewing and evolving a "real" business information system.

It is critical to remember that the goal is not to "make" the application but to prototype the design. The prototype serves as the mechanism to validate the design. If the design is inappropriate then throw the prototype away, modify the design and regenerate the prototype.

3.4 Step 4: Evolve the Specification Through Prototyping

Specification evolution through prototyping has as its goal the creation of a valid requirements specification. That is, one that mirrors the needs and requirements of the enterprise such that, when implemented, it only has to be implemented once. Taking the time to do it right the first time is always cheaper.

Step 4.1: Demonstrate Prototype

The process of creating demonstration scenarios requires knowing the decision domains of the persons who are in the audience, which means knowing their subordinate mission areas in detail. These can be known by using the Metabase to print out the database domains for the missions of the enterprise. Missions lead to organizations Organizations lead to functions. These four, missions, organizations, functions, and database domains are the decisions domains of those involved in the prototype demonstrations. Those involved in the prototype should have their Positions registered in the Metabase as shown in Figure 12. It also means reviewing their current set of automation assists, the current set of management goals and objectives. In short, it means knowing what will make them successful to their management.

The entire prototype's demonstration should be divided into a grand and then smaller objectives that are easy to present, to comprehend, and to propose reactions or changes. Each small objective should be cast as a scenario.

Every scenario must relate to a specific business problem that is solved or avoided. Further, the benefits in terms of increased quality, lowered risk, increased performance and lowered costs must be palpable. If the persons participating in the scenario do not understand that the specification evolution team has satisfaction of the participants' needs and goals as its primary objective, participation will be surface level at best.

The preparation time for the prototype demonstrations should range from 20:1 to 40:1. That is, 20 to 40 hours preparation for each hour of prototype demonstration.

A key component of any prototype demonstration is test data. Prototype demonstration test data should be so realistic that the prototype demonstration team should be "accused" of stealing the data from the demonstration attendees. During a 1970s use of these requirements evolution techniques with a large urban school system's management information system's specification, the prototype team met in a conference room and determined the demographics of the school system's population including the types and quantities of schools, teachers, education programs, and other characteristics critical to the realistic understanding of the database and the management information system under development. The data was encoded to mirror these pre-determined characteristics and loaded into the prototyped management business information system's database.

During the demonstrations that were conducted with users from the large urban school systems, some of the demonstration attendees became highly agitated and the manager of the prototype team got several letters that directly accused the team of stealing real data.

During the prototype demonstrations, feed-back forms should be filled out by every attendee. Solicited should be the attendee's name, position, level in management, decision domains, and how the prototype did or did not:

- Support specific decision domain.

- Save time (what, how, and how much).

- Save money (how much, and why).

- Reduce risk (which kind, how and what benefitted).

- Increase quality (what kind, how, by how much, and what benefitted).

Specific suggestions should be solicited as to different process functionality, database data, missing or inappropriate data fields, window design, and the like. The prototype demonstration team should review the comments and determine exactly what and how the specification prototype should be modified to meet the unfolding and/or changed requirements of the prototype audience. Letters/memos should be sent to all prototype attendees thanking them for their contribution.

One more time: It is critical to remember that the goal is not to "make" the application but to prototype the design. The prototype serves as the mechanism to validate the design. If the design is inappropriate, throw the prototype away, modify the design and regenerate the prototype.

Step 4.2: Evolve Prototype

For the purpose of demonstrating the process of specification evolution, presume that a key result of a review was the need to install a new database table, Distributor, as a method of identifying the source of the movie. This is not a Distributor of movies to individual stores, but distribution of the movie itself to the Movie Rentals Corporation's main distribution center. The steps to accommodate this new capability are the traditional set:

- Add the table Distributor to the dictionary.

- Modify the Movie table to add the Distributor-Id column.

- Create the relationship and referential integrity between Distributor and Movie.

- Generate and then modify, as appropriate, the browse and update.

- Create and/or modify reports.

- Adjust the prototype demonstration scenarios.

Figure 45 presents the new database graphic. It contains the Distributor table right below Movie. To have the metadata that supports the production of the diagram, the Distributor table had to be defined, the columns and keys allocated and the relationships established between Distributor and Movie.

If this were a "one-off" effort then there would no need to create additional metadata in the Metabase. But since this is an integrated effort, where the results are to be available for use by other projects in the enterprise, the first step is to create additional metadata. This is accomplished by importing the entity Distributor from the Specified Data Model into the Movie Sales schema in the Implemented Data Model. The next step is to add the

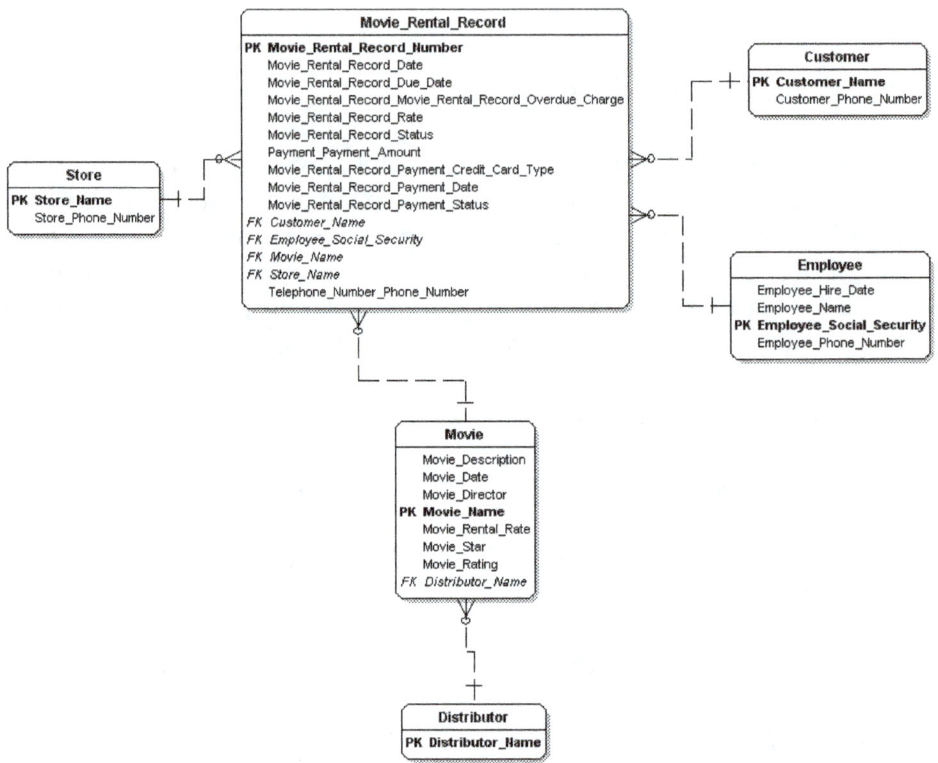

Figure 45. Modified movie sales data model.

foreign key relationship between the newly created table, Distributor and Movies. The next step is to create a new Operational Data Model and export that model to SQL DDL. These steps took about 10 minutes.

Figure 46 presents the window through which the Specified Data Model's entity, Distributor was imported into the Implemented Data Model. Figure 47 presents the foreign key creation window. Figure 48 shows the Operational Data Model's window for importing the movie sales replacement data model into the Operational Data Model from the Implemented Data Model.

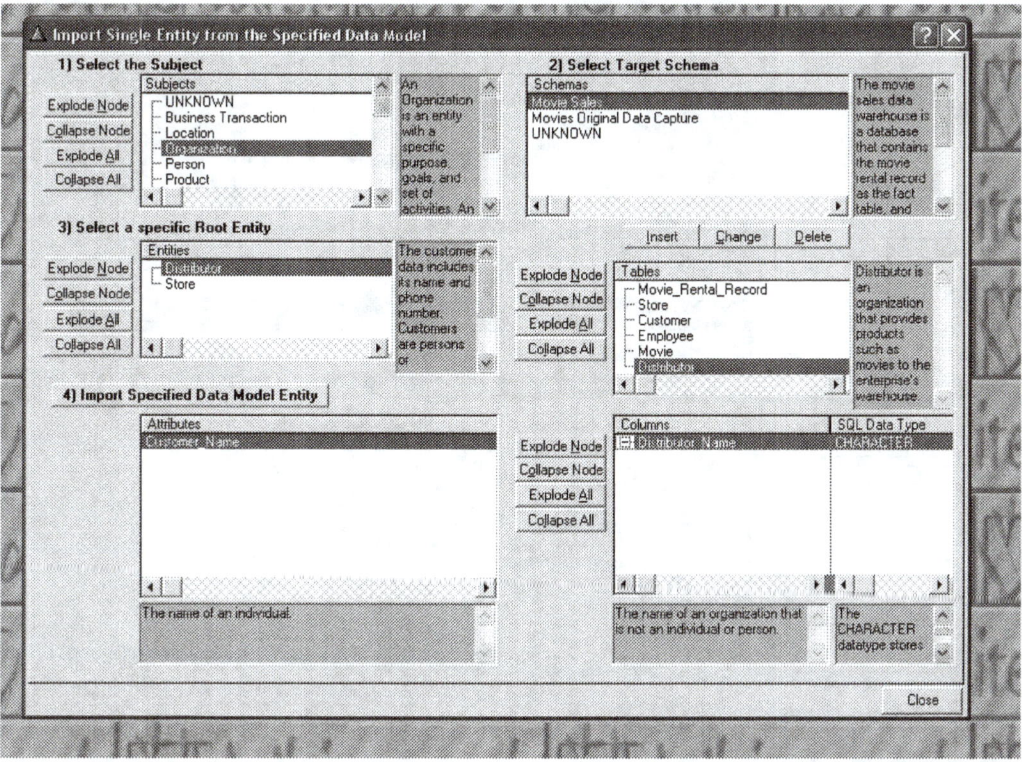

Figure 46. Screen for importing a single entity from the specified data model into the implemented data model.

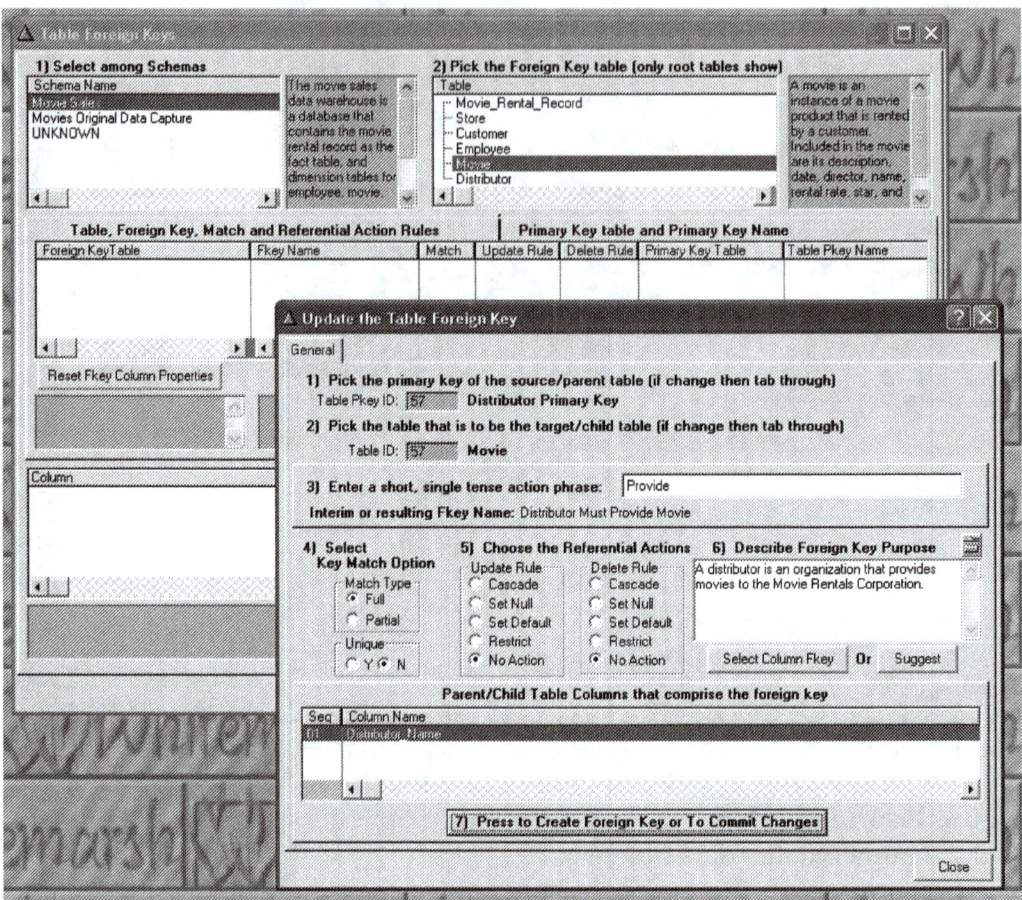

Figure 47. Foreign key creation screen.

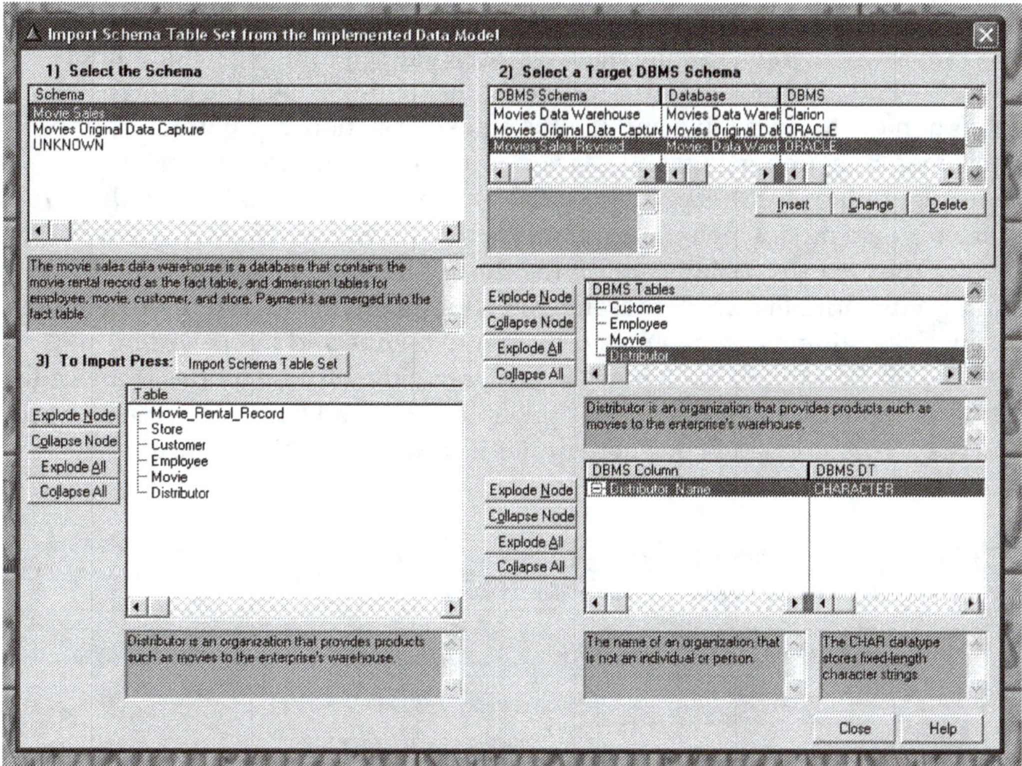

Figure 48. Schema import screen from Implemented to Operational Data Models.

With respect to the actual database application, invoke the Metabase procedure to generate a single database table into Clarion's data definition language and import that into Clarion. At this point, create the foreign key column in the Movies table and the foreign key relationship within Clarion. The generation, importing, and Clarion foreign key creation step takes just about 30 minutes. At this point both the Metabase's data model metadata and Clarion's data model metadata are in synch.

The next step entails modifying the application for the menu, browse, and update form. Figure 49 presents the window involved with modifying the menu. The main frame's menu is broken into menus and items within menus. The first round of changes was to move the browse entries from under "Browse" and to put all the dimension tables under a Dimensions menu item and the Movie Rental Record item under its own name. Now, since

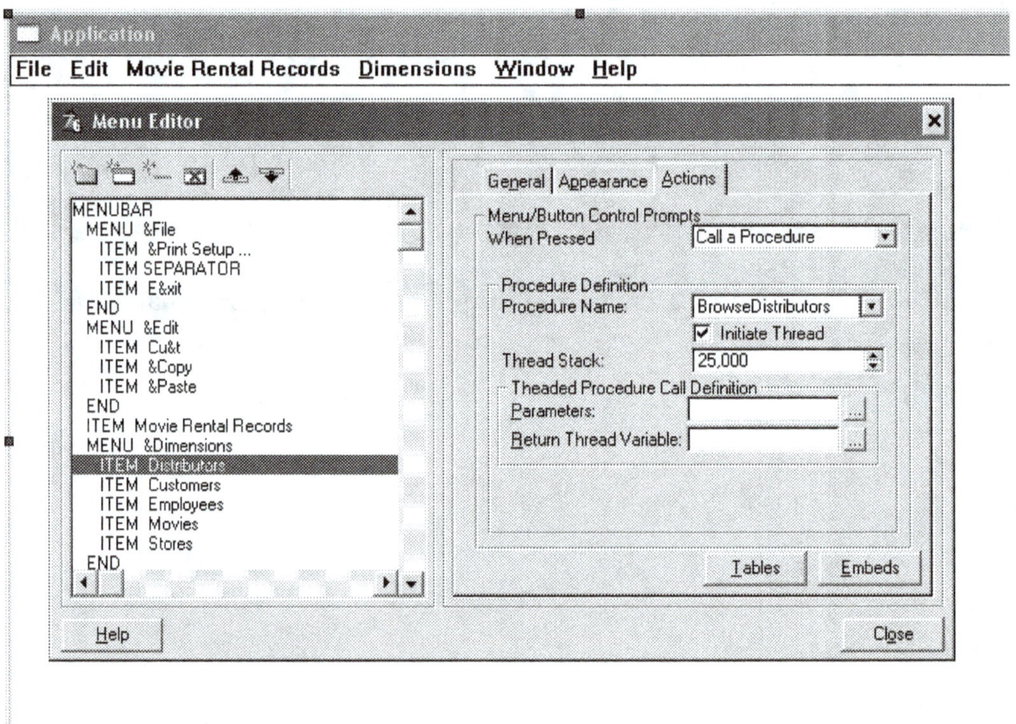

Figure 49. Movies application menu modification process.

Distributor is also related to Movie, it is placed in the Dimensions menu item. This new entry is shown in Figure 49.

Figure 49 also shows where the Distributor browse's name is placed in the menu. Getting to the menu's metadata starts with the application tree, then double-clicking the main module, and then selecting edit-menu. The new menu item is placed in alphabetical order. The right-side browse instructs Clarion what to call when the menu's item, Distributor, is pressed. This instruction is entered under the Actions tab. The procedure, BrowseDistributor, is named, and is to operate under its own thread. After "Ok-ing" out of this process the application tree is redisplayed. The tree, shown in Figure 50 shows the Distributor process as a "To-do" item.

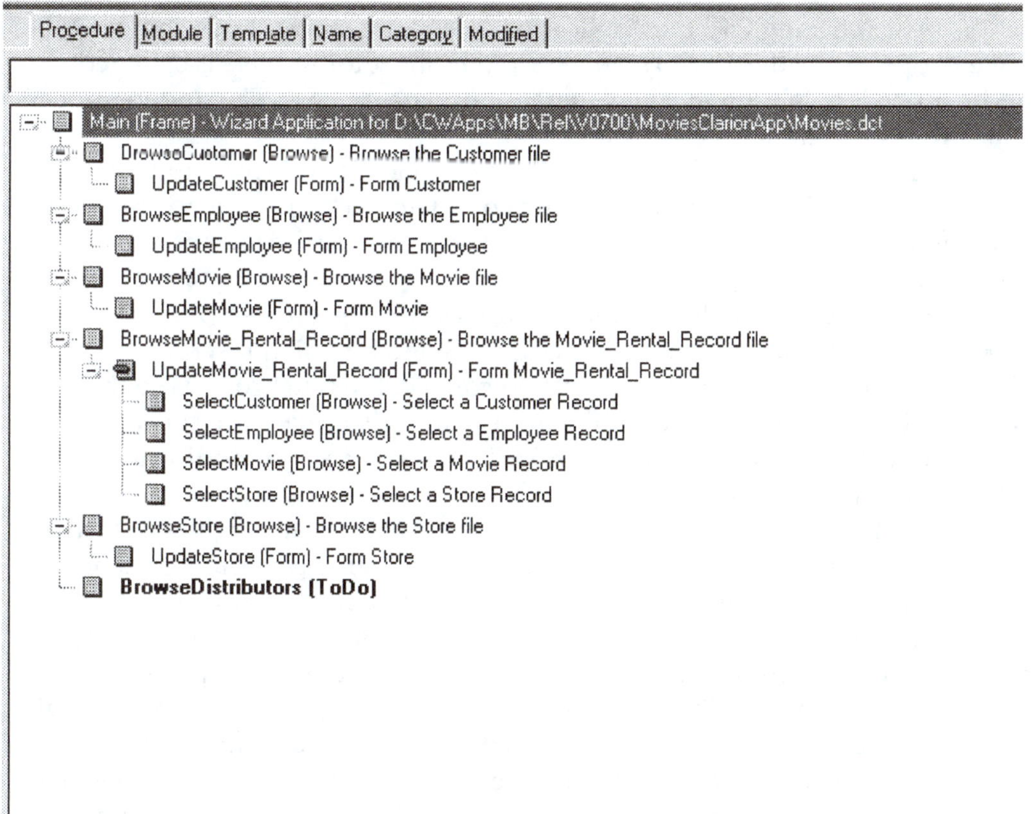

Figure 50. Modified application tree for the new distributor module.

Actually making the Distributor browse and the associated update window is rather simple. Just double-click the "To-Do" procedure from Figure 50, and then select the Browse Wizard generation template. The Browse Wizard selection is shown in Figure 51.

Figure 52 shows the window that contains the start of metadata generation. By clicking a series of "nexts," and identifying the Distributor table, the Clarion software then creates all the metadata necessary to enable Clarion to generate the computer code that will list and update distributors.

After the metadata generation process is complete, the Clarion window that enables Distributor browse editing is presented. This is shown on Figure 53. No changes are necessary. The generated Distributor browse window is shown in Figure 54.

After clicking OK, the application tree reappears and two things will have happened: 1) the To-Do status for the Distributor browse is changed, and 2) there is an automatically generated update process. The update process is just fine so no updates are needed.

The remaining step is to modify the Movies browse and update windows. Once those modifications are complete, the application is ready to demonstrate again. Once familiar with Clarion, these steps take no more than 60 minutes.

Figure 55 shows the initially generated Movies browse. The modifications that are made are to make the window taller, insert a Distributor browse above Movies, and to connect the two browses so that when a distributor is selected only that distributor's movies are shown. The resulting window is shown in Figure 56. This specific set of modifications takes only about ten minutes.

Modifying the Movies update window involves adding the Distributor field, and then establishing the referential action (value cannot be zero or blank) between the Movies record and the Distributer record. The original Movies update window is provided in Figure 57. The modified Movies update window is shown in Figure 58, which shows the newly placed Distributor field. Figure 58 also shows the window for adding the referential action between movies and distributor. This window shows the actions at the bottom, and the actions always take place when the Distributor window field is selected. If it is blank upon selection then the Distributor select process executes just like in the Movies Rental Records. At that point the movies application has been modified. It can then be regenerated.

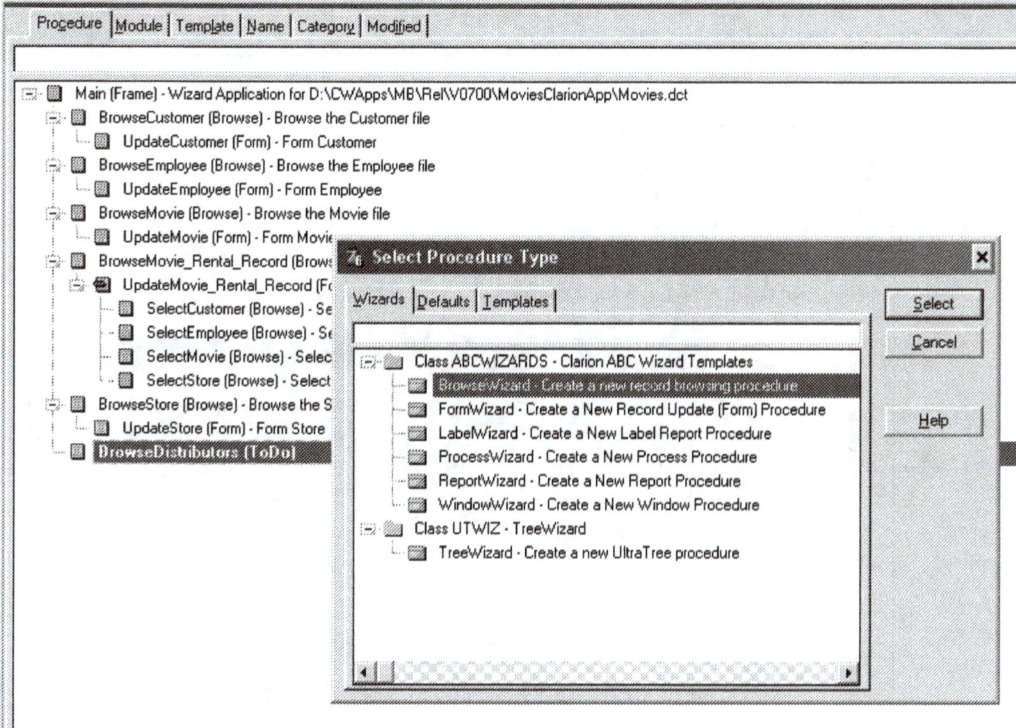

Figure 51. Selecting the browse wizard generation template.

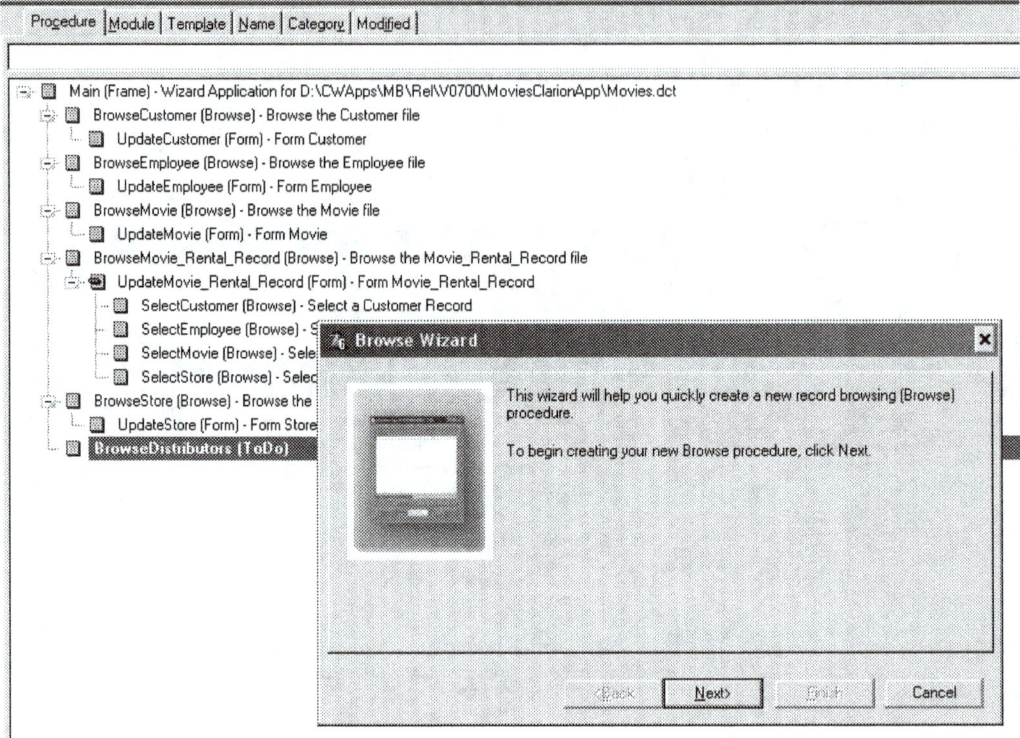

Figure 52. Starting the distributor code-generation process.

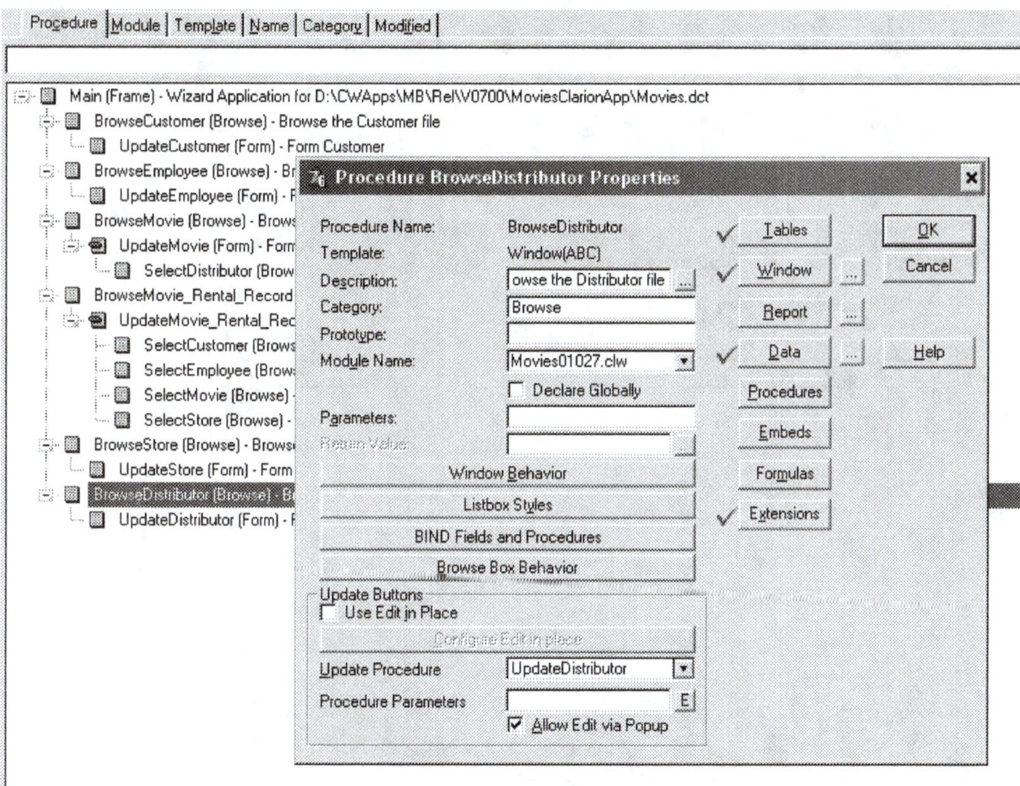

Figure 53. Ready to modify distributor generated window.

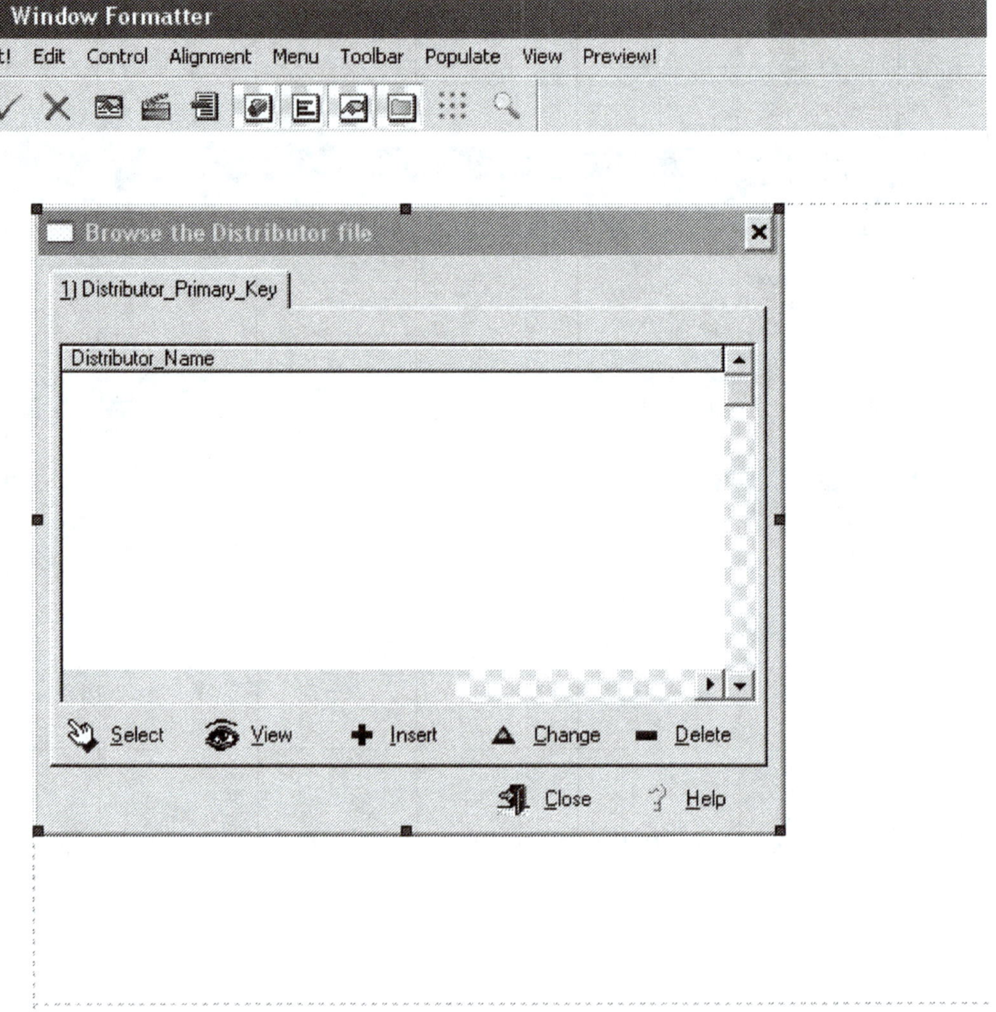

Figure 54. Newly generated, unmodified distributor browse.

Once the application is generated, all the movies records are going to have to be modified to hold the value of one of the distributors. At the outset, add several distributors so there is a basis for updating the movie records. Make one of the distributors be "Unknown," and then link all the movie records to the "Unknown" distributor. Finally, in the actual application, proceed to update the movie records and assign them to a "known" distributor.

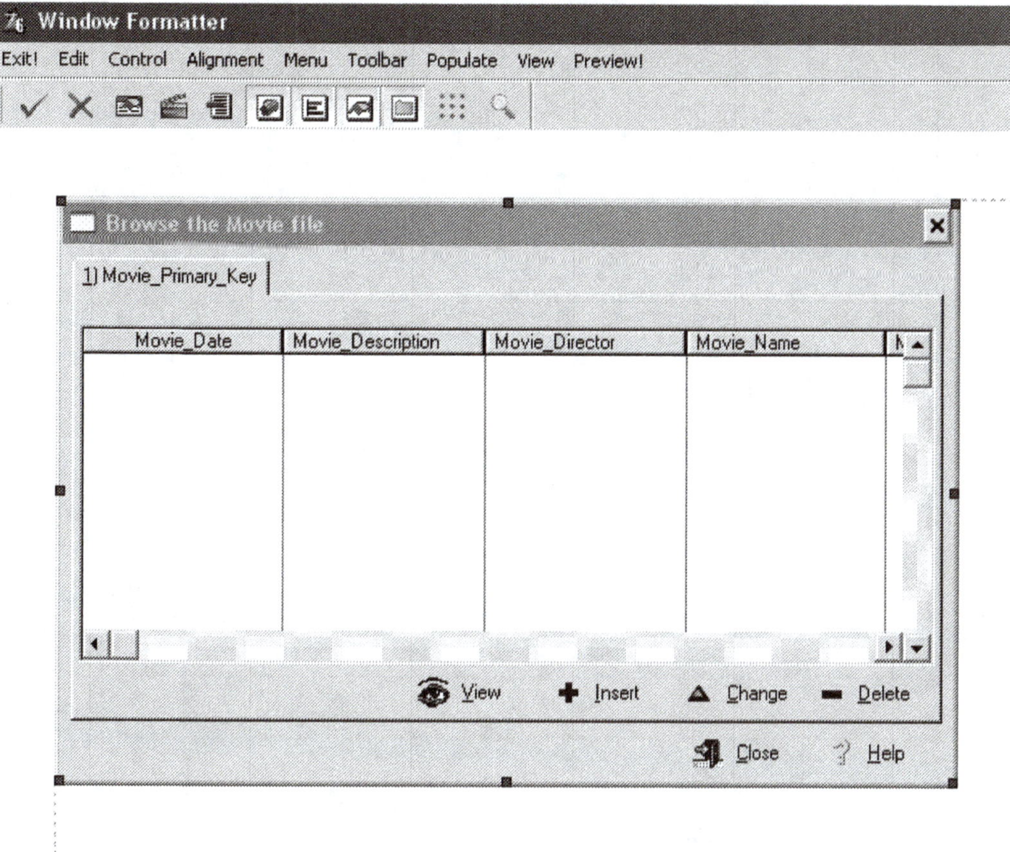

Figure 55. Initially generated movies browse.

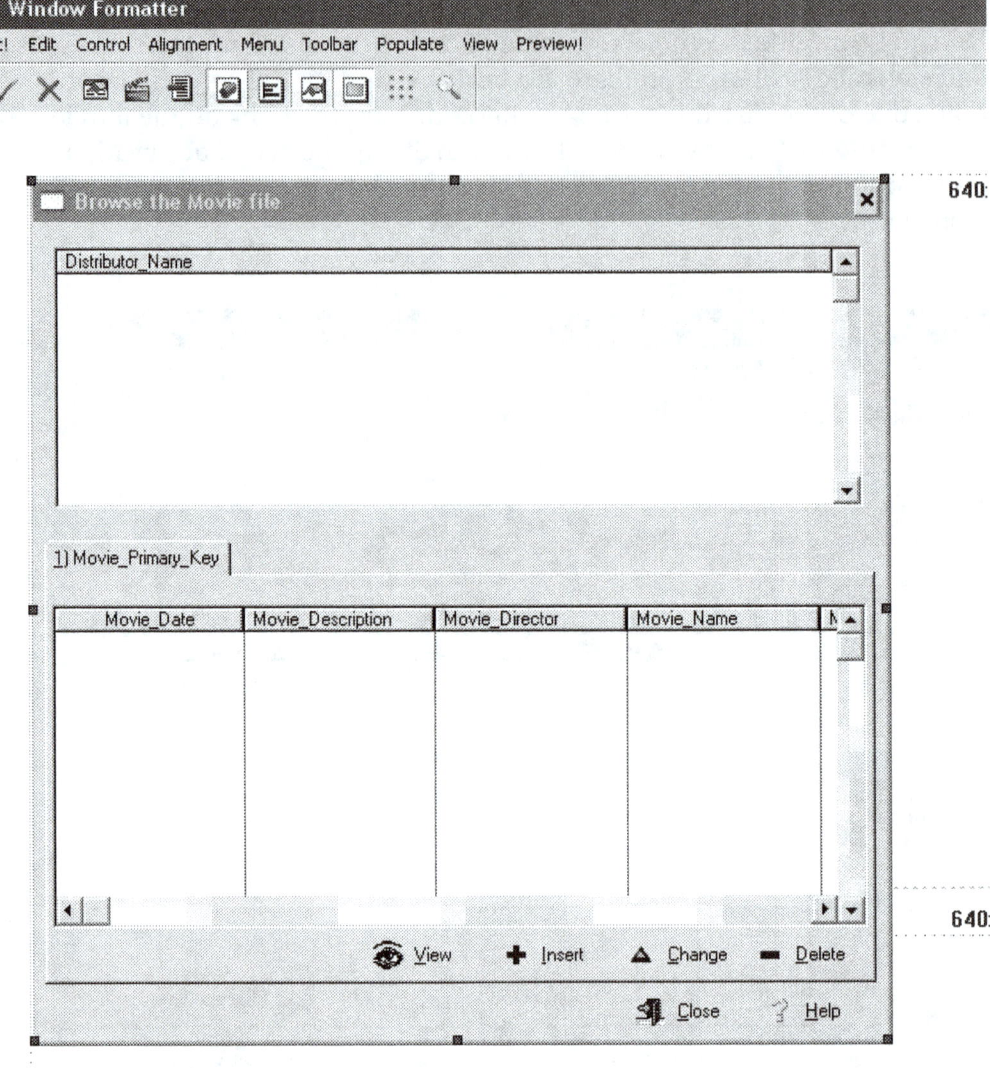

Figure 56. Modified movies browse.

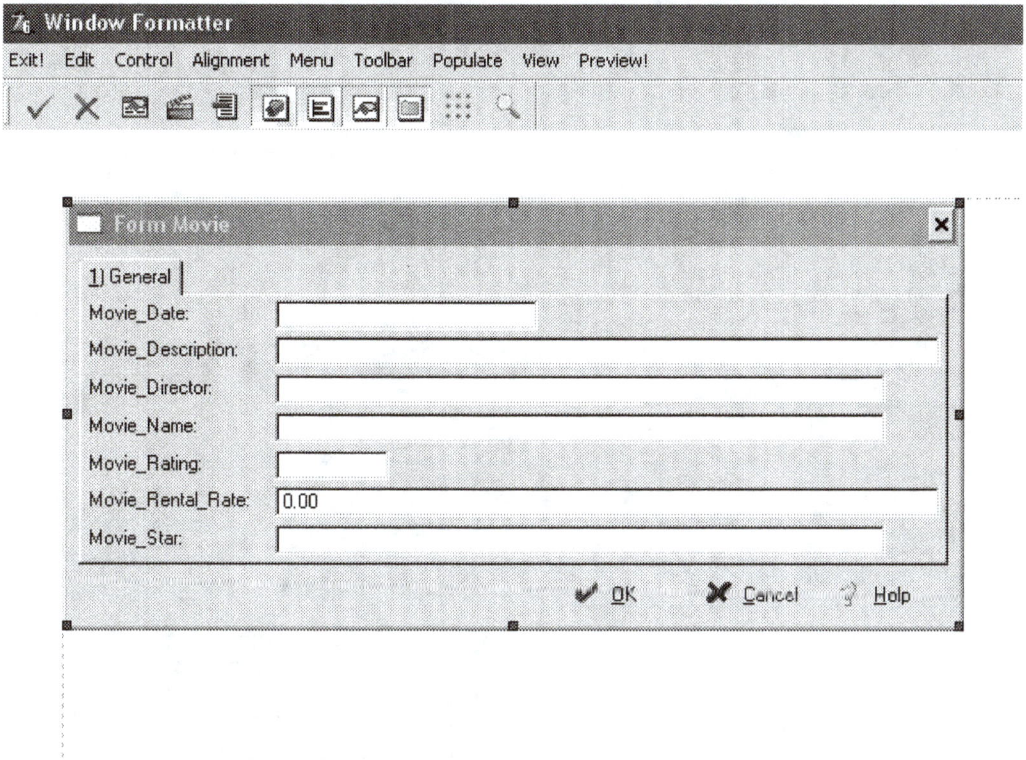

Figure 57. Initial Movies update screen.

The final set of activities is to either modify or create new reports. The processes to accomplish this is the same as previously presented.

All in all, the process to add a new table, modify the application's menu, add its browse, update and reports should take no longer than two hours per new table. That presumes, however a table design. So, if a prototype is demonstrated in a morning session, and during the afternoon the database design changes are formulated, it is quite practical to presume that a modified prototype could be presented the next morning. If the changes are more substantive, for example, if an entire new set of tables is discovered, or if tables must be injected within an existing hierarchical sequence of tables, the effort will naturally take longer. The longer time, will be in hours rather than in staff-weeks.

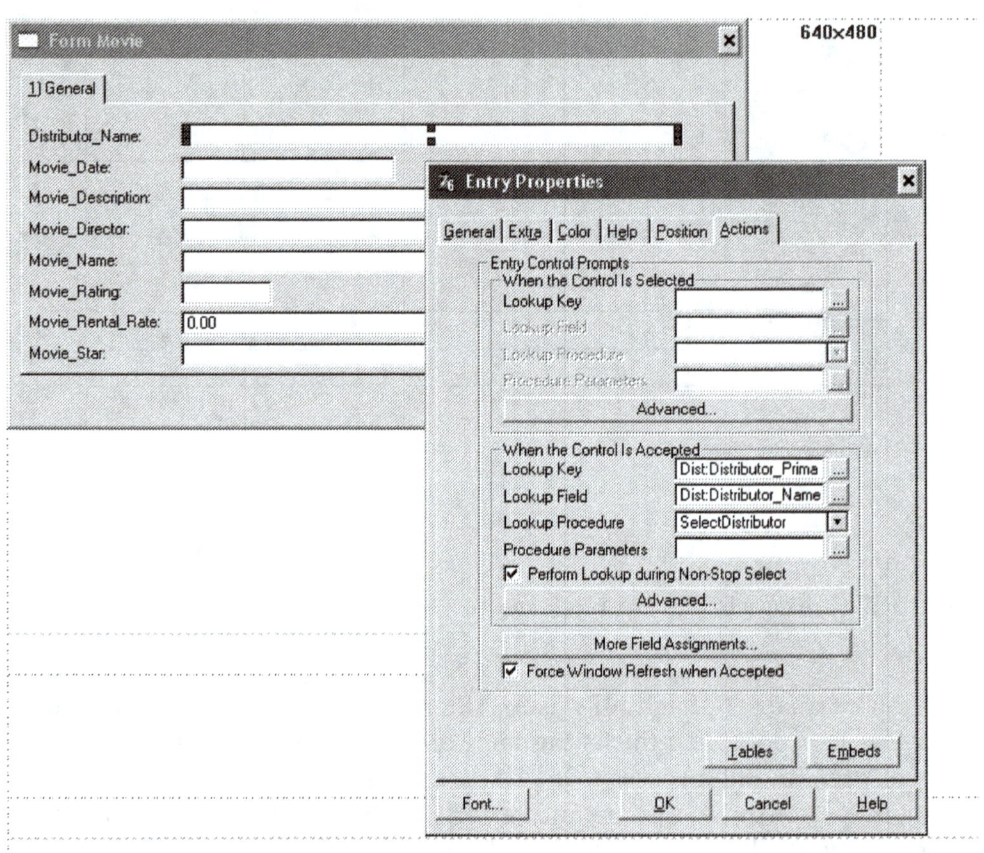

Figure 58. Entry of referential actions specifications on movies update screen.

If this process is repeated two or three times per week for a period of about a month it is very likely that the application's specification, that is, the database design and fundamental process logic will have progressed to a level that is equivalent to several years of normal evolution.

Step 4.3: Achieve Benefits From Prototyping

The benefits derived from the process of requirements evolution through prototyping cannot be overstated. It is a well-known mantra that every dollar spent in requirements' changes saves $100 for the same changes during design and saves $1000 during normal business information system evolution of a production class business information system. While that mantra has been known for years, no tools really existed that would make the requirements changes practical to accomplish.

With business information systems generators such as Clarion, it is practical to create entire business information systems that can be demonstrated and evolved. Given that these prototypes are integrated within Metabases, the mantra can be accomplished.

Figure 59 presents the overarching formula for business information systems life cycle costs. The formula basically states that if $100K is spent during Requirements Analysis and Function-Design, about $400K more will be spent during Detailed Design, Code & Unit Test, business information system Test, Deployment, Documentation, and Training. About five times more than the first $500K will be spent for business information system's evolution and maintenance. Traditionally, the cry has been to cut the first box, Requirements Analysis and Function Design. That however merely exacerbates the second box by making it 6, 7, 8, or more units because of all the necessary rework caused by an adequate requirements analysis.

Further, the costs for evolution and maintenance rise because the business information system has been quickly processed through its Requirements Analysis and Functional Design stage. But with the use of tools like the Metabase and business information system generators like Clarion, a more highly refined business information system (data and process models) emerges from the first stage. So, while this stage may cost the same, much more is accomplished. The business information system requirements appear not as version one, but as maybe version 8, 9, or 10.

Systems Development Life Cycle Costs

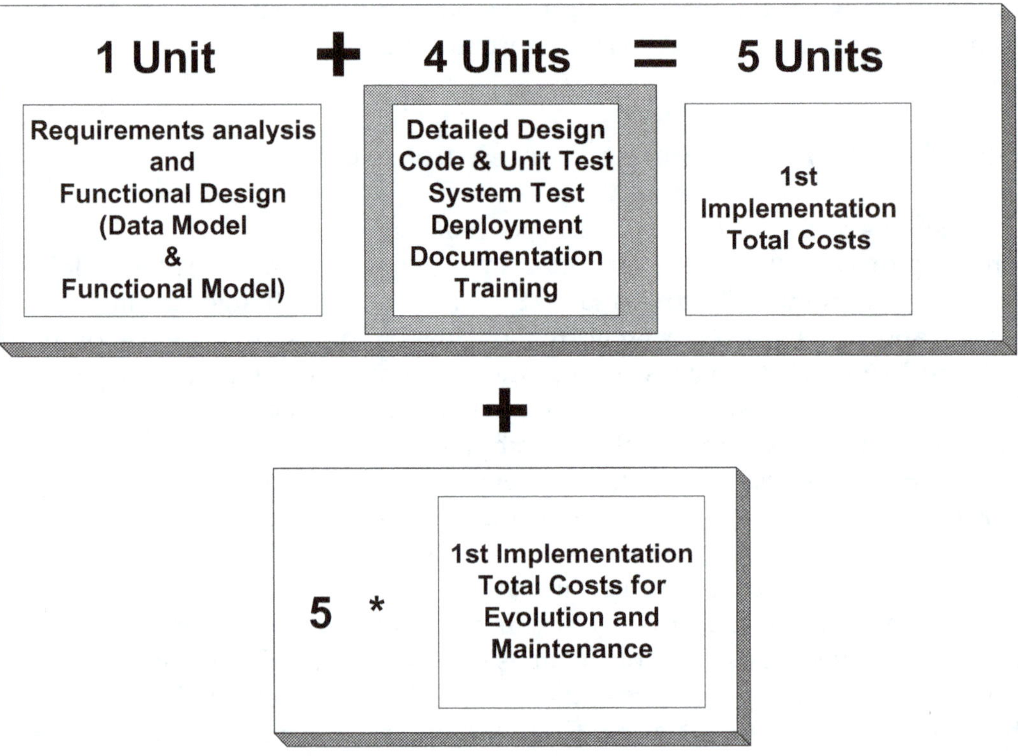

Figure 59. Critical components of the systems development life cycle.

Again, because of the Metabase and business information system generators, the second box can be radically reduced from maybe 4x to at most 2x. Because the business information system emerges from the requirements' stage at version 8, 9, or 10, it is more than possible to reduce the quantity of major evolutions from five to two or at most three. The overall effect is dramatic. If through traditional methods, a business information system originally cost $400K in stage one, its life cycle costs approached $12 million. Through the use of Metabase and business information system generators, stage two can be reduced to 2x, and life cycles cost's stage can also be reduced to 2x. That means that the overall life cycle costs can be reduced to $3.6 million. That's a savings of about 66%.

Once the requirements are both valid and finalized, Step 5, Create Request for Proposal can begin.

3.5 Step 5: Create Request for Proposal

The role of a request for proposal under this approach is non-traditional. Traditionally, the requirements development organization creates a requirements specification, issues the specification to a number of business information systems development organizations, receives proposals from these organizations, selects a winner and then provides funding to the winning organization as it creates the business information system.

Subsequent to the delivery, the business information systems development organizations perform warranty maintenance for a period of time, and thereafter, make functional changes on a fee for service basis. Under the traditional approach, there are three main types of procurement alternatives:

- Firm fixed price.
- Time and materials.
- Cost plus fixed fee.

Under the firm-fixed-price approach, whenever there is a requirements change, the contract's funding is increased and the original delivery date is slipped. Under the time-and-materials approach, whenever there is a requirements change, the contract's funding is increased and the original delivery date is slipped. Finally, under the cost-plus-fixed-fee approach, whenever there is a requirements change, the contract's funding is increased and the original delivery date is slipped. Different? Not much.

While the costing and fee structure may be different, the ultimate result is the same. That is, under any of the three request for proposal procurement alternatives, all the risk for proper specification is with the requirements development organization. Whenever there are new or changed requirements, the business information systems development organizations immediately request a contract modification which almost always means a schedule slip coupled with an increase in funding. All the risk is with the requirements development organizations, and the relationship with the business information systems development organizations is almost always adversarial.

Under the approach in this book, the procurement paradigm is fundamentally changed. Traditionally, the system development organization only received a large volume of requirements. It was up to the business information system development organization to figure out everything else and then implement the system. The Preface to this book exemplifies the traditional approach.

Rather than adversarial, the role of the requirements development organization's procurement group is to promote maximum involvement by the business information systems development organization including:

- Providing technical support for the already proven to be valid technical specification including a complete database design and all process and report specifications.

- Providing a completely working prototype of the business information system.

- Performing functional demonstrations of the prototype.

- Providing access to the Metabase.

- Developing and iterating a complete set of functional conformance tests that ensure acceptable business information system performance.

- Performing conformance testing and certification of the developed business information system so it can be accepted and put into production.

The implementing organization may be given the latitude to choose the implementation platforms, hardware, operating system, telecommunications and interoperability environments, and database management business information system.

The obligations of the business information systems development organizations under this approach are:

- Develop the production system.

- Perform conformance tests provided by the requirements development organization prior to delivering the system to the requirements development organization.

- Provide a set of training, documentation, and technical support.

The request for proposal needs to clearly set out this strategy for "procurement" and invite the business information systems development organization to compete for the work. The main content of the request for proposal should contain descriptions of the problem to be solved, the mission, business organizations, business functions, all interrelationships among these missions, organizations, and functions, the database design, and the working prototype, examples of the functional conformance tests that must be accomplished, proposed calendars and schedules that participants would be expected to meet.

The request for proposal should include the Metabase system itself along with the contained metadata so that the business information system development organization can employ it to store all the metadata products developed as the business information system is implemented. It is through the Metabase that the requirements development organization receives all work products and assesses the proposed functionality of the solutions.

In addition, the request for proposal should contain a complete copy of the methodology the requirements development organization employs to track the development and progress of the business information systems development. If the methodology is comprehensive enough, the business information systems development organizations will probably immediately adopt it as their methodology for accomplishing the work.

If both the requirements development organization and business information systems development organizations are working off the "same sheet of music," the overall process will be smoother.

3.6 Step 6: Evaluate Proposal Responses

Vendor responses should contain:

- Descriptions of the business information system's design and development strategies.

- Methodologies and quality controls that the vendor are to undertake.

- The management controls that would be placed on business information systems development to ensure quality product development.

- Proposed schedules.

- The expected quantity and duration of meetings with the requirements development organization staff.

- References of past efforts of a similar nature that ensure the requirements development organization that the vendor will complete the effort.

These types of proposal materials are critical because vendors (internal or external) are largely on their own to produce products. Vendors that place too few demands on the requirements development organization's staff are naive implementers and will likely fail in the business information system's implementation. If a business information system implementing organization has a "don't call us, we'll call you" approach, that vendor should be disqalified.

3.7 Step 7: Award Contract

For external business information system development organizations, a formal contact should be created. For internal organizations, *contract* is certainly the wrong word. The proper phrase should either be "cooperative agreement" or "memorandum of understanding." Notwithstanding the name of the agreement, the content should be what is contained in Section 3.6 above.

Once a vendor is selected, a contract or memorandum of understanding can be scripted that enables vendor access to materials and key members of requirements' development organization. These individuals resolve ongoing detailed design and implementation problems, progress status, and the testing of early releases of products.

These group meetings enable staff from the intended requirements development organization to be aware of progress and to factor the impending availability of products into their budget cycles.

3.8 Step 8: Manage Contractor

Contractor management within this type of cooperative arrangement is also unique. Instead of just managing the expenditure of funds and the receipt of large volumes of opaque deliverables, the best type of arrangement is a series of meetings over a period of months. During these meetings, the vendor works with requirements development organization addressing in-progress work, Metabase data updates, demonstrations, development of test data and functional test scenarios. The Metabase should either be kept current by the vendor, or the vendor should submit deliverables in the form of Metabase metadata loads. Under either scenario, the requirements specification and the prototype are current with the actual implementation. This is critical because it is from the Metabase that the conformance tests are generated.

The vendor also addresses vendor-surfaced anomalies, proposes resolutions, develops and promulgates functional-process handbooks and/or user guides, and training materials. The working relationship between the two teams should be such that it's difficult to know who works for whom.

3.9 Step 9: Test Conformance to Prototype

The final step is conformance testing. The need for conformance testing is to simply answer the question: How will the requirements development organization know if they receive a properly working software business information system? Traditionally, the answer has always been, *caveat emptor*. To resolve healthy scepticism, the requirements development organizations has to develop a set of functional acceptance tests. These tests, if valid and comprehensive were almost always very expensive to build.

Conversely, tests that are cost effective to build and quick to accomplish are almost always invalid. Consequently, requirements' development organizations often cycled through a series of almost-useful products which required them to develop extensions, ancillary support business information systems, and the like. All these work-arounds for missing functionality are not cost-effective nor satisfying to any of the involved parties.

The benefits from a comprehensive and valid set of conformance tests are compelling, and include:

- All parties, that is, the requirements development organization and the business information systems development organization, all know that there is an agreed-to minimum essential and testable functionality that must be performed.

- The requirements development organization knows that all products sold to it are capable of a minimum essential set of functionality.

The requirements development organization and supporting user-group committees are responsible for developing a set of standardized conformance tests that meet the needs of all requirements development organizations across all levels in support of internal business information system functionality and data interchange functionality.

If a prototype exists along with mission, business organizations, business functions, and database design, the fundamental basis for conformance tests already exists. During the business information system implementation process, if these artifacts are constantly updated, the basis for the conformance tests is also being updated.

At the end, the business information system development organization has to merely satisfy the requirements development organization that the business information system accomplishes all the functionality represented through the metadata contained in the Metabase.

How this is done is quite simple. The metabase has facilities that allow the processes of the business information system to be allocated to the Mission-Organization-Function triples. If all are allocated, and if all are satisfactorily implemented, the conformance tests are largely accomplished.

There must also be conformance tests for performance, ease of use, documentation, training, hotline support, and human factors engineering. All these are necessary to develop and demonstrate as well.

3.10 Nine-Step Approach Summary and Conclusion

This chapter presented a nine-step approach through displays from the Metabase and the Clarion environment to actually illustrate the accomplishment of the steps. The key characteristic of this 9-step approach is that it represents a significant change in responsibilities. Traditionally, almost all the nine steps are contracted to a business information systems development organization. Too often, this results in cost overruns, late deliveries, and diminished capabilities. In contrast, the approach moves the responsibility to the requirements development organization where it always rightly belonged.

The first seven steps are totally the responsibility of the requirements development organization. Step eight involves the information systems development organization as it implements the business information system. Step nine, Conformance Testing, is the responsibility of the requirements development organization.

The main objective is to enable functional users to advance their awareness of their information technology requirement, and to evolve this awareness through prototyping until it is ready for information technology to implement: one time and correctly.

Experience on many projects have shown that too much is expected from business information system development organizations. In addition, the GAO studies of information technology failures show that most causes of business information system failures occur outside the control of information technology organizations.

Even if the entire enterprise adopted and followed a knowledge worker framework, this model will probably not solve all the problems associated with business information systems. That's because most requirements' development organizations have a long-standing tradition of autonomous development of business information systems. These almost always result in stove-pipes of metadata, databases, and business information systems. The autonomous approach prevents the effective deployment of an enterprise-wide business information system design and implementation strategy that has define-once, use many times as its founding principle for all work products. In contrast to the autonomous, stove-pipe approach, this nine-step approach has the benefits listed in Table 17.

Nine Step Approach to Business Information Systems Development		
	Step	**Benefit and/or Description**
1	Mission Development	Missions provide the overarching framework for the entire enterprise. Missions are accomplished by Organizations through Functions, and further refined into database domains. All databases and business information systems are established within this enterprise architecture framework. This sets every effort squarely within the business's architecture.
2	Database Design	Database designs are built from within the enterprise architecture. Metadata is used to ensure enterprise-wide data structures and semantics. Database designs are based on enterprise-wide data elements, data models of concepts, DBMS independent models, and finally DBMS dependent models. This enables maximum metadata re-use, data interoperability, and semantic harmonization.
3	Prototype Generation	Prototypes, set within the enterprise architecture, and which are built through maximally reusable metadata, represent business information systems set within the context of recognized functions. Through business information system generating the prototype, maximum efforts can be expended on getting a full set of requirements, and minimum efforts can be expended on the creation of the business information system.
4	Specification Evolution	Specification evolution is critical because it enables the complete set of requirements to be teased out. Through the use of business information system generators, the ability to proceed from one iteration to the next is easy and can be accomplished in hours to days versus weeks to months. This enables a first real implementation from a version 10 prototype. Prototyping also greatly reduces the quantity of evolutions during a business information systems life cycle.

Nine Step Approach to Business Information Systems Development		
	Step	**Benefit and/or Description**
5	Request for Proposals	A request for a proposal is a formal specification of what is desired to be implemented. The document should contain all the metadata and the prototype that were created in first four steps. The document should contain a requirement for being able to evolve the specification of the business information system being implemented. The document should contain the method through which the requirements development organization monitor and evaluates the accomplishments of the business information systems development organization. Another component of the document should be the specifications of the conformance tests, based on the prototype and other requirements that are to be accomplished as the basis of business information system acceptance.
6	Proposal Evaluation	The proposal evaluation process should be engineered to determine how well, when, and for what cost a business information systems development organization will implement the business information system. The proposal evaluation process ultimately produces an agreement between the requirements development organization and the business information systems development organization regarding the implementation process, schedules, costs, reviews, and deliverables.
7	Contract Award	The contact award is the event whereby the accord reached in the prior step becomes the blueprint for action between the requirements development organization and the business information systems development organization. The key components of the contact are the deliverables' specifications, time-lines, costs, and agreements on the obligations of both the requirements development organization and the business information systems development organization.
8	Contractor Management	Contractors, whether in-house or from outside the enterprise need to be managed by the requirements development organization. By management, it is not meant that daily activities need to be monitored but rather, there is joint participation in the success and/or problems associated with the effort.

Nine Step Approach to Business Information Systems Development		
	Step	**Benefit and/or Description**
9	Conformance Testing	Once the business information systems development has completed, the execution of the conformance tests form the basis for acceptance by the requirements development organization.

Table 17. Benefits from the nine step approach to business information systems development.

3.11 Questions and Exercises

1. Do you have a 9-step like process at your enterprise? How is it similar or different overall?

2. What is the role of missions? How are they the same or different from functions?

3. Why should you have both missions and functions? Why are mission documents strategic, and function documents tactical or operational? Are there some missions that are accomplished by the same functions? What would be examples?

4. What is the role of organizations? Do you have them cross referenced to missions? What are examples of different cases of mission-organization cross references that would be considered good or bad?

5. What is the role of functions. How do they differ from missions? Do you have functions cross referenced with mission-organization pairs? What are examples of different cases of mission-organization and function cross references that would be considered good or bad?

6. What does the book mean by "data is executed policy?" Is that true? What does that mean in regards to how database should be engineered? How stable should database designs be?

7. Does the database design strategy provided in this book make sense from an enterprise-wide viewpoint?

8. Do you have mechanisms to create enterprise-wide data elements and data models of concepts that can be used over and over to standardize parts of database designs? What's the value? How does that impact the time and effort to design databases?

9. Does it make sense to have five data model generalization levels? Are any really not needed? Which ones and why? How would your data engineering environment change if you had all five levels in your enterprise?

10. What strategy would you create/impose to accomplish data standardization? How would the five data model generalization levels help? Explain what value these levels would have Does it make sense to re-engineer your existing data models? What would be the benefit to a project, to a functional area, and to the enterprise?

11. What is your definition of a prototype? How is it similar or different than the book? Are your prototypes data-driven? Process-driven? What's the difference? Why is one preferred over another?

12. How is the use of the database design an assist in creating a prototype? Why must the database design be in third normal form? What is the effect if the database is not in this form?

13. Why can't the business information system generator infer a particular behavior model with the business information system generator imports the data model? Why does the business information system generator come up with an every-which-way-but-loose design?

14. Why is it critical that the business information system generator create an application design metadata layer first rather than just directly creating steams of program code?

15. What would happen to the prototyping process if you didn't have the application design metadata layer?

16.   What is the process you would construct to validate the prototype?

17.   What should the real objectives be from a prototype demonstration?

18.   What are the most likely results from the prototype generation process?

19.   What is the role of test data in the prototyping process? How should the test data be constructed?

20.   What are the differences between a prototyped application and a real production-ready application? How does the prototype help? How does the prototype set up a false expectation of "ready-prototype-n-go?" How would you correctly set expectations?

21.   What components should there be in an request for proposal (RFP)?

22.   What role should each component play?

23.   What is the real objective of the RFP? What kind of interaction should there be between your organization and the vendors during the RFP and proposal process?

24.   What are the factors that should be evaluated in each proposal? How would you rank the items that are evaluated. Why is the determined rank for each make it more valuable than an item on a lower rank and less valuable than an item on a higher rank?

25.   What should be in a vendor contract?

26.   What should be the basis of a "good deal?"

27.   What should your interaction be with the vendor during a contract's performance?

28.   What should the role of the metabase be during contract performance? Should the metabase be kept up-to-date? Should the prototype be kept up to date?

29.   How should conformance tests be constructed? What role would the Metabase play? What role would the prototype play? How can test/demonstration data be updated?

30.   How detailed should conformance tests be? Should the tests be pass/fail?

31.   How could the conformance tests be turned into "user performance" tests for training and testing the competence of users? What role would the Metabase and the Prototype plan in user conformance tests?

4

Business Information Systems Planning

This chapter presents an overview of the Whitemarsh Business Information Systems Plan process[16]. It does no good to know how to implement business information systems if you do not know which ones to implement and in which sequence.

Over the past 10 years, starting in the late 1990s, there has been a dramatic increase in the use of Enterprise Resource Packages (ERP). These are comprehensive database and business information system implementations across broad functional areas. Consequently, many of the newly created database and business information systems are derivative business information systems, not one-off business information systems that start from blank slates. Because of this very significant change, enterprise-wide database and Business Information Systems Plans are more important than ever, and the very metadata created during the development of these plans needs to be stored in the Metabase so that impact analyses can be quickly developed and accomplished.

4.1 Rationale for a Business Information Systems Plan

Every year corporations and other types of organizations spend about 5% of their gross income on business information systems and their supports. If the

---

[16]. There are a significant quantity of materials, that is, books, courses and papers, on the Whitemarsh website dealing with a comparative analysis of Information Systems Planning approaches, and a significantly greater exposition of the Whitemarsh approach. The Whitemarsh approach was created specially to overcome the shortcomings of the other approaches.

enterprise spends from $300-700 million, that implies an information technology budget of about $15,000,000 to $35,000,000! A significant part of those funds support enterprise database, a philosophy that enables corporations to research the past, control the present, and plan for the future.

Even though a business information system costs from $1,000,000 to $10,000,000, and even through most chief information officers (CIOs) can specify exactly how much money is being spent for hardware, software, and staff, CIOs cannot however state with any degree of certainty why one business information system is being done this year versus next, why it is being done ahead of another, or finally, why it is being done at all.

Many enterprises do not have model-based business information systems development environments that allow business information system designers to see the benefits of rearranging a business information systems development schedule. Consequently, the questions that cannot be answered include:

- What effect will there be on the overall schedule if a business information system is purchased versus developed?

- At what point does it pay to hire an abnormal quantity of contract staff to advance a schedule?

- What is the long term benefit from 4GL versus 3GL?

- Is it better to generate 3GL than to generate/use a 4GL?

- What are the real costs of distributed software development over centralized development?

If these questions were transformed and applied to any other component of a business (e.g., accounting, manufacturing, distribution and marketing), and remained unanswered, that unit's manager would surely be fired!

Not only are answers to these questions needed NOW!, they are also needed quickly, cost effectively, and in a form that they can be modeled and changed in response to unfolding realities. This chapter provides a brief review of a successful 10-step strategy that answers these questions.

Too many organizations have only a vague notion of the names and interactions of the existing and under development business information systems. Whenever they need to know, a meeting is held among the critical *few*, an inventory is taken, interactions confirmed, and accomplishment schedules are updated.

This ad hoc Business Information Systems Plan was possible only because all design and development was centralized, the only computer was a main-frame, and the past was an acceptable prologue because budgets were ever increasing, schedules slippages were not fatal, and information was not part of the corporation's critical edge.

Well, today is different, really different! Budgets are under pressure, and slipped schedules are being cited as preventing business opportunities. Confounding the computing environment are different operating systems, DBMSs, development tools, telecommunications (LAN, WAN, Intra-, and Inter-net), and distributed hard- and software.

Rather than having centralized, long-range planning and management activities that address these problems, today's business units are using readily available tools to design and build ad hoc stop-gap solutions. These ad hoc business information systems not only do not interconnect, support common semantics, or provide synchronized views of critical corporate policy, they form the almost impossible to comprehend confusion of business information systems and data from which business information systems order and semantic harmony must spring.

Not only has the computing landscape become profoundly different and more difficult to comprehend, the need for just the right information at just the right time is escalating. Late or wrong information can be worse than no information.

Business information system managers need a model of their business information systems environment; a model that is malleable. As new requirements are discovered, budgets modified, new hardware/software introduced, this model must be such that it can reconstitute Business Information Systems Plans in a timely and efficient manner.

4.2 Characteristics of a Quality Business Information Systems Plan

A quality Business Information Systems Plan must exhibit five distinct characteristics to be useful. These five are presented in the Table 18.

Characteristic	Description
Timely	The Business Information Systems Plan must be timely. A business Information Systems Plan that is created long after it is needed is useless. In almost all cases, it makes no sense to take longer to plan work than to perform the work planned.
Useable	The Business Information Systems Plan must be useable. It must be so for all the projects as well as for each project. The Business Information Systems Plan should exist in sections that once adopted can be parceled out to project managers and immediately accomplished.
Maintainable	The Business Information Systems Plan must be maintainable. New business opportunities, new computers, business mergers, etc. all affect the Business Information Systems Plan. The Business Information Systems Plan must support quick changes to the estimates, technologies employed, and possibly even to the fundamental project sequences. Once these changes are accomplished, the new Business Information Systems Plan should be just a few computer program executions away.
Quality	While the Business Information Systems Plan must be a quality product, no Business Information Systems Plan is ever perfect on the first try. As the Business Information Systems Plan is executed, the metrics employed to derive the individual project estimates need to be refined as a consequence of new hardware technologies, business information system generators, techniques, or faster working staff. As these changes occur, their effects should be installable into the database that supports Business Information Systems Plan computation. In short, the Business Information Systems Plan should be a living product. It should be updated with every technology event, and certainly no less often than quarterly.
Reproducible	The Business Information Systems Plan must be reproducible. That is, when its development activities are performed by any other staff, the Business Information Systems Plan produced should essentially be the same. The Business Information Systems Plan should not significantly vary as a consequence of the assigned staff.

Table 18. Characteristics of a quality Business Information Systems plan.

Whenever a proposal for the development of a Business Information Systems Plan is created, the plan must be assessed against the five characteristics cited in Table 15. If any of the characteristics cannot be achieved in an appropriate way, then the entire set of funds for the development of a Business Information Systems Plan is at risk.

4.3 Business Information Systems Plan Within the Context of the Metadata Environment

A Business Information Systems Plan is the plan by which the databases and business information systems of the enterprise are accomplished not only in a timely manner but also in a business-need order. A high-level Business Information Systems Plan stylized process is depicted in Figure 60. A key facility through which the Business Information Systems Plan process obtains its "data" is the Metabase.

The overall process of Business Information Systems Planning is conveyed through the following story. Persons, through their positions within

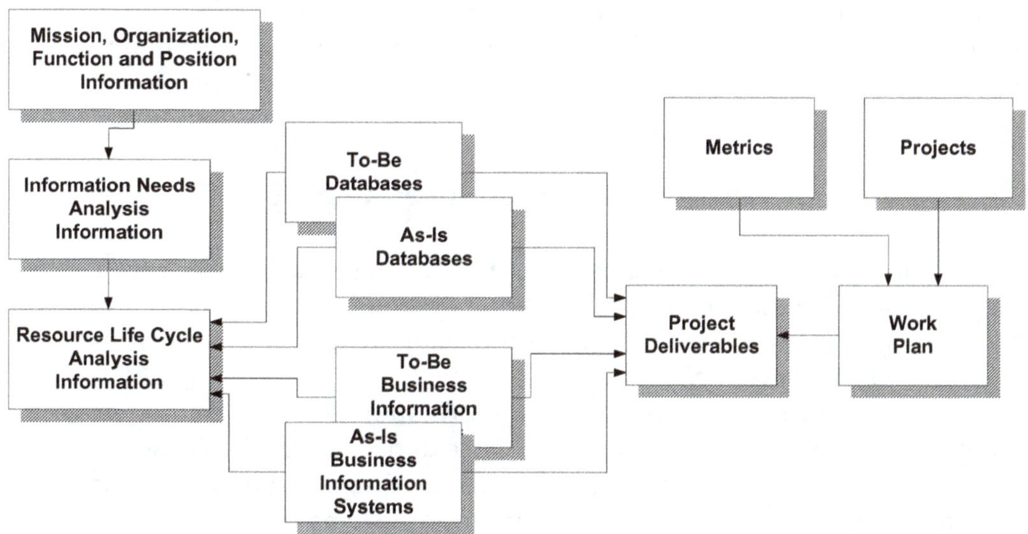

Figure 60. High-level view of metabase meta entities involved in information systems planning.

an organization, perform their organization-based functions in support of enterprise missions. Missions, organizations and functions all frame the enterprise.

From a foundation of missions, the information needs of the various positions and even persons occupying positions are determined. Information needs reflect the value-states of certain enterprise resources such as finance, people, and products. Enterprise resources too are determined within the scope of the missions.

Resources are defined in a life cycle manner such that the various Resource Life Cycle node value states are created through the execution of business information systems and data from databases. The databases and business information systems that should exist should be only those necessary to provide the information needed to support Resource Life Cycle states.

The goal of the Business Information Systems Planning process is to identify the operation, use, and and sequence the databases and business information systems necessary to operate the enterprise in a satisfactory manner. From that sequence flows the database and business information system creation and maintenance sequence.

Finally, project management exists to support the timely and appropriately sequenced accomplishment of all enterprise architecture, Business Information Systems Plans, database, and business information systems projects.

4.4 The Business Information Systems Plan Steps

The Business Information Systems plan project determines the sequence for implementing specific business information systems. The goal of the strategy is to deliver the most valuable business information system at the earliest time possible in the most cost-effective manner.

The end product of the Business Information System Planning project is a Business Information Systems Plan. Once deployed, the business information systems department can implement the plan with confidence that they are doing the correct business information systems project at the right time and in the right sequence. The focus of the Business Information Systems Plan is not one business information system but the entire suite of business information systems for the enterprise. Once developed, each identified business information system is seen in context with all other business information systems within the enterprise. The ten steps[17] for the Business Information Planning process are provided in Table 19.

Business Information System Plan Development Steps		
Step	**Name**	**Description**
1.	Create the mission model	The mission model, generally about 30 pages presents end-result characterizations of the essential raison d'etre of the enterprise. Missions are strategic, long range, and apolitical because they are stripped of the "who, how, and technology."
2.	Develop a high-level data model	The high-level data model is an Entity Relationship diagram created to meet the data needs of the mission descriptions. Only high-level attributes, keys, and relationships are required.
3.	Create the Resource Life Cycles and their nodes	Resources are drawn from both the mission descriptions and the high level data model. Resources and their life cycles are the names, descriptions and life cycles of the critical assets of the enterprise, which, when exercised achieve one or more aspect of the missions. Each enterprise resource "lives" through its Resource Life Cycle.
4.	Allocate precedence vectors among Resource Life Cycle Nodes	Tied together into an enablement network, the resulting Resource Life Cycle network forms a framework of enterprise's assets that represent an accomplishment-order and set of inter-resource relationships. The enterprise "lives" through its Resource Life Cycle network.
5.	Allocate existing business information systems and databases to the Resource Life Cycle Nodes	The Resource Life Cycle network presents a "lattice-work" onto which the "as is" business information systems and databases can be "attached." See for example, the meta model in Figure 60. The "to-be" databases and business information systems are similarly attached. "Difference projects" between the "as-is" and the "to-be" are then formulated. Achievement of all the difference projects is the achievement of the Business Information Systems Plan.

---

[17] These ten steps were initially formulated at the MITRE Corporation for an internal information systems planning project. Significant contributors to the successful accomplishment of the MITRE Information Systems Planning project were Dagmar Bogan and Stan Hopkins.

Business Information System Plan Development Steps		
Step	**Name**	**Description**
6.	Allocate standard work break down structures to each Resource Life Cycle Node	Detailed planning of the "difference projects" entails allocating the appropriate canned work breakdown structures and metrics. Employing work breakdown structures and metrics from a comprehensive methodology supports project management standardization, repeatability, and self-learning.
7.	Load resources into each work breakdown structure node	Once the required project resources are determined, these are loaded into the project management meta entities of the Metabase, that is, metrics, project, work plan and deliverables. The meta entities are those inferred by Figure 60.
8.	Schedule the Resource Life Cycle Nodes through some project management package facilities.	The entire suite of projects is then scheduled on an enterprise-wide basis. The PERT chart used by project management is the "PERT" chart represented by the Resource Life Cycle enablement network.
9.	Produce and review the Business Information Systems Plan	The scheduled result is predicable: Too long, too costly, and too ambitious. At that point, the real work starts: paring down the suite of projects to a realistic set within time and budget. Because of the metadata environment (see Figure 6), the integrated project management metadata (see Figure 60), and because all projects are configured against fundamental business-rationale-based designs, the results of the inevitable trade-offs can be set against business basics. Although the process is painful, the results can be justified and rationalized.
10.	Execute and adjust the Business Information Systems Plan through time.	As the Business Information Systems Plan is set into execution, it is inevitable that technology changes will occur that affect resource loadings. In this case, only steps 6-9 need to be repeated. As work progresses, the underlying metadata built or used in steps 1-5 will also change. Because a quality Business Information Systems Plan is "automated" the recasting of the Business Information Systems Plan should only take a week or less.

Table 19. Business Information Systems Plan development steps.

Collectively, the first nine steps take about 5,000 staff hours, or about $500,000. Compared to an information systems organization budget $15-35 million, that's only about 3.0% to 1.0%. If the information technology budget is 5% of the enterprise then any information systems plan effort is really just "noise" compared to the overall enterprise budget.

If the pundits are to be believed, that is, that the right information at the right time is the competitive edge, paying for a business Information Systems Plan that is accurate, repeatable, and reliable has a small price and a high pay-off.

4.4.1 Step 1: Create Mission Model

The mission model step should already be accomplished. So, other than to preform some review and minor revision there is no additional work to accomplish.

4.4.2 Step 2: Build the High Level Data Model

As in the mission step above, this work should have already been accomplished. So, other than to perform some review and minor revisions there is no additional work to accomplish.

4.4.3 Step 3: Create Resources and the Resource Life Cycles[18]

As a brief review, Missions are the idealized characterizations of end results of the visionary state of the operating enterprise. Database Object Classes, founded squarely on missions are the high-level declarations of the data required to reflect the achievement of the mission's vision. Resources and their life cycles are the names, descriptions, and life cycles of the critical assets

---

[18] The Resource Life Cycle Analysis monograph, authored by Ron Ross and Wanda Michaels was published in 1992 by Database Research Group, Boston MA. Ron can be reached at www.BSRsolutions.com

of the enterprise, which when exercised achieve one or more aspects of the missions. Each life cycle is composed of Resource Life Cycle Nodes.

A mission might be human resource management, wherein, the best and most cost effective staff are determined, acquired and managed. A Database Object Class that is squarely based, for example, on human resources would be Employee. Within the Database Object Class, Employee, are all the data structures, procedures, integrity constraints, table and Database Object Class procedures necessary to "move" an Employee object through its many policy-determined states. A resource might also be named employee, and would set out for the employee resource the life cycle stages that reflect the employee resource's "journey" through the enterprise. While an enterprise may have 50 to 150 Database Object Classes, there are seldom more than 20 resources.

Enterprises build databases and business information systems around the achievement of the life cycle states of its resources. Business information systems execute in support of a particular life cycle stage of a resource (e.g., employee promotion). These business information systems cause the databases to change the value-state of database objects to correctly reflect the resource's changed state. The state of one or more database objects in the database is the proof that the resource's state has been achieved. Resources become the lattice work to which database and business information systems are allocated. Table 20 presents the basic components of resources and their life cycles.

The ultimate goal of Resource Life Cycle Analysis is the identification and description of the major resources essential to the enterprise's survival. The ultimate goal of the Business Information Systems Plan is the identification and accomplishment-sequencing of the business information systems projects required to implement the enterprise resources in the most effective manner possible.

Resources and Resource Life Cycles	
Critical Components	**Definition**
Resource	A resource is an enduring asset with value to the enterprise
Resource Life Cycle	A Resource Life Cycle is the linear identification of the major states that must exist within life of the resource. The life cycle of a resource represents the resource's "cradle to grave" set of state changes.
Precedence Vector	A precedence vector is a relationship between two nodes of different Resource Life Cycle that indicates that the target Resource Life Cycle Node is enabled in some significant way by the source Resource Life Cycle Node.
Resource Life Cycle Node Matrix	The Resource Life Cycle Node matrix is the set of all resources, their life cycles and the precedence vectors among the nodes. Properly drawn the Resource Life Cycle Node Matrix resembles a PERT chart.

Table 20. Resources and Resource Life Cycles.

Step 3.1: Determine the Resources

The enterprise's product and/or service resources are defined; they may be either concrete or abstract. Ron Ross provides two guidelines to assist in resource identification:

- Define the product or service that constitute the enterprise's resources from the customer perspective.

- Define the resource as it is managed between the enterprise and its customers.

In addition, the characteristics of a resource are presented in Table 21.

Resource Characteristics	
Characteristic	**Definition**
Basic	The resource must exist for the enterprise to exist.
Complex	The resource requires development and management.
Valuable	The resource must be protected, exploited, and/or leveraged by the enterprise.
Enduring	The resource exists beyond business cycles.
Shareable	The resource is shared by different functions of the enterprise.
Structured	The resource can be described and organized.
Centralized	The resource can be controlled and monitored centrally, even if distributed in creation or use.

Table 21. Resource characteristics.

Additional tests for resources are:

- The resource must be monitored and forecasted. By the time the resource is required, it is too late to be produced.

- The resource must be optimized. The resource is of such a cost that an unlimited supply is not possible.

- The resource must be controlled and allocated. The resource is desirable and necessary, and must be shared among components of the enterprise.

- The resource must be tracked. Each stage of the resource is important to the enterprise, including its demise.

Step 3.2: Determine the Resource Life Cycles

The second step is to determine a life cycle for each resource. Each node in the life cycle represents a major state change in the resource. The state change is accomplished by business information systems and is reflected through the enterprise's Database Object Classes (conformed into databases). Figures 61, 62, and 63 developed in support of an enterprise database project for a state-wide court business information system, show the Resource Life Cycles for , Case, Court's Personnel, and Document.

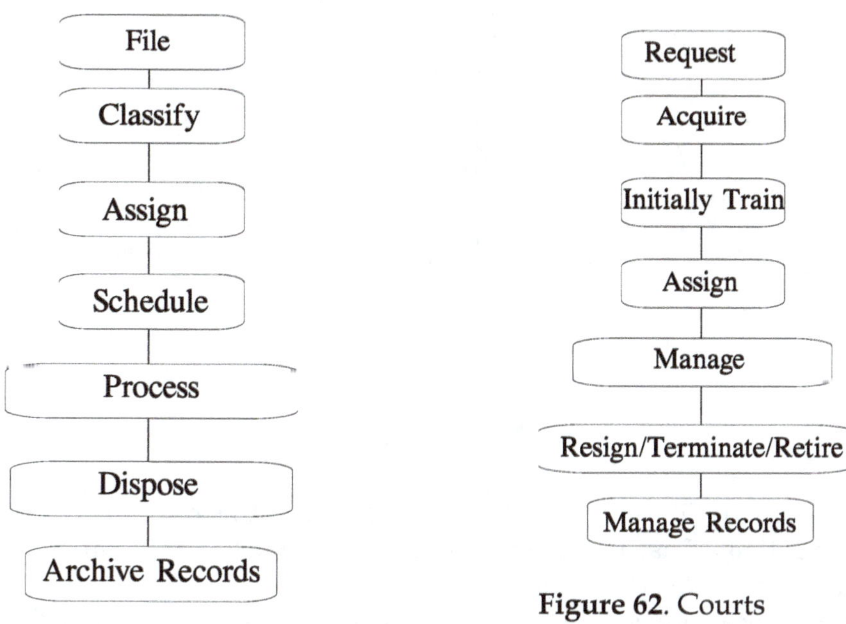

Figure 61. Case.

Figure 62. Courts Personnel.

4.4.4 Step 4: Allocate Precedence Vectors among Resource Life Cycle Nodes

After the resources and life cycles are complete, precedence vectors are established. There are actually two types of precedencies: Within the Resource Life Cycle chain and between Resource Life Cycle Nodes of different resources. Precedencies *within* the Resource Life Cycles are established during the Resource Life Cycle Analysis. These are the lines that connect one node to

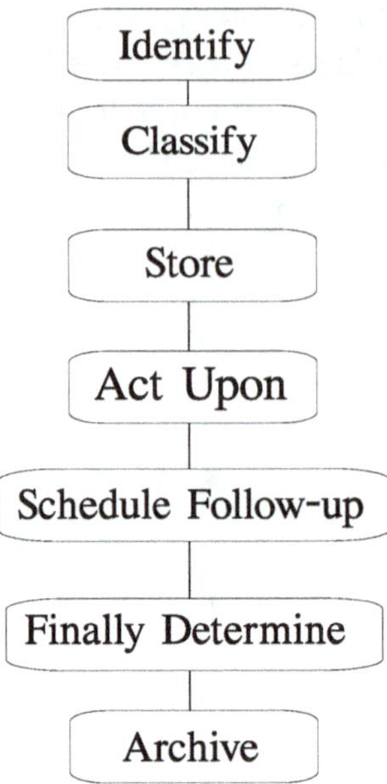

Figure 63. Document.

the next. In Figure 61, File and Classify are connected in this manner. What is being implied is that a Case must first be Filed within the Court before it can be Classified by the Court Personnel.

A precedence between resources is created when a Resource Life Cycle state, that is, a specific life cycle node, cannot be effective or correctly accomplished unless a different Resource Life Cycle's node state from a different Resource Life Cycle has been established or completed. Figure 64 illustrates this case. The Resource Life Cycle, Court Person, has the node, Assign, as the source of the precedence vector to the Resource Life Cycle, Case and the node, Classify. The meaning here is that a court person must be assigned before a case can be classified. A precedence vector is drawn from an enabling Resource Life Cycle Node to an enabled Resource Life Cycle Node.

The most difficult problem in establishing the precedence is the mind set of the analyst. The life cycle is *not* viewed in *operational* order, but in *enablement* order: that is, what Resource Life Cycle state must exist before the next Resource Life Cycle state is able to occur. This is a difficult mind set to acquire, as there is a natural tendency to view the life cycle in operational

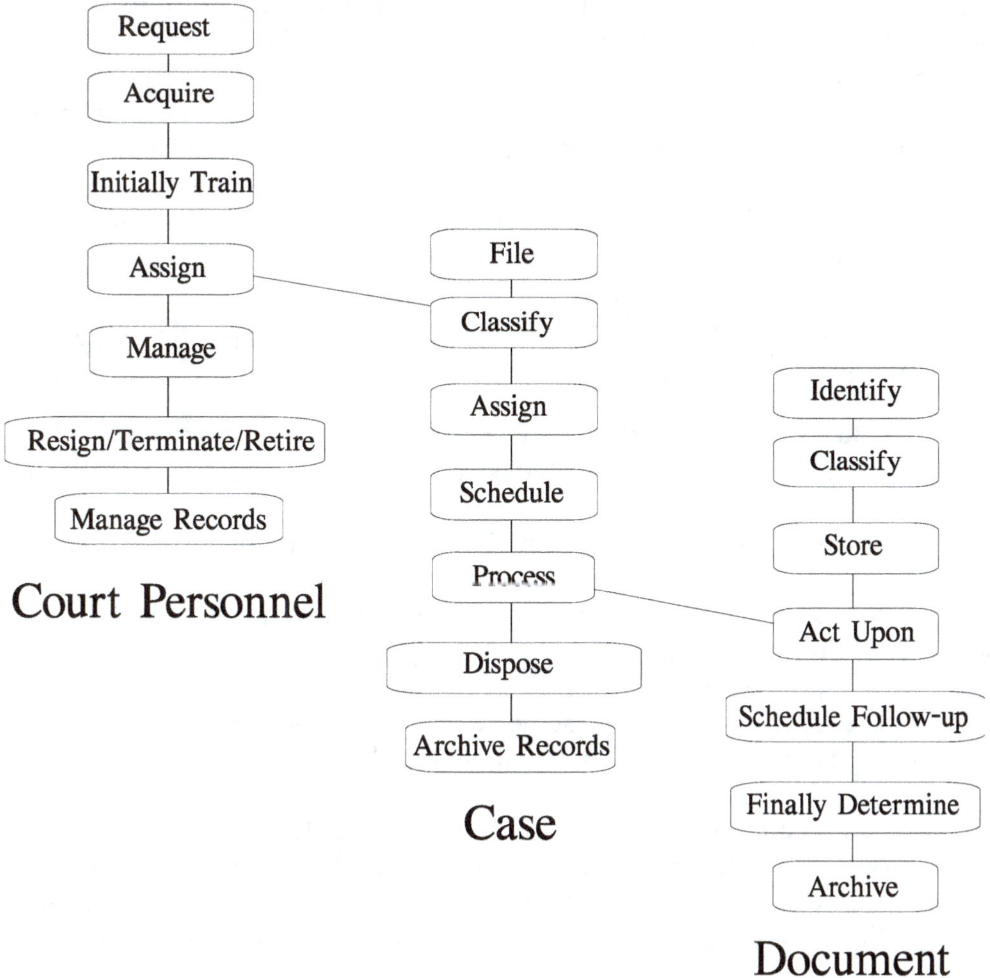

Figure 64. Precedence vectors among resource life cycles.

order. The test of precedence is: What enables what, and what is it enabled by what?

For example, project establishment precedes the award of a contract. This does not seem natural, since a project would not operationally begin until after a contract is awarded. However, there must be an established infrastructure to create the project and to perform the work prior to the contract award. A workforce must be in place to perform work along with the ability to assign work to the employee on the contract, and the ability to bill the customer. Therefore, project establishment enables the contract accomplishment.

There are three possible meanings for enablement. That is, a Resource Life Cycle state precedes another Resource Life Cycle state because:

- The accomplishment of the preceding Resource Life Cycle state saves money.

- The Resource Life Cycle state leads to rapid development of another Resource Life Cycle state.

- The Resource Life Cycle state permits faster, more convenient accomplishment of another Resource Life Cycle state.

If one or more of those meanings exist, then a precedence vector should be created.

Two alternatives exist relative to the existence of the enterprise: newly established or existing. Experience shows the preferred perspective is that of an already-existing enterprise.

Resource Life Cycle Node states may or may not exist during a life cycle, or events may occur in parallel. For example, an employee may receive an award, but then again, may never receive an award. An employee may work before and after a security clearance is granted. The strategy to deal with parallel or optional Resource Life Cycle Node states is to create a single stream of Resource Life Cycle Nodes in which none are parallel or optional by "pushing down" the parallel or optional Resource Life Cycle Nodes to a lower level.

Figure 64 presents the Resource Life Cycle network for Documents, Cases, and Court Personnel. The enablement stories for this figure are presented in Table 22.

Enablement Vector Stories				
Source		**Target**		
Resource Life Cycle	**Node**	**Resource Life Cycle**	**Node**	**Enablement Effect**
Court Personnel	Assign	Case	Classify	Court Personnel Assignments enable Case classification
Case	Process	Document	Act upon	A case process enables Document actions.

Table 22. Resource life cycle precedence vector enablement stories.

4.4.5. Step 5: Allocate Business Information Systems and Databases to the Resource Life Cycle Nodes

Once a Resource Life Cycle network has been created, it is stored into the Metabase. Once there, its lattice can be employed to attach the databases and business information systems. Databases and their business information systems exist within a data architecture framework. The five distinct database architecture classes:

- Original data capture.
- Transaction data staging area.
- Subject area databases.
- Data warehouses (wholesale and retail (a.k.a. data marts)).
- Reference data.

These database architecture classes are illustrated in Figure 1. Each architecture class is briefly described in Section 2.4.1. Each of these database architecture classes is described in Attachment 2. A more detailed description of these data architecture classes is provided through the Whitemarsh website.

Most Resource Life Cycle Nodes contain at least one original data capture database application. The data from these original data capture databases should be pushed to their respective transaction data staging area databases.

Once there, various subject area databases pull the data to build the longitudinal and broad subject area databases. It is likely that there is one subject area database for one or more resources. Data from the subject area databases, also called operational data stores by Bill Inmon, is again pulled to create one or more data warehouse databases.

Most databases employ one or more reference data tables as standard semantics for selection, control-breaks and printing.

Databases and business information systems exist in two forms: "as-is" and "to-be." An "as-is" database or business information system, as its characteristic implies, represents the existing state of the information technology assets. A "to-be" database or business information system is a proposal for some technology improvement, functional enhancement, or an under-way project effort.

Step 5.1: Allocate Existing (As-is) Databases or Files to Resource Life Cycle Nodes

Within the class of existing databases or files, there are three prototypical examples:

- A file for every distinct process or purpose.
- A single database for all reasons.
- Multi-data architecture database classes.

Knowledge about these existing set of databases and files should already reside in the Metabase. If their metadata is not in the Metabase, these databases and files must be discovered. A good way is to research all the reports produced by the business information systems department and allocate the file or database that was employed to produce the report to the Resource Life Cycle Node that best fits the representation of the data.

Once all the databases and files are allocated, reports can be produced by the Metabase that show Resource Life Cycle Nodes that have a "bountiful" quantity of databases and files (not a good sign) and those that have no allocated databases or files (also not a good sign). In the later case, there probably are databases and files but they are either "private" or undiscovered. Either case is also "not a good sign."

In any case, allocating them to Resource Life Cycle Nodes is a matter of distilling the intended purpose of the database or file, and creating the relationship. It is likely that some files or databases will be allocated to multiple nodes and even to different nodes of different life cycles. The quality of mapping relationships is inversely proportional to the encapsulation of the data to the Resource Life Cycle Node. For original data capture databases or files, there should be few multi-node mappings. For data warehouse databases there will probably be many multi-node mappings.

Step 5.2: Allocate Existing (As-Is) Business Information System to Resource Life Cycle Node

Within the class of existing business information systems, there are three prototypical examples:

- Monolithic mainframe with manual sub business information systems for workflow.

- LAN-based, workflow, client/server, and Internet-based business information systems architecture.

- Commercial Off-the-shelf software (COTS).

As above, knowledge about these existing business information systems should already reside in the Metabase. If their metadata is not already in the Metabase, these business information systems must also be discovered. Similar to databases and files, a good way is to again research all the reports produced by the business information systems department and allocate the business information system that produced the report to the Resource Life Cycle Node that best fits the representation of the data.

Again, similar to databases and files, once all the business information systems are allocated, reports can be produced by the Metabase to show the Resource Life Cycle Nodes that have a "bountiful" quantity of business information systems (not necessarily a good sign) and those that have no allocated business information systems (also not a good sign). In the later case, there probably are either business information systems that are either "private" or undiscovered, or the set of activities necessary to accomplish the work implied by the Resource Life Cycle Node is being accomplished manually.

In any case, allocating them to Resource Life Cycle Nodes is a matter of distilling the intended purpose of the business information system and then creating the relationship. It is likely that some business information systems will be allocated to multiple nodes and even to different nodes of different life cycles. The quality of mapping relationships is inversely proportional to the encapsulation of the business information system to the Resource Life Cycle Node. For original data capture business information system, there should be few multi-node mappings. For data warehouse databases there will probably be many multi-node mappings.

Step 5.3: Allocate Future (To-Be) Databases to Resource Life Cycle Node

Within the class of existing databases or files, there are three prototypical examples:

- A file for every distinct process or purpose transformed to a single database for all reasons.

- A single database for all reasons transformed to multiple databases fitting within the five database architecture classes.

- A file for every distinct process or purpose transformed to multiple databases fitting within the five database architecture classes.

It is important to note that none of the options propose the creation of a standard access file. This is because all permanent data should be defined as databases, whether they are single table databases or many hundred-table databases. DBMSs provide many features that greatly benefit persistent data such a standard data definition language, backup and recovery, audit trails, security, ad hoc query language access and update, and sophisticated report writer access.

The metadata for the existing databases or files should already be in the Metabase as a consequence of Step 5.1. The purpose and scope of the future databases merely have to be defined in terms of names and descriptions of Database Object Classes and not any of the Database Object Class details.

Step 5.4: Allocate Future (To-Be) Business Information System to Resource Life Cycle Node

Future business information systems, if properly proposed have three components:

- The existing environment description.

- The future environment description.

- A high level strategy for accomplishing the transformation from the existing environment to the future environment.

Within the class of future business information systems there are three prototypical examples:

- Monolithic mainframe with manual sub business information systems with standard data access and COBOL that are transformed to LAN-based, workflow, client/server, and Internet.

- Monolithic mainframe with manual sub business information systems transformed to commercial off the shelf (COTS) software.

- Monolithic mainframe with manual sub business information systems with standard access and COBOL transformed to same but with DBMS access.

Any of these alternatives could be enhanced by either Internet or Intranet access. This type of access, if the proper software development environment ha been employed, is a paradigm shift only if the business information system is batch. If the business information system was already on-line through terminals, PCs, or is client/server, the Internet or Intranet should only be a presentation layer shift.

In any case, the high level metadata for the three components that comprise the future business information system must be collected and stored in the Metabase. The first set of metadata should already be in the Metabase as a consequence of Step 5.2. In addition, all future business information systems should be cast in terms of future databases.

Step 5.5: Configure Business Information Systems Plan Projects

Configuring Business Information Systems Plan projects consist of determining the full set of requirements and selecting the first cut preferred alternative for carrying out the transformation from the "as-is" environment to the "to-be" environment. The considerations that must be reviewed and addressed are distinct for databases and for business information systems. Figures 65 and 66 provide the three prototypical alternatives for each and then the assessment areas that must be addressed.

The final outcome is a full understanding of the proposed future project. This full understanding is employed in the next step, Allocating Standard Work Breakdown Structures to each database and business information system project. Thereafter, each proposed project is input to a project management system and scheduled.

As expected, the items dealing with database or file transformations are primarily centered around identifying the correct set of activities associated with successful database projects. Similarly, the assessment areas regarding business information systems deal mainly with the process, database interface, and presentation layer considerations associated with reading, updating through Database Object Classes, and writing data. Each assessment area should be supported by an already existing work breakdown structure and a set of experience-based metrics.

A key consideration in any transformation from an existing set of databases and business information systems is the movement of a maximum quantity of functionality to inside the boundary of the DBMS. Whenever a routine is outside the purview of the DBMS, it must be implemented exactly the same from within every different environment that may employ it.

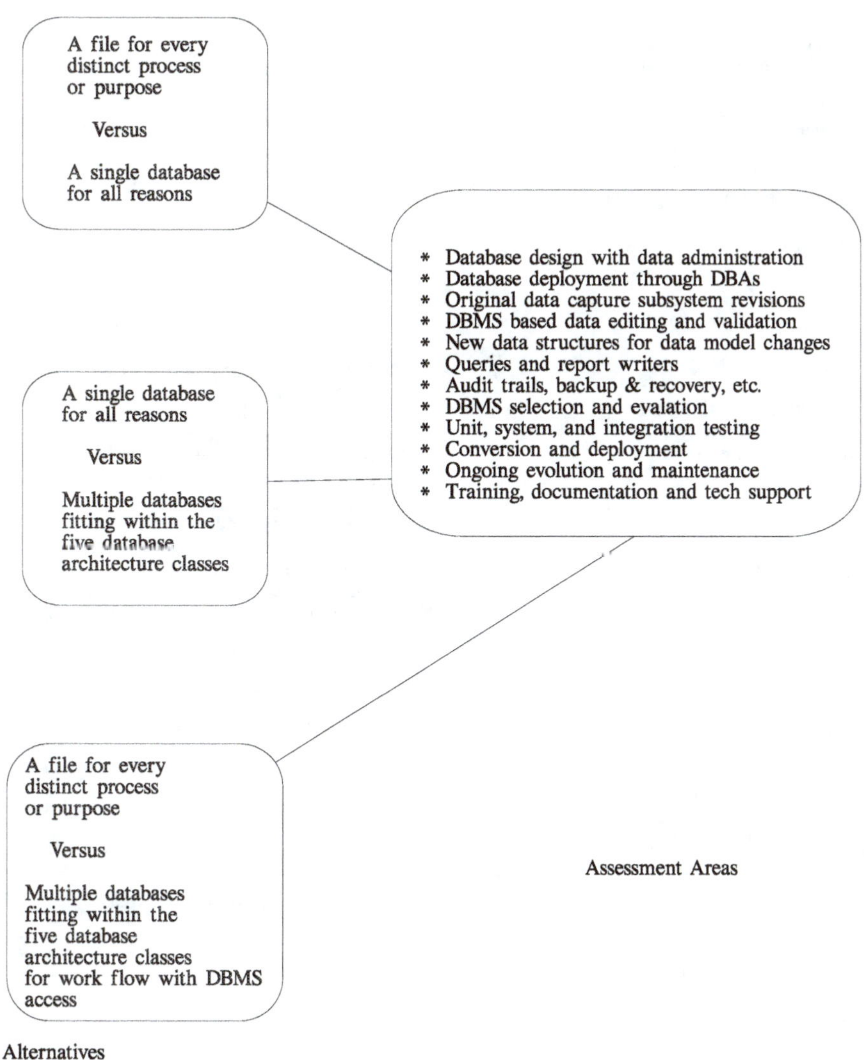

Figure 65. Alternatives and assessment areas necessary to determine preferred project for database or file transformations.

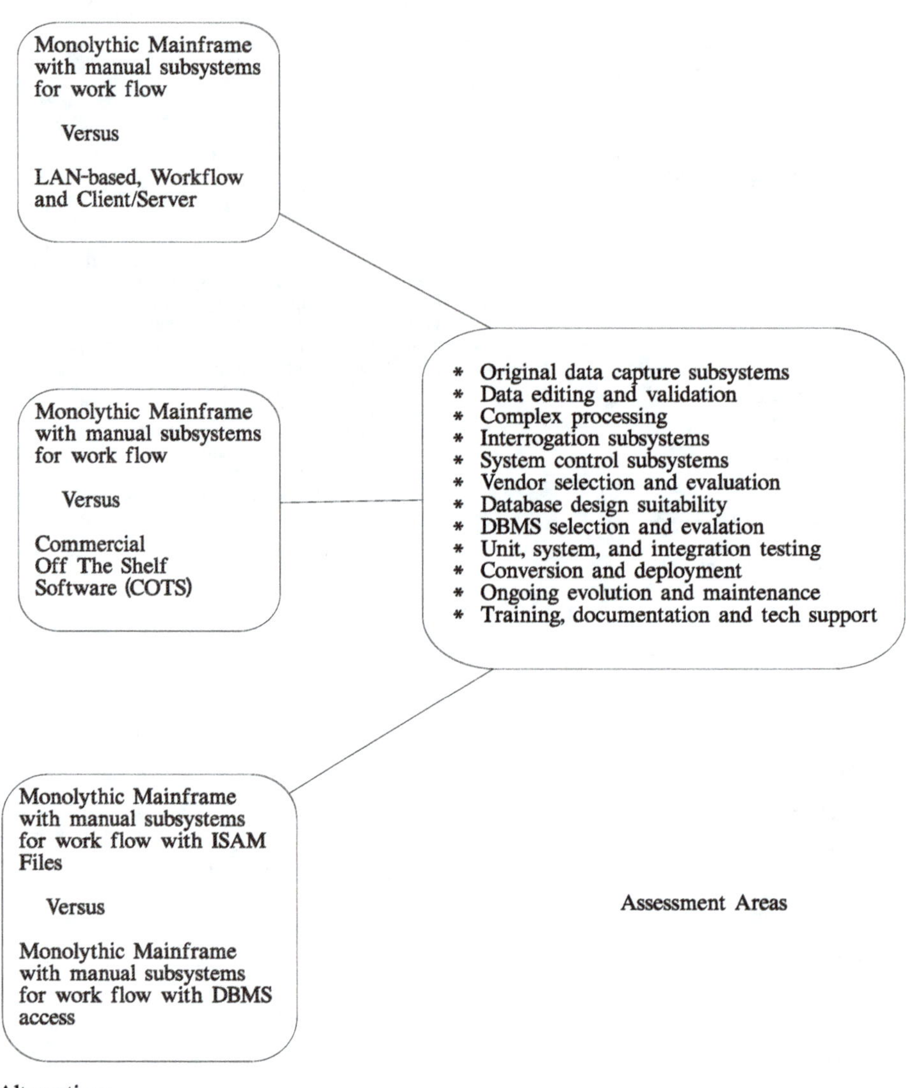

Figure 66. Alternatives and assessment areas necessary to determine preferred projects for business information systems.

For example, if data integrity rules are created and executed from within a 3GL COBOL program, there must absolute assurance that these same data integrity rules are defined and acted upon in exactly the same way if an update is carried out through a 4GL program or a DBMS vendor's query language. Since that would be very difficult indeed, it is wisest for the enterprise to implement data integrity rules within the domain of the DBMS

4.4.6 Step 6: Allocate Standard Work Break down Structures to Each Business Information Systems and Database Project

The key reason for having a well-engineered check list for identifying the types of work involved in either a database or business information system project is the ability to use canned work breakdown structures. When these work breakdown structures are coupled with experience-honed metrics that are embedded in a project management system that "self-learns" from on going projects, accurate, reliable and repeatable project plans can result.

Figure 67 presents a very high level view of how project management and the projects associated with Resource Life Cycle Nodes are interrelated. In actuality, there are many more tables within the Whitemarsh project management software. But, from this perspective, when the assessment checklist is compiled, the specific work breakdown structures that are applicable are selected from the project template table. The are five distinct classes of projects are:

- Administration and management.
- Specification.
- Implementation.
- Operation and maintenance.
- Multiple category.

The lists that follow provide the names of all the different projects for which Whitemarsh has standard work breakdown structures and metrics.

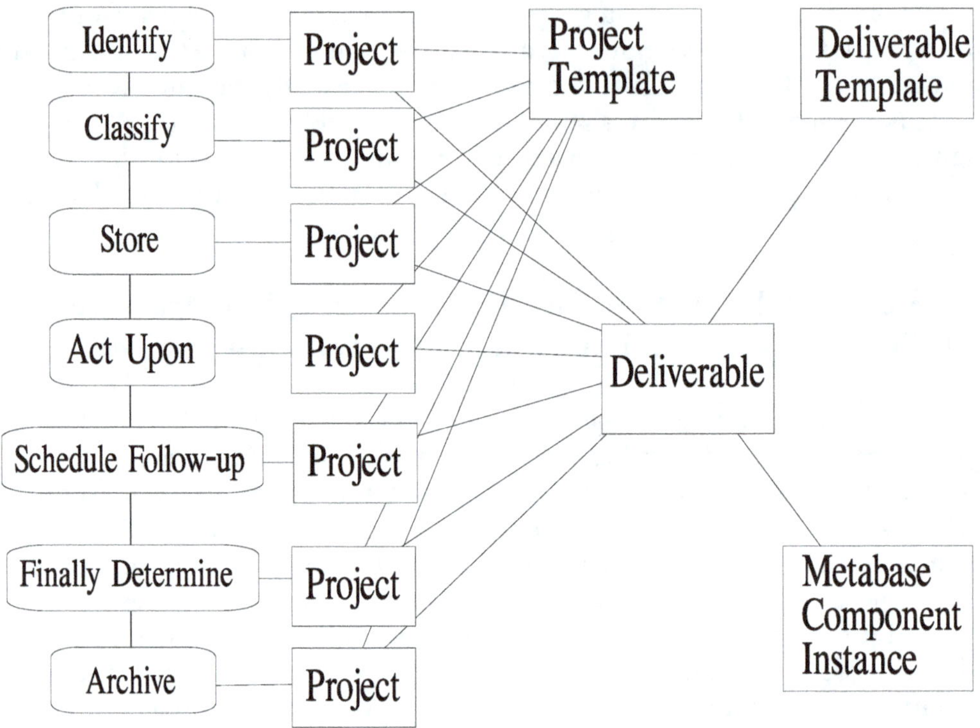

Figure 67.   Projects allocated to resource life cycle nodes with deliverables and project templates.

Administration and Management

- Administrator Documentation
- DBMS Selection and Evaluation
- Repository Selection and Evaluation
- Enterprise Model Audit
- Business Information Systems Plan
- Repository Development
- Standard Estimation

Specification

- Conceptual Specification
- Database Process Model
- Data Element Model
- Specified Data Model
- Functional Area Specification
- Functional Commercial Off The Shelf Selection
- Functional Prototype
- Implemented Data Model
- Impact on Enterprise Model
- Implementation Strategy
- Mission Model
- System Control Requirements

Implementation

- Functional Area Implementation
- Functional Commercial Off the Shelf Software Implementation
- Operational Data Model
- DBMS Schema and View Development
- DBMS Physical Database Specification and Implementation
- Interrogation Development
- Business information system Control Implementation
- Business information system Documentation
- View Data Model

Operation and Maintenance

- Emergency Maintenance
- Application Optimization Assessment
- Standard Maintenance
- Business information system Evolution
- Repository Evolution

Multiple Category

- Data Collection and Validation Business Information Systems
- Data Conversion
- Training
- Warehouse

4.4.7 Step 7: Load Resources into Each Project

Once the work breakdown structures are selected, the task list and associated deliverables and metrics are automatically brought into the Whitemarsh project management system. When the quantities for each deliverable type are determined, the overall gross hours estimate for the project are computed.

The gross hours estimate is finalized (either upwards or downwards) by the selection of work environment factors (e.g., nobody even knows who the users are (that's a costly work environment factor)), and also by the specific persons assigned who have varying levels of capabilities in certain experience levels (e.g., someone is assigned to create the data model who doesn't know the meaning of the term, "ER diagram" (that's another costly staffing factor)).

The value in having a highly engineered work environment and staffing experience factors that adjust the gross hours is that project managers can then relay back to management the exact reasons why a project will cost more or less than another project of even the same construct and size.

The resources are exported from the Whitemarsh project management system to a text file that is able to be loaded into a project management system such as Microsoft Project so that PERT, Gantt, and CPM charts can be produced. This is necessary because the purpose of the Whitemarsh project management system is to support the planning of projects on an enterprise-wide basis rather than the scheduling of individual projects.

4.4.8 Step 8: Schedule through a Project Management Package

Project management systems like Microsoft Project, Welcom's Open Plan Professional, or Primavera's P3e all require PERT (activity network charts) to effectively schedule an entire Resource Life Cycle Node network of assigned projects.

When work breakdown structures are brought into such a project management system, they are treated as self-contained subprojects within the overall Resource Life Cycle Node network of projects. Figure 68 shows a Resource Life Cycle Node network. The Resource Life Cycles are depicted from their first to last node in a top-down fashion. The precedence vectors are shown from one node of a Resource Life Cycle to another node of a different Resource Life Cycle. Multiple precedence vectors do not exist between Resource Life Cycles. When this Resource Life Cycle Node network is turned

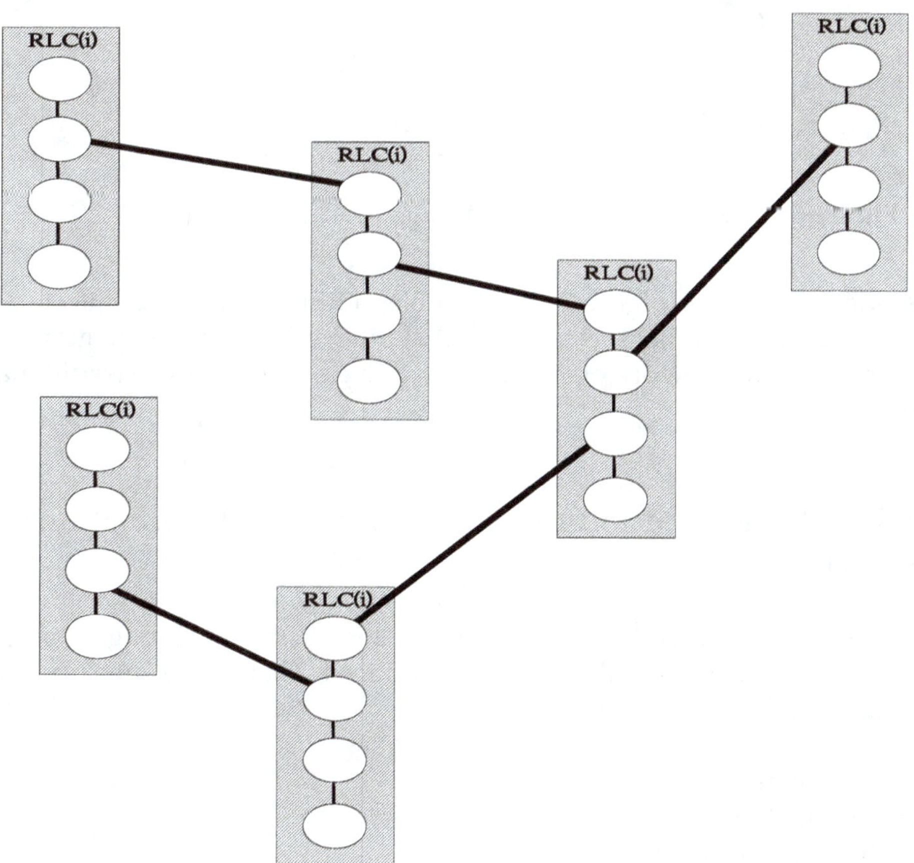

Figure 68. Resource life cycle network.

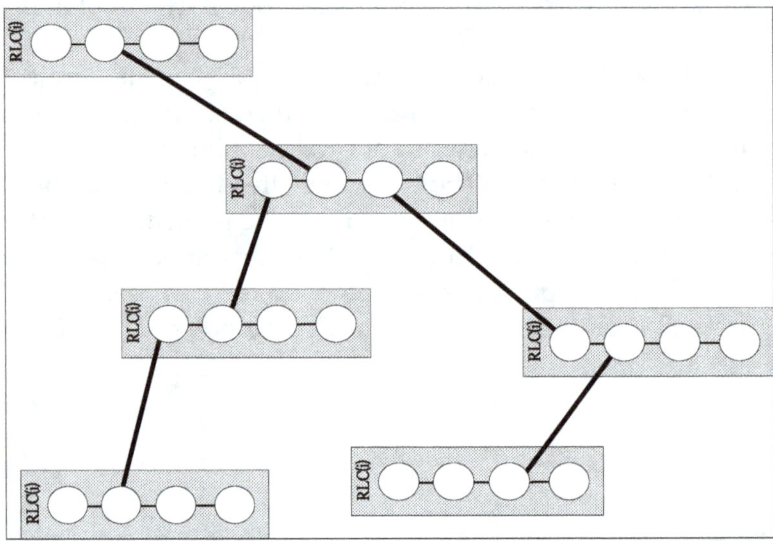

Figure 69. RLC network seen as a PERT chart.

on its side, as shown in Figure 69, it resembles a PERT chart. The chart naturally contains parallel sets of nodes that intersect. From this diagram it is easy to see that the network of Resource Life Cycle Nodes can be traditionally scheduled.

4.4.9 Step 9: Produce and Review the Business Information Systems Plan

When the resource-loaded network of projects is scheduled through a project management system, normal results are produced. That is, the enterprise is faced with the requirement for:

- Infinite resources.
- Infinite time.
- Infinite computer capacity and speed.
- Zero time allocated by "management" to accomplish all the work.

The Business Information Systems Plan produced by this technique is no more able to be accomplished *on the first pass* than is any other Business Information Systems plan. Now, where the Whitemarsh Business Information Systems Planning approach starts to become very different from traditional Business Information Systems Plans is that the Whitemarsh Business Information Systems Plan is fundamentally just data (actually, metadata) within a database. Because the Whitemarsh Business Information Systems Plan is "data," it can be reported, queried, updated, recalculated, and reprinted any number of times with only reasonable effort.

A second key distinction is that the data that supports the Business Information Systems Plan is primarily contributed by and supported by management. After all, it is their missions, their database domains, their Database Object Classes, their resources, their Resource Life Cycles, and their precedence vectors among the Resource Life Cycles. The only parts that are truly owned by information technology are the proposals for information technology projects that transform an "as-is" database or business information system to a "to-be" database or business information system.

Since "management" is the source of the business information systems projects, as they should be, the key questions that management must answer in order to bring the Business Information Systems Plan within the boundaries of "mere mortals" are:

- What really needs to be done? (That's expressed as the allocated databases and business information systems against the Resource Life Cycle Nodes.)

- When is it appropriate to do it? (That's expressed through the enablement vectors.)

- Why does it benefit the enterprise? (That's expressed as the resources and their life cycle nodes.)

In support of answering these questions, and being able to adjust the Resource Life Cycle network, precedence vectors, resource loadings and the like, the following should be considered:

- Determine essential results versus optional results.

- Re-examine and adjust precedence vectors to minimize critical path sequences.

- Examine and adjust benefits derived from technology because benefits are soft or can be postponed.

- Examine and adjust technology for each business information system implementation, that is:

  - Old technology will suffice.
  - 4GL versus 3GL.
  - Business information system generator versus 4GL/3GL.
  - Package versus (4GL/3GL/Business information system generators).

These questions can only be answered within a team relationship between business management and the technical staff. As management makes new assertions or adjustments, the Business Information Systems Plan team can adjust assumptions, work breakdown structures, levels of staff skill, quantities of staff, contractor resources, and the like. As these change, the Resource Life Cycle Node resource-loaded network that has been loaded into the project management system can be rescheduled. Iteratively, a realistic schedule will emerge. One that will not be pleasing to all, but fully justified and understood. It will not be a business Information Systems Plan that is based on magic or that is shrouded in technical mystery. Once the finalized Business Information Systems Plan is generated, the following work products will have been produced:

- Mission, organization, and function descriptions.

- Database domains and entity relationship diagrams.

- Database Object Classes.

- Resources, life cycles and precedence vectors among the Resource Life Cycles.

- Identified and allocated "as-is" and "to-be" databases and business information systems.

- Workplans.

- Loaded Resources.

- Complete Schedules.

- Technology choices.

- Benefits.

While each one of these items has value in its own right, collectively, there exists a Business Information Systems Plan that is enterprise-wide, grounded squarely on the enterprise's missions and resources and is accurately scheduled with experience-honed work plans.

4.4.10 Step 10: Execute and Adjust the Business Information Systems Plan Through Time

Enterprises, once they evolve beyond their first round of business information systems, find themselves transformed from a project and package mentality to a release mentality. See for example, Section 2.7 and Figure 10.

Through this approach to developing a Business Information Systems Plan, the majority of the work contributes to the planning-work of other activities. As each project is started, the output of the Business Information Systems Plan, that is, work plan, resource estimates, and the like will provide a quick start for the project. As projects are accomplished, any refined estimates, technology break-throughs achieved and the like will cause an automatic back-flow to the very metadata from which the Business Information Systems Plan was created. In short, as project work is complete, the basis of the Business Information Systems Plan is also becoming automatically updated. Generating a new Business Information Systems Plan is merely the process of reviewing the existing set of Resource Life Cycles and their networks, adjusting work plans and revisiting the technology assumptions for any unstarted projects and then reproducing the Business Information Systems Plan.

4.5 Business Information System Plan Summary

This chapter presented an overview of the Whitemarsh Business Information Systems Plan process. This approach is needed because it does no good to know how to implement business information systems well if you do not know which ones to implement and in which sequence.

As a consequence of Enterprise Resource Packages (ERP), many newly created database and business information systems are derivative business information systems, not one-off business information systems. Movement is from fewer but bigger stove-pipe business information systems to many and smaller business information systems that are related to the ERP environments. Because of this very significant change, enterprise-wide Business Information Systems Plans are more important than ever, and the very metadata created during the development of these plans needs to be stored in the Metabase so that impact analyses can be quickly developed and accomplished.

In summary, any technique employed to achieve a Business Information Systems Plan must be accomplishable with less than 3% of the information technology budget. Additionally, it must be timely, useable, maintainable, able to be iterated into a quality product, and reproducible. Information technology organizations, once they have completed their initial set of databases and business information systems will find themselves transformed from a project to a release environment.

The continuous flow environment becomes the only viable alternative for inventorying, interrelating, and moving the enterprise forward. It is precisely because of the release environment that enterprise-wide Business Information Systems Plans that can be created, evolved, and maintained are essential.

While the Business Information Systems Plan is critical to the business-sense sequencing of business information systems projects, it is not enough. Project management is critical as well. For an enterprise to be a Level 5 organization, the Software Engineering Institute of the Carnegie Mellon University states that the environment must be "self-correcting." Whitemarsh project management as described in the next chapter enables self-correcting.

4.6 Questions and Exercises

1. Does your organization have a business information system plan? If yes, why? If no, why not? What is the effect on orderly business information system development without an business information system plan?

2. Is the business information system planning process formal? If yes, who participates? By what methods and procedures does one participate? How do you interrelate all the business information systems in regards to the business information system plan?

3. Has your organization abandoned a business information system planning process? If yes, why? What was wrong? What has been the replacement process for business information system planning? Compare and contrast the old and new approach.

4. Compare and contrast the steps within the book's business information system planning process with yours? The same? Different? What's extra? What's missing?

5. What role would standardized methodology and metrics play in the development of your business information system plan?

6. What is the value of the Resource Life Cycles Analysis as a framework for allocation your inventory of databases and business information systems?

7. Have you used something like a Resource Life Cycles Analysis network to engineer and interrelate the build and maintenance sequence for your database and business information systems?

8. Is there value from having business information systems allocated to only one Resource Life Cycle Node? Does that make the node an agent of achieving business information system based coupling and cohesion?

9.   When would a business information system be assigned to multiple nodes on the same Resource Life Cycle or to different Resource Life Cycles? Should such situations be "accidental" or to serve a well-defined engineering and architecture purpose?

10.   When would a database be assigned to multiple nodes on the same Resource Life Cycle or to different Resource Life Cycles? Should such situations be "accidental" or to serve a well-defined engineering and architecture purpose?

5
Project Management

This chapter, Project Management, presents an overview of the Whitemarsh's approach to project management. It is illustrated through key windows from the Whitemarsh project management system. Whitemarsh's approach is a difference in kind as it manages deliverables not work plans, and enables enterprise-wide project management through the use of project, deliverable, and task templates coupled with person-based skill inventories and work environment factors. Thus, while every project is different, each is built from commonly found (define once, use many times) building blocks. The entire Whitemarsh environment meets a key Software Engineering Institute critical success factor, self-correcting. The Whitemarsh approach to project management is especially important because it is set within the context of other enterprise metadata and all the projects that are identified, in development, in production, or in maintenance across the enterprise.

5.1 Why Project Management is Important

Project Management is important because almost all enterprises suffer from one or more of the following problems:

- Inaccurate estimates.

- Conflicting priorities among projects.

- Inability to deal with varying levels of work conditions, staff skills, and the like.

- No intra- and inter-project reporting.

Simply put, a common lament is that while there are projects everywhere, the ability to effectively manage these projects on an individual or enterprise-wide basis is nowhere.

For example, studies by have shown that many, if not most, knowledge worker projects exhibit these characteristics: over budget, under specified, delivered late, and fail to meet organizational expectations. While not all reasons for failure can be laid at the foot of project management, too many can. Among the underlying reasons are invalid work plans, insufficient time for requirements changes, and inexperienced or mis-allocated staff resources.

The United States Government' General Accounting Office (GAO) has been studying information technology projects for a number of years, and a review of eight GAO studies clearly shows that the main reasons why business information systems fail has nothing to do with information technology. Again, while not all the reasons are specifically related to project management, some of the reasons have to do with critical components of project management. These include invalid work plans, insufficient time for requirements changes, and inexperienced or mis-allocated staff resources.

As a consequence of market pressures and corporate mergers, two classes of project management systems exist today:

- PC based or low-end packages.
- Server based or high-end packages.

PC based project management systems are typified by Microsoft's Project (www.microsoft.com) or Time Line Solution's product, Time Line (www.tlsolutions.com). Server based project management systems are typified by Primavera (www.primavera.com) and Welcom Software (www.welcom.com).

While the high-end packages are designed for very large, complex projects of thousands of nodes, and while the low-end packages are well suited for scheduling a single project of relatively simple complexity, both the high end and low end solutions do not really address the problems associated with:

- Disjoint projects.
- Management of generally uncontrolled resources.
- Repeatability of projects.

- Use of enterprise-wide metdata.
- Incorporation of learned experience into the project estimation cycle.

Many knowledge worker projects involve persons from within different organizations over whose time the project manager may not have direct control. Thus, the best the project manager can do is to request participation and to create approximate schedules that show deliverables from these semi-controlled participants.

If the knowledge worker project manager creates elaborate project schedules based on many layers of intricately crafted activity networks, then while they look magnificent the instant they are first created, these project plans cannot withstand assaults from all the schedule conflicts. Once these assaults are underway, the project manager has to continuously adjust the layers of project activity networks, resource estimates, parallel and serial paths, etc. Soon the project manager's life is consumed by project management rather than project accomplishment. The dilemma becomes:

- Accomplish the project, or
- Plan the project's accomplishment.

All too often, project planning is discarded because the project management system, initially thought to be the savior from chaos actually has become another source of chaos. The castle of project management becomes the project manager's dungeon wherein time is the dungeon master, the PERT charts are the shackles, the schedule is the rack, and the evolving requirements are the torture.

To be successful at knowledge worker project management, an approach must:

- Concurrently manage disjoint projects.

- Seamlessly employing and updating enterprise-wide metadata.

- Manage generally uncontrolled resources.

- Enable maximum re-use of past efforts.

- Incorporate learned experiences.

- Not require a full-time project planner.

- Support what-if resource allocation scenarios.

- Enable management to know about and view all projects and resources across the enterprise.

- Support the presentation of projects individually, or from the perspective of a business-defined set of priorities.

5.2 Whitemarsh Project Management Environment

Whitemarsh project management is based first and foremost on a database design. The general "life cycle" of Whitemarsh project management is:

- Employ project, deliverable, and task templates to plan projects.

- Plan and estimate projects in a gross way and accommodate different work environment factors.

- Staff projects and generate schedules.

- Record progress towards deliverable accomplishment.

- Re-plan projects as needed.

- "Learn" from actual durations from accomplished deliverables.

Whitemarsh project management does not, however, support the creation of:

- Very precise parallel and serial networking of projects or tasks.
- Very detailed and precise scheduling.
- Gantt, PERT or CPM diagram production.

These three activities are the proper activities of both low-end and high-end project management systems. In support of these systems, the Whitemarsh project management system is engineered to be able to generate output data files that can be input into these business information systems. These systems can be used to create very precise schedules, activity diagrams and the like. Whitemarsh holds however, the proposition that if accomplishing these three activities were THE basis for successful project management, there would be no need for Whitemarsh project management. While very precise schedules, activity diagrams and the like are important, it seems clear that these features have little or nothing to do with project management success.

In contrast, Whitemarsh believes that project management success is predicated on different activities, which are:

- Continuous optimization of repeatable projects.

- Accommodation of various work environments and factors within these environments.

- Adjustment of project schedules based on differing staff and skill levels.

- Capturing actual work accomplishment metrics that support earned value analysis and reporting.

The project management database design employed by Whitemarsh has been implemented several times as the basis for project management over the past 15 years. Whitemarsh believes that the "design bugs" are worked out. Whitemarsh project management serves the need of the independent project manager who has to accomplish the definition, management and reporting of diverse and possibly disjoint projects with staff of varying skill levels within mixed work environments that are generally not within direct control. Whitemarsh believes that this type of knowledge worker environment is the rule, not the exception.

5.3 Whitemarsh Project Management, a Difference in Kind

A key difference between the Whitemarsh project management approach and others is that the Whitemarsh approach concentrates on the management of "nouns" while other project management approaches focus on the management of "verbs." Clearly, there is no one sacred, perfect way to produce a deliverable (i.e., the nouns). If the focus of project management is to identify and control the "methods" (i.e., the verbs) by which deliverables (nouns) are produced, then to have enterprise-wide project management and/or to have enterprise-wide metrics, the enterprise must first carve-into-stone the processes by which work is done. Not only is this impossible, it is highly undesirable. It is impossible because it is inconceivable that there is only one way to accomplish any product. It is also undesirable because it is insulting to project staffs to presume to control their every technique, process and step. Not only can't this be done, no one will allow it to be done.

In contrast to managing "verbs," Whitemarsh project management manages "nouns." It does this by collecting the quantities of resources expended to produce deliverables. Whitemarsh project estimates are therefore based on the staff hours required to produce deliverables rather than to accomplish tasks.

This technique enables different styles of project management to be employed or be set one against the other by comparing the resources expended to produce deliverables. There might be one project template for mainframe development, another for micros, and finally a methodology for web-based business information systems even though all the deliverables might be essentially the same. Alternatively, there might be multiple project templates that produce the same set of deliverables to serve the needs of different styles or techniques as might be the case for the data-driven and process driven approaches.

Additionally, the Whitemarsh project management approach enables enterprise-wide project reporting in terms of the cost and effort to produce deliverables versus the accomplishment of activities. As work techniques improve, either through the increased skill of staff, or through the adoption of different techniques, the efforts remain comparable because it is the quantity of resources expended to produce the deliverables that are compared. Not compared are the activities because one project's activities are different than another. The best that could be reported is that the activities associated with one deliverable appear to be better than another set because the resources expended on the first deliverable are fewer than the second deliverable.

To illustrate, when you go into a grocery store and buy an apple, the cost is expressed in terms of the product you are buying, the apple. While you may wonder how much the various activities cost that ultimately produce the apple, fundamentally, you probably do not care. When you go to five different stores and compare the cost of apples (given a standard for equating quality), again you are only comparing the cost of the deliverable, the apple. If one store spends 10% for transportation and another spends 8%, you probably don't care. It's the final cost of the apple that matters, nothing else. So also should it be with project management. The only thing that should matter is the final cost of the deliverable. Nothing more, and nothing less.

However, if you are a wholesale apple buyer that deals with a co-operative and by contract, you have to pay every apple grower the maximum cost incurred by any one member of the cooperative, you have a real incentive to look "behind" the costs of the deliverables (the apples) to find the different underlying processes that make the costs different. Even then, the goal then is to find the lowest-cost set of activities, and to highly recommend that set of activities to all members of the cooperative so that your costs for the deliverable–as a buyer–will go down. So, while there may be an interest in activity-sets, they are not the driving force. So too with Whitemarsh project management wherein the cost of deliverables rather than the cost of methods is the driving force.

Whitemarsh project management enables melding project templates with selected:

- Task templates–that is, the enterprise's techniques, methods or work breakdown structures that have been proven of the years to accomplish in work the most cost effective manner.

- Deliverable templates–that is, the enterprise's specifications of and unit effort metrics required to accomplish the components of its Knowledge Worker's products.

The resulting Project Templates are specially tuned into "real" projects by determining the quantity of deliverables, and affecting the resulting "norm" estimates through:

- Work environment factors–that is, the effects from varied work environments on the creation of deliverables according to certain task templates.

- Staff–that is, the effects from persons and their varying types and degrees of skills on the rate of production of deliverables according to the task templates.

Collectively, these four project management components are an exemplary use of the database fundamental, *define once, use many times.* Whitemarsh believes it has achieved the ability to have maximum reuse with minimum original, one-off effort.

5.4 Architecture and Concept of Operations

Whitemarsh Project Management is squarely founded on a database application that captures and manages the data critical to effective project management. The database's design is depicted in Figure 70, and consists of a number of tables. All these tables are traditional and are interconnected through one-to-many relationships except for those tables that show a one-to-many relationship from the table to itself. Organization (upper right) contains such a relationship. This relationship means that the table contains subordinate organizations. For example, an Information Technology organization may contain the Information Resource Management organization, which in turn may contain the Data Administration organization, and the Database Administration organization. The seven recursive tables are:

- Contract.
- Deliverable.
- Deliverable Template.
- Organization.
- Project Template Type.
- Task.
- Task Template.

The tables from Figure 70 are also divided into six distinct clusters, which are:

- Contracts, organizations and contract [staff] resources.
- Resources.
- Project, Deliverable, and Task Templates.

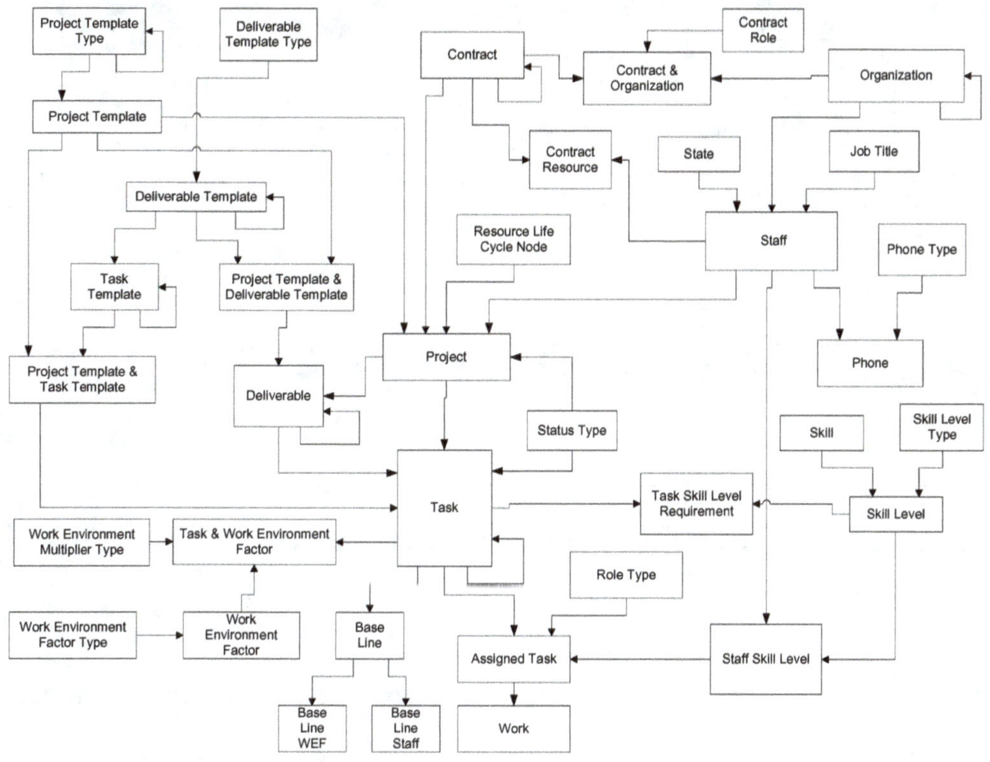

Figure 70. Overall database architecture for Whitemarsh project management.

- Project Staff.
- Project Building and Estimation.
- Project Work.

Since each table cluster is described in great detail in the Whitemarsh Project Management document, only an overview is presented here.

In general, the *Contracts, Organizations, and Contract [staff] Resource* cluster of tables represents the environment within which projects take place.

The Resource Life Cycle Node table represents the target of the project, that is, the specific Resource Life Cycle Node benefitted by the project. For example, from Figure 61, the project may be for Case Assignment or Case Processing.

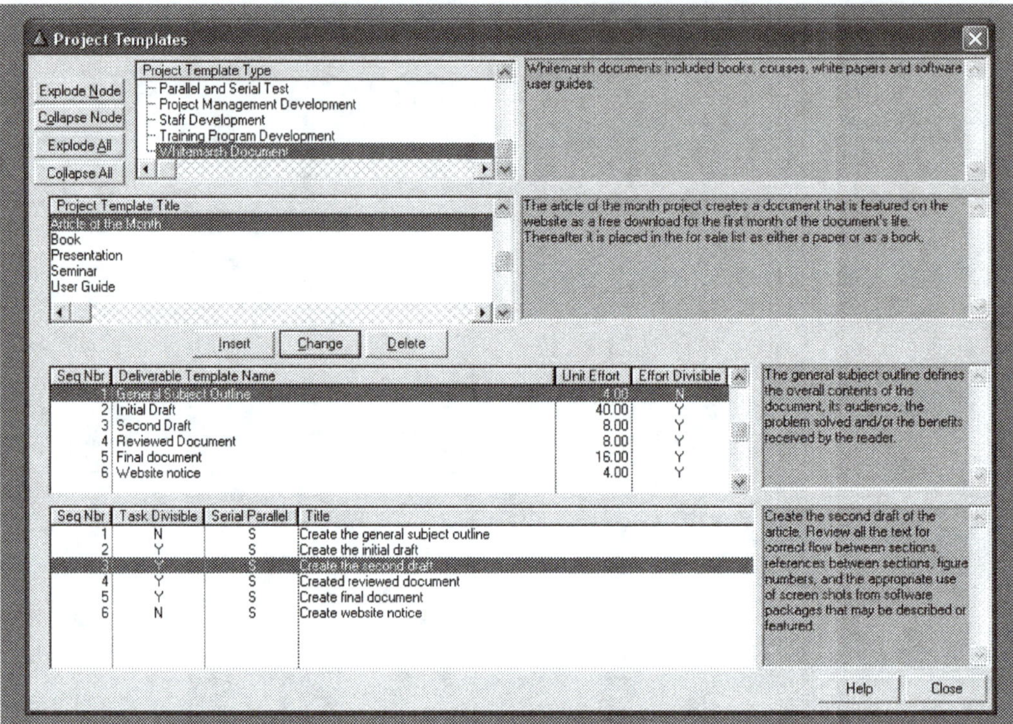

Figure 71. Project template list of the Whitemarsh project management system.

The *Projects, Deliverable, and Task Template* table cluster enables the definition of the templates employed in the actual building of projects. Defined across the enterprise, these templates enable standard project execution and accomplishment measurement.

Project templates are defined and stored in the project management database. Figure 71 presents a project template list. The top-most browse of the window contains the project template types. Each project template type can have multiple project templates.

Project templates are related to task templates and deliverable templates through many-to-many relationships. This permits a particular deliverable template, for example, Project Plan, to be allocated to multiple projects. Similarly, the task template, Develop Project Plan, can be contained in multiple projects. The goal here is: Define once, use many times.

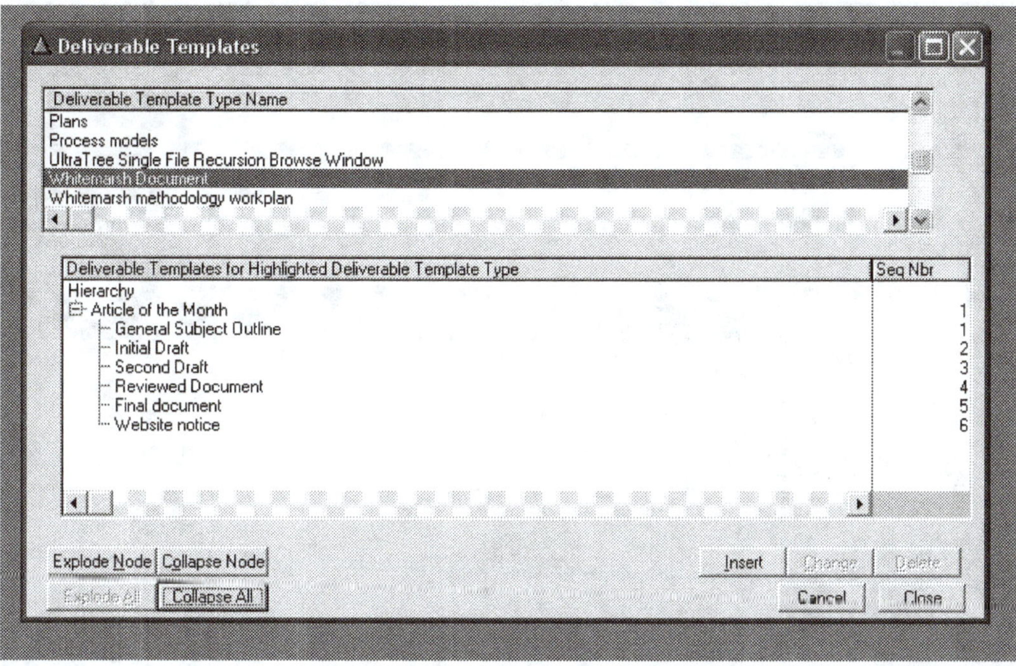

Figure 72. Deliverable template for a specific deliverable template type.

As stated above, the Whitemarsh project management system is based on deliverable templates, which are presented in Figure 72. The top browse is a list of the deliverable template types. The bottom browse is the hierarchical list of deliverable templates within the types. In this particular example, Whitemarsh has a deliverable template type, Whitemarsh Document. The related deliverables template is *Article of the Month*. For this deliverable template, the subordinate deliverables represent the product milestones in the creation of the Article of the Month.

The information that is stored about a deliverable template is presented in Figure 73. The most important information is the unit effort required to accomplish the effort, the sequence number of the deliverable within the deliverable template type, and whether the effort is divisible among those assigned to complete a single unit of the deliverable. For example, it is unlikely that the deliverable, Defined Data Element, would be divisible, whereas, Project Plan might be. In this example, the back window

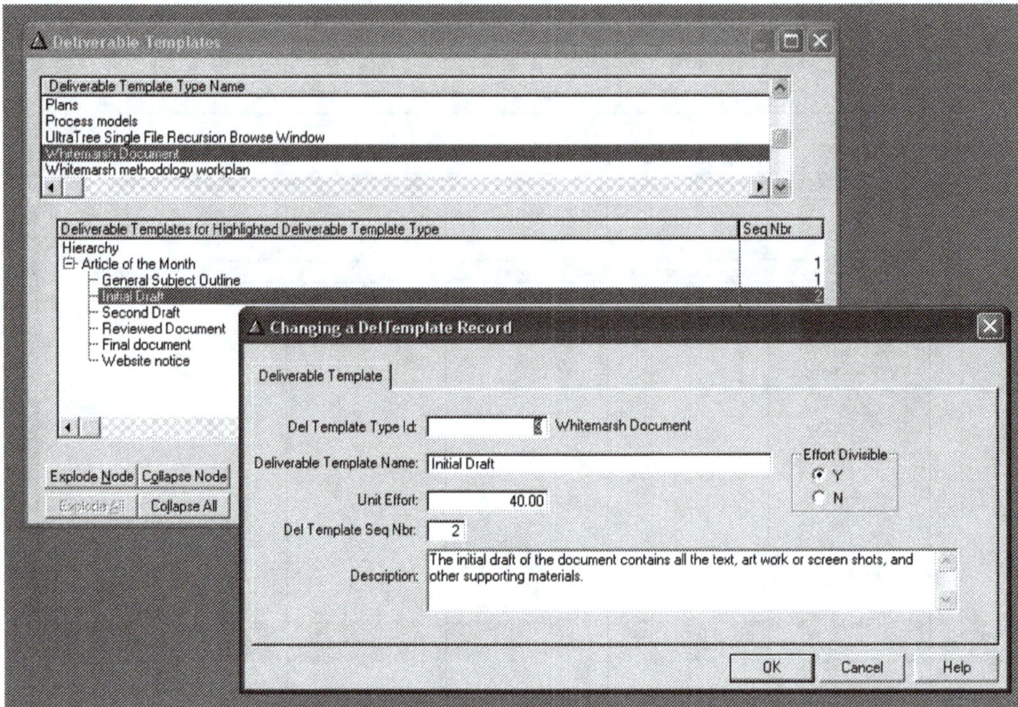

Figure 73. Information captured about deliverable templates.

shows the list of subordinate deliverable templates (General Subject Outline...
Website Notice) and the front window shows for Initial Draft the information
that is captured to describe what is meant by the deliverable template, Initial
Draft.

Deliverables are related to project templates through a many-to-many
relationship. This enables enterprise-wide reports of project work by
deliverable template type and deliverable template.

Figure 74 displays the task templates. As can be seen, tasks can contain
subtasks to any depth. The only caution is that every task that represents a
leaf must be resourced to have a complete project plan. The level of detail
should be carefully chosen to ensure that the project is able to be scheduled in
a finite time. Project templates are allocated task templates through many-to-
many relationships. This enables enterprise-wide reports of resources
expended across all projects by certain task templates.

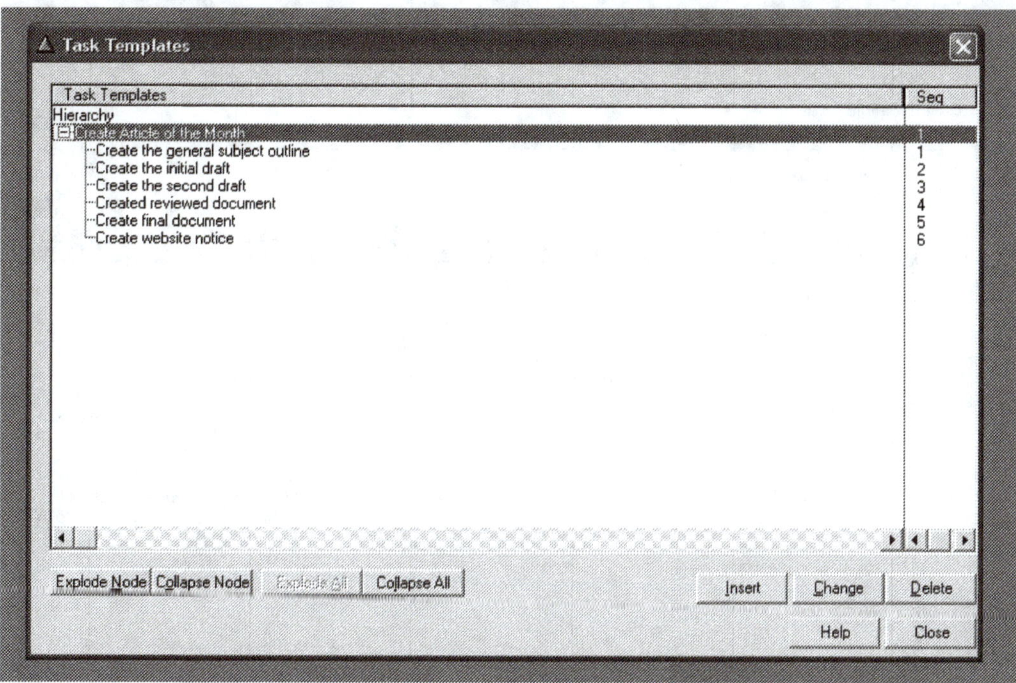

Figure 74. Task template list.

The information captured in the task template is presented in Figure 75 and consists of the deliverable template that is being produced, the task title, description, task sequence number within its task parent, whether the task's effort is divisible, and finally, whether the tasks that are "children" of this task are accomplished serially or in parallel.

The *Project Staff* table cluster enables the inclusion of the staff as resources for a contract, and also permits the specification of the specific types and performance ratings of skills that a person may bring to a specific project.

The *Project Building and Estimation* table cluster represents the tables that support building projects. Projects and associated tasks are initially created through the use of the Project Deliverables, and Tasks Templates. Once projects and associated tasks are created, they are modified by attaching work environment factors and specific skill-level-based staff assignments. Only then can task and project resources be computed.

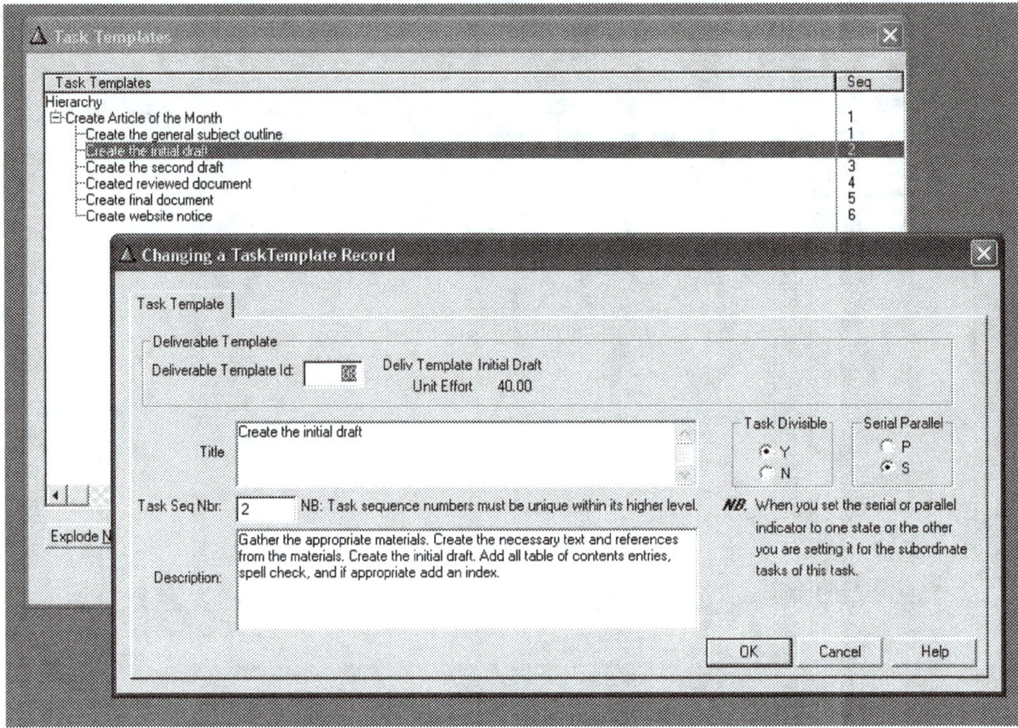

Figure 75. Information captured about task templates.

Figure 76 presents the Projects browse. This browse contains the list of projects, and associated with each project the list of the project's tasks and deliverables.

Of especial interest is the Build Project Tasks and Deliverables button. Once the basic project data, including the project's template is entered and committed to the database, the newly created project is listed. At that time, the Build Project Tasks and Deliverables button is pressed. Since the project template has been allocated the set of task templates and deliverable templates, all the necessary information to populate the project's tasks and deliverables exists.

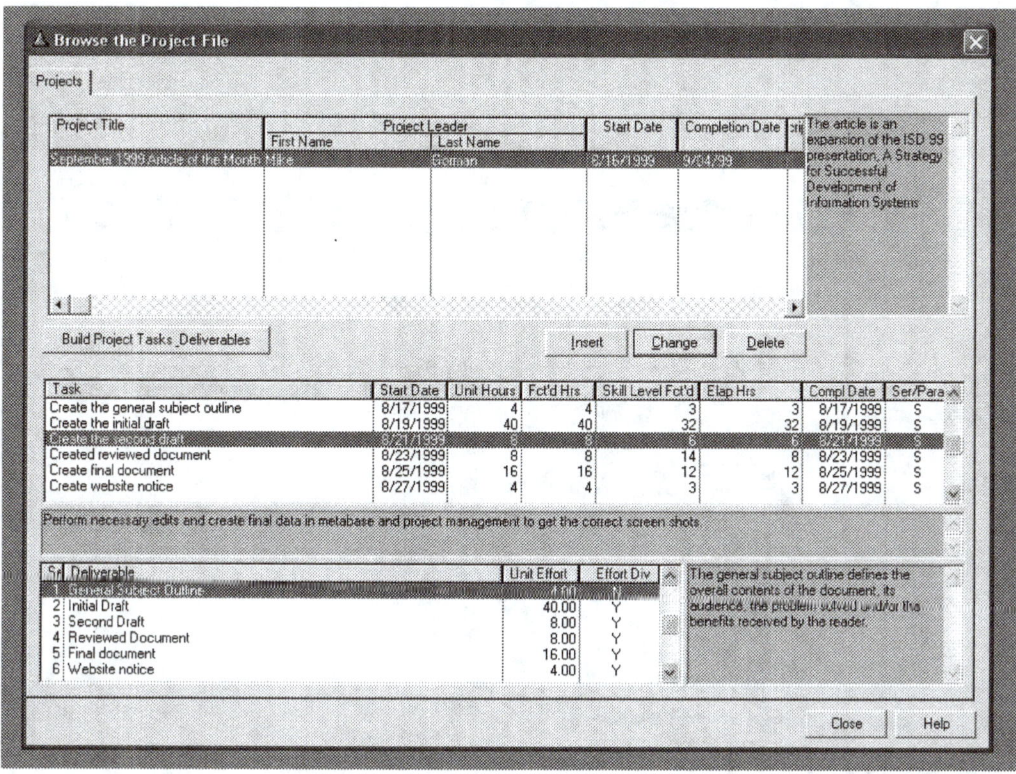

Figure 76. Project list with associated tasks and deliverables.

In Figure 77, when a project is initially created, it shows zeros for the three hours fields in the lower left part of the window. These numbers change only after individual tasks are updated. Deliverables cannot be updated. Only tasks that are leafs can be updated with resources. For example, Create Reviewed document can be assigned work as it does not contain subordinate tasks. If a task is preceded by a "+" sign then it contains subordinate tasks and cannot be updated.

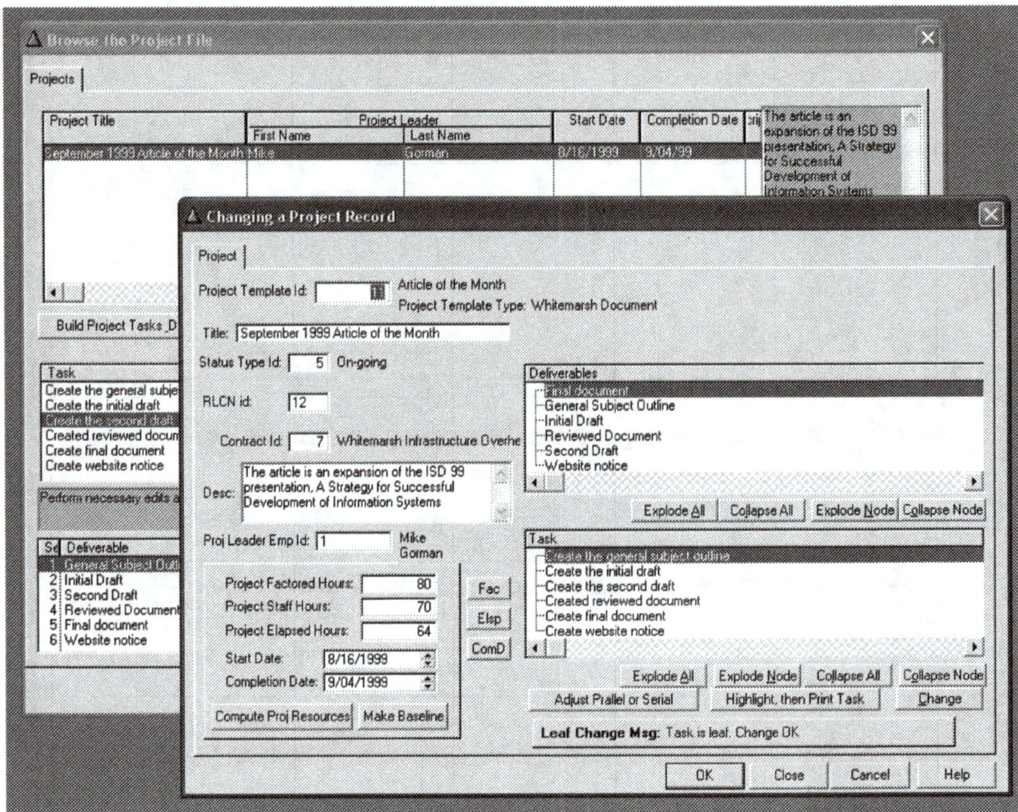

Figure 77. Project update screen.

Figure 78 contains the information for a project's task. First, the task is located and the update button is pressed. The information that can be entered is the task's local title and description if it is to be different or more localized than that provided by the task template. Entered as well is the quantity of deliverable units. In this particular example, the task title name has been left the same, but the task's description has been localized to describe the exact work that must be done by the assigned staff.

The most important information that can be entered for a task are its work environment factors. A list of environmental factors is provided in Table 14. In Figure 78, the entered data shows that the work environment factors have no effect. Thus, the multiplier is 1.0. If there are more than one

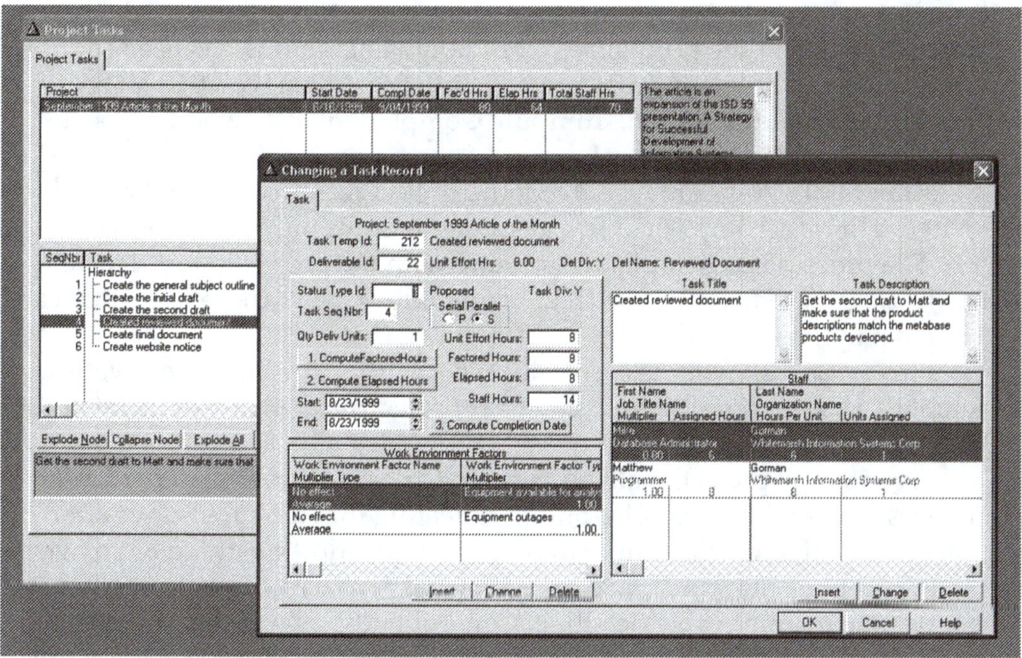

Figure 78. Task update screen.

multiplier, the effect is their multiplicative summation. Once all the work environment factors are entered, the effect on the deliverable template's unit effort hours (multiplied by the quantity of deliverable units) is computed by pressing the Compute Factored Hours button. In this example, the factored hours stay the same, that is, 8.

The next information entered are the staff members (including their skill and skill levels) who are to work on the task. Additionally, persons can be assigned to work part time (by percent). The window shows that two people are to work on the effort. In this case, one staff member is considered an expert (multiplier of 0.8) and the other is a journeymen (multiplier 1.0). Once all the staff are assigned, the Computer Elapsed Hours button is pressed. Depending on a set of rules, the work is divided among the workers. In this example, since there is only one deliverable unit, they work together on the one work unit. This means that the expert works for around 6 hours and the journeyman works for 8 hours on the task. While the total staff hours is 14, the longest work effort is 8 hours, or two staff days. But, since August 27 is a Friday, the work cannot be finished until August 30. The reason the elapsed hours answers often do not appear to compute correctly is that partial days are not assigned, and the productive work hours in each day has been set to 6, and weekends and holidays must be taken into account. Given that a task start date is entered, the button, Compute Completion Date, when pressed computes the end date for the task.

After all the tasks are resourced, the project resources as a whole are computed. This is accomplished by pressing the Compute Proj Resources button. The process is accomplished starting with the project's start date and first task and proceeds to the last task, taking into account those tasks that can be done in parallel.

Finally, as task work is accomplished, the *Project Work* table is valued. As actual work is accomplished, it can be reported through any of its related tables.

As with any project, reality sets in. In the case of creating a particular Whitemarsh paper there was also another meeting that took four days after the start date of the Article of the Month project. In addition, there were two more interruptions that consumed an additional four days. That meant 8 work days lost with an unmovable deadline. Consequently, as with most project efforts, long days were put in, and weekends (including Labor Day weekend (how appropriate)) were worked. Simply put, just because an effort is stored in a project management system and is scheduled, doesn't mean that reality is suspended. Traditional remedies, that is, nights and weekends occur.

5.5 Whitemarsh Project Management Summary

This chapter presented an overview of the Whitemarsh's approach to project management. This was illustrated through windows from the Whitemarsh project management system.

Whitemarsh's approach is a difference in kind as it manages deliverables not solely work plans and enables enterprise-wide project management through the use of project, deliverable, and task templates coupled with person-based skill inventories and work environment factors. Thus, while every project is different, each is built from commonly found (define once, use many times) building blocks. The entire Whitemarsh environment meets a key Software Engineering Institute critical success factors, self-correcting.

The Whitemarsh approach to project management is especially important because it is set within the context of other enterprise metadata and all the projects that are identified, in development, in production, or in maintenance across the enterprise.

Because Whitemarsh project management system is implemented as a database application, it supports the following:

- Projects and project statistics of a certain project template.
- Projects and project statistics within certain [business area] resources.
- Projects and project statistics by deliverable types.
- Projects and project statistics by organizational units.
- Projects and project statistics by specific project staff members.
- Projects and project statistics by certain types of skills.
- Projects and project statistics according to certain status types.
- Projects and project statistics according to certain work environment factors.

5.6 Questions and Exercises

1. How is your project management environment engineered? Can the enterprise see across all your projects? Can you compare and contrast all your projects? Work breakdown structures, staff assigned performances? Work environment factors?

2. Isn't project management just another form of metadata? Shouldn't project management metadata just be another part of your overall metadata environment? Shouldn't project management metadata be integrated with all other metadata?

3. Is the project management database open? That is, accessible through an "ODBC" for report writers like Crystal Reports and/or 3GL programming languages?

4. Have you used or do you know that there are 3rd party PERT and CPM chart maker vendors that can import and export project management metadata?

5.   Is your project management environment such that you can record deliverables-status-based updates to the project management data?

6.   What is the role of standardized methodology and metrics within project management? How have they helped or hurt?

7.   Do you keep and affect project management estimates by the work environment factors? What are your work environment factors? Has exposing them and their effects within project management estimates caused changes in the work environment factors?

8.   Do you keep and affect project management estimates by the staff performance? What are your staff performance factors? Has exposing them and their effects within project management estimates caused changes in the staff skills and associated performances?

9.   What is or should be the role that project management plays with respect to other metadata such as databases, business information system plans, and Resource Life Cycle Analyses?

6
Summary and Conclusions

This chapter brings forth the features, advantages, benefits, conclusions and future actions necessary from adopting this approach to database and business information systems development. There is no down-side to its adoption.

The overall information technology organization, and the functional organizations that are supported by this approach are more productive, less costly, higher quality, and lower risk because more work is done in a non-redundant, integrated manner. More work products are able to be re-used because they are created with re-use in mind, stored in a metadata format, and reside in a multiple-user Metabase that has an enterprise-wide perspective. Data semantics are able to be harmonized which eliminates whole classes of data transformation and reloading business information systems and logic. Again, there is no downside to adoption providing doing more, faster at a lower cost and risk are the objectives.

6.1 The Preface

From the scenario described in the preface, the government agency was caught in a requirements-failure cycle. They hired a contractor who came in and did a traditional requirements analysis. After about a year of detailed design, coding, unit testing, and business information system testing, the business information system was delivered to the government agency. The government agency shrieked in horror. What had the contractor done? That is not what the agency had said. Not what they had wanted. How could this happen? So the contractor was promptly fired. This cycle repeated three more times.

A study was conducted on the process. Afterwards, a meeting was called with the government agency's heads. The agency was eager to know not only what went wrong but who to blame. The answer was a shock. It was the agency that was at fault, not the contractors. Of course the agency angrily protested the findings. The requirements-failure cycles and showed that during every cycle, the perception of what the problem was and therefore what the solution should be had changed.

It was never a case of the contractor getting the requirements right. Rather it was the case of the government agency knowing what requirements it actually wanted. When the contractor talked to different government staff, the answers were different not just from one staff member to another, but from previous answers provided by the same government staff over the different cycles. The objective, a successfully developed business information system, was impossible to achieve.

The remedial plan was to conduct a workshop that caused the creation not only of the specifications of the business information system to be produced, but also of the prototype. The specifications were stored in a 1980s version of the Metabase so that the repository could be included in a subsequent implementation contract as the specification of what needed to be done.

At the end of the week, the specification, the metadata, and a high-level prototype were complete. The agency's information technology department took the result and increased it with one or two more levels detail, including evolving the prototype. The implementation contract was let and the business information system was developed, tested, and accepted by the agency.

Ultimately, the prototype of the requirements, and the iteration of the prototype teased out all the requirements from the functional experts and were properly reflected in the overall specification that became the prototype.

6.2 The Problem

At the outset of this book, the typical conditions surrounding business information systems efforts were presented. That is, that 31% of a class of business information systems efforts failed outright; another 53% were challenged (late, greater than budgeted, and fewer features than promised), and only 16% were delivered on-time, within budget, and with features as promised.

It was also cited that the top three reasons the uncovered for successful business information systems were:

- User Involvement
- Executive Management Support
- Clear Statement of Requirements

And, the three top reasons cited by executives for business information systems failures were:

- Incomplete Requirements
- Lack of User Involvement
- Lack of Resources

Finally, it was shown in a review of the GAO studies of business information systems' failure show that new requirements during business information systems development are such a common occurrence that they must be considered intrinsic to the business information system development process.

The solution accomplished for the government agency dealt with the three success factors. First, users were heavily involved from the very start and were key drivers of the solution. Second, it was the agency's executive who drove the workshop. Leadership was never in doubt. Third, because of the iterated prototype, the requirements became exceptionally clear.

The requirements, as stored in the Metabase along with the prototype became the technical specifications of the request for proposal.

6.3 Essentials for Information Technology Success

There are eight environment essentials for business information system development success. These are:

- Knowledge Worker Framework.
- Data-driven Methodology.
- Database Object Classes.
- Data Architectures.
- Business Information System Generators.
- Metabase Environment.
- Discrete and Release Development Environments.
- Metrics and Work Environment Multipliers.

Of these eight, three deserve a special summary. The first is the Knowledge Worker Framework. It identifies the different major classes of activities and products that have to be created in support of enterprise, database, and business information systems development. Table 6 presents in percents, the allocation of reasons for failure that occur when these activities and products are not accomplished. The most surprising part of the allocation is that 95% of all business information systems fail for reasons outside of information technology.

The second is the use of business information system generators to accomplish prototyping. Needed also is the reorientation from a stove-pipe project-based mentality to a "release" mentality to enable capabilities across multiple business information systems to advance in a coordinated fashion.

The third is the use of metrics and work environment factors because most information technology projects within a class are really just methodology-clones of one another. Thus, project-accomplishment manufacturing is clearly possible by standardizing the "what" and the "how" of work.

6.4 Nine-Step Approach

The nine-step approach was presented through displays from the Metabase and the Clarion environment. This clearly moves this approach from the land of theory to the real-world. A key characteristic of this 9-step approach is that only the last two steps require the involvement of information technology. The main approach enables functional users to advance their awareness of their information technology requirement, to evolve this awareness through prototyping until it is ready for information technology to implement, and to implement it one time and correctly.

The nine-step approach represents a significant change in responsibilities. From the preface example, there are cost overruns, late deliveries, and diminished capabilities. In contrast, this 9-step approach moves the responsibility for the critical-to-success steps to the requirements development organization where it always rightly belonged.

The first seven steps are the responsibility of the requirements development organization. The business information systems development organization implements the business information system within Step 8. Step 9, Conformance Testing, is the responsibility of the requirements development organization. The division of labor is based on subject matter expertise. The benefits from this nine-step approach has the benefits listed in Table 23.

Nine Step Approach to Business Information Systems Development		
	Step	**Benefit and/or Description**
1	Mission Development	Missions provide the overarching framework for the entire enterprise. Missions are accomplished by Organizations through Functions, and further refined into database domains. All databases and business information systems are established within this enterprise architecture framework. This sets every effort squarely within the business's architecture.
2	Database Design	Database designs are built from within the enterprise architecture. Metadata is used to ensure enterprise-wide data structures and semantics. Database designs are based on enterprise-wide data elements, data models of concepts, DBMS independent models, and finally DBMS dependent models. This enables maximum metadata re-use, data interoperability, and semantic harmonization.
3	Prototype Generation	Prototypes, set within the enterprise architecture, and which are built through maximally reusable metadata, represent business information systems set within the context of recognized functions. Through business information system generating the prototype, maximum efforts can be expended on getting a full set of requirements, and minimum efforts can be expended on the creation of the business information system.
4	Specification Evolution	Specification evolution is critical because it enables the complete set of requirements to be teased out. Through the use of business information system generators, the ability to proceed from one iteration to the next is easy and can be accomplished in hours to days versus weeks to months. This enables a first real implementation from a version 10 prototype. Prototyping also greatly reduces the quantity of evolutions during a business information systems life cycle.

Nine Step Approach to Business Information Systems Development		
	Step	**Benefit and/or Description**
5	Request for Proposals	A request for a proposal is a formal specification of what is desired to be implemented. The document should contain all the metadata and the prototype that were created in first four steps. The document should contain a requirement for being able to evolve the specification of the business information system being implemented. The document should contain the method through which the requirements development organization monitors and evaluates the accomplishments of the business information systems development organization. Another component of the document should be the specifications of the conformance tests, based on the prototype and other requirements that are to be accomplished as the basis of business information system acceptance.
6	Proposal Evaluation	The proposal evaluation process should be engineered to determine how well, when, and for what cost a business information systems development organization will implement the business information system. The proposal evaluation process ultimately produces an agreement between the requirements development organization and the business information systems development organization regarding the implementation process, schedules, costs, reviews, and deliverables.
7	Contract Award	The contact award is the event whereby the accord reached in the prior step becomes the blueprint for action between the requirements development organization and the business information systems development organization. The key components of the contact are the deliverables' specifications, time-lines, costs, and agreements on the obligations of both the requirements development organization and the business information systems development organization.

Nine Step Approach to Business Information Systems Development		
Step		**Benefit and/or Description**
8	Contractor Management	Contractors, whether in-house or from outside the enterprise need to be managed by the requirements development organization. By management, it is not meant that daily activities need to be monitored but rather, there is joint participation in the success and/or problems associated with the effort.
9	Conformance Testing	Once the business information systems development has completed, the execution of the conformance tests form the basis for acceptance by the requirements development organization.

Table 23. Benefits from the nine step approach to business information systems development.

6.5 Business Information Systems Plan

It does no good to know how to implement business information systems well if you do not know which ones to implement and in which sequence. Business Information Systems Plans are more important than ever, and the very metadata created during the development of these plans needs to be stored in the Metabase so that impact analyses can be quickly developed and accomplished.

These plans must be timely, useable, maintainable, able to be iterated into a quality product, and be reproducible. This book's approach enables business information system plans that fulfill these five characteristics.

6.6 Project Management

The Whitemarsh approach is a difference in kind because it manages deliverables versus work plans and time consumed. It enables enterprise-wide project management through the use of project, deliverable, and task templates coupled with person-based skill inventories and work environment factors. While every project is different, each is built from commonly found (define once, use many times) building blocks. The entire Whitemarsh environment meets a key Software Engineering Institute critical success factor, self-correcting.

The Whitemarsh approach to project management is especially important because it is set within the context of other enterprise metadata and all the projects that are identified, in development, in production, or in maintenance across the enterprise.

Because Whitemarsh project management system is implemented as a database application, it supports the following:

- Projects and project statistics of a certain project template.
- Projects and project statistics within certain [business area] resources.
- Projects and project statistics by deliverable types.
- Projects and project statistics by organizational units.
- Projects and project statistics by specific project staff members.
- Projects and project statistics by certain types of skills.
- Projects and project statistics according to certain status types.
- Projects and project statistics according to certain work environment factors.

6.7 Way Ahead: BLUF

Th U.S. Army uses a starter slide for many of its briefings. The slide's header contains the string, "BLUF." Here's this book's BLUF. With this approach you can both save at least 40% on all your business information systems' development but also you can create these business information systems within an enterprise-data framework. As stated many times in this book, there is no down-side to this approach. It is squarely based on database's first principle: Define once, use many-times. That's this book's BLUF. BLUF, in the Army means, Bottom Line Up Front.

It is hoped that careful consideration will be given to this book and that it will be applied to bring about some reality to the myth of data processing. That is, all things in a blink of an eye. If you are a member of a project team, accomplish the book's lessons. When you are successful and you manager wants to know why, have him/her read the book. If you are a project manager, make sure your project adopts the methods in the book so you can have a positive impact on your organization. When you boss notices and asks what you are doing differently, give him/her the book to read. In short, keep passing this book to higher levels in your organization until enterprise-wide changes in the business information system development are accomplished.

Feel free to contact Whitemarsh and to provide feedback. Whitemarsh welcomes opportunities to practice what it preaches. For example, Whitemarsh can deliver this book through a highly intensive workshop, or through casual consulting arrangements. Whitemarsh's warranty is that its products cause increased quality, lowered risk, increased velocity and lowered costs.

6.8 Questions and Exercises

1. Can you and/or your organization relate to the scenario that is presented in the Preface? What can you do about it? How has such a scenario affected your organizations ability to create systems and meet new business opportunities?

2. Are your top three success factors different? If so, how and why?

3. D you relate to the "problem" set out in Chapter 1? What can or have you done about it? Has it helped? Explain.

4. Which of the eight "essentials" is the most important? How are they all interrelated? Can you really have a first-class and highly productive information technology organization without these eight "essentials?" Are any missing? What are they?

5. Does the 9-step approach make sense? Under what conditions would you not do this 9-step approach? Are there classes of information technology systems for which the approach just doesn't apply? Explain?

6. How does the decision to procure COTS affect the 9-step approach?

7. Can you safely buy COTS without the 9-step approach? If yes, how? If no, what's the effect on the COTS procurement process?

8.   Have you used this 9-step approach? How does it compare with other approaches you have tried?

9.   Can you have a quality-engineered information technology organization without business information systems plans? What's the effect of having business information system plans? What's the effect of not having business information system plans?

10.   How is this book's project management similar or different from what you've used? Faster or slower? Cheaper or more expensive?

Attachment 1
Knowledge Worker Framework
Rows and Columns Description

The Knowledge Worker Framework is essentially an architectural framework that, from Wikipedia, is "… a skeleton upon which various objects are integrated for a given solution." In this case, the scope of the integrated solution is the "knowledge worker." And in the case of the Knowledge Worker Framework, the "object" may be a representation of a real object such as a mission, or may be a wholly contained architecture such as the enterprise architectures, Database Object Classes, and the data architectures.

A quick review of all the cells in the Knowledge Worker Framework, presented in Table 3, shows that not all the cells are represented in the architectures listed in Table 2. That's acceptable because not everything has to be represented in one architecture or another. An architecture is intended to have high cohesion and low coupling. Each of the architectures above exhibit those characteristics in that they can stand alone and are not dependent on one another.

These architectures are however interconnected, and the mechanism of connection is the Metabase database. In Whitemarsh, this metadata database is called a Metabase. Whitemarsh has been using the string, Metabase, since the early 1980s, and has been designing and building Metabase systems for more than 30 years. Metabases are neither unique nor new. They are however essential to a well ordered, efficient and effective knowledge worker environment in our enterprises.

Databases are commonly seen as the intersection of collections of tables. If a database had only one function-based and narrowly focused collection of tables, it would be called a stove-pipe database. Collections of stove-pipe databases commonly suffer from differently named and discordant semantics for the same thing, and the same names for different things. For example, Region Id in one database is the country's Tax Id number assigned to the corporation. In another database, Region Id might be an auto-generated integer number. In a third database, Region Id might be a crafted code representing a geographic region of the country.

In other databases there are many different names for a person's gender. Notwithstanding that the meaning is easily discovered, some of these value domains are M and F, Male and Female, 0 and 1, and 1 and 2. If combined all together without "scrubbing" a real mess would result, including the fact that in this example there are only seven distinct gender codes.

Analogously to real-data databases, the metadata databases that contain the metadata-based artifacts of all these architectures must be melded, have consistent semantics, and all overlaps merged. It is thus just not enough to have collections of architectures. If they are unintegrated, redundant, and semantically discordant, they are just stove-pipes, but of metadata.

Enterprises commonly create computing supports for knowledge workers under the assumption that the functions they perform and the organizations through which they act are fixed and seldom change. Not only are these assumptions wrong, but when the functions and organizations do change, computing environment changes seldom keeps pace because they are time consuming to specify, difficult to implement, and slow to accomplish. Slow-to-react computing environment changes, therefore, become the very reason why information technology support to business functions and organizations cannot keep pace with the demands of change. What is needed are computing environments that are object-oriented, sensitive to knowledge worker functions and organizations, and that can react to the demands of change in a timely fashion.

What follows is a brief explanation of the Knowledge Worker Framework through an explanation of the rows and the cells belonging to each of the rows. Following the row explanations are the column explanations. While the content of the individual cells are essentially the same, they are presented somewhat differently because in a row-based perspective, for example, the business row, proceeds from missions through organizations, while the column perspective, for example Database Object Class, proceeds on a row by row basis from the "birth" or discovery of Database Object Classes through to the operating enterprise. Ultimately, however, there are not conflicts.

A1.1 Knowledge Worker Framework Rows

The rows of the Knowledge Worker Framework are largely borrowed, with slight modification, from the Business Information Systems Architecture Framework of John Zachman. The Zachman framework's columns are the six interrogatives but set into a particular order of What, How, Where, Who, When, and Why. The Zachman framework, as illustrated at:

www.frameworksoft.com, contains illustrative cell contents that imply products required for business information systems.

The Whitemarsh Knowledge Worker Framework did not adopt the Zachman framework columns. This difference is not to just be different for difference's sake, but a difference that resulted from a through analysis of the reasons for information technology systems' failure. The analysis was made of reports from the United States General Accountability Office (GAO) on large-scale information technology system failures. Eight multi 100 million dollar U.S. Federal agency information technology system efforts were studied. Once the reasons for information technology system failure were uncovered, they were allocated to the Zachman framework. From the allocation, it became quite clear that the Zachman framework addressed less than 10% of the reasons for information technology system failure. The failure was not because of the row, but because of the columns, and the artifacts implied by the columns.

The Knowledge Worker Framework, in contrast to the Zachman framework, was created "bottom-up" after 25+ years of research and refinement into the creation of a methodology to serve the needs of knowledge workers in database centric environments. When the reasons for information technology system failure were allocated to the Knowledge Worker Framework, the reasons were all addressed. This should not come as a surprise because the Knowledge Worker Framework was not invented. Rather, it was derived over many years of iteration and refinement, and was specifically targeted to the knowledge worker's scope.

The sections that follow present the rows of the Knowledge Worker Framework along with a description of each row.

A1.1.1　　Scope Row

The Scope row discovers, enumerates, interrelates, and, at a high level, details the contents of the six columns. Thus, discovered, enumerated, interrelated, and described are the enterprise's missions, Database Object Classes, Business Information Systems, business event interfaces, business functions, and organization.

Missions are the essence of the business. Accomplished well, missions are timeless and are independent of both "who" and "how." It is from a foundation of missions that the rest of the 35 cells are developed. While missions are created top-down, their completeness and content are validated through both organization and functional analysis. Organizations are bureaucratic groupings of individuals that generally have a common objective and are evaluated as to cost and effectiveness in the completion of their mission. Functions are the human activities that are accomplished by the organizational staff in support of mission accomplishment.

Database Object Classes are the major business-based groupings of enterprise data that proceeds through a well ordered set of states. Business information systems are identified, briefly described and are related to the Database Object Classes.

Business events represent the intersections between [human] functions performed by enterprise staff from within their organizations and the business information systems. Business events are triggered by functions and are set within both calendar and business cycles.

Missions and organizations are interrelated. Functions are related to the mission-organization pairs. Database domains (not listed) are derived from missions and are analyzed to support the discovery of Database Object Classes.

Through this top row an analyst is able to say which organizations perform which functions, and which business events need assists from business information systems to employ which business data all in support of enterprise mission. This row, across all the columns tells a complete story.

A1.1.2　　　Business Row

The Business row details the objects that have been discovered and presented in a high-level way from the first row. In addition to further detailing, the Missions, Business Organizations, and Business Functions are all set within hierarchies.

The Organization cell additionally shows organization charts, and job descriptions. The Business Functions and Business Events cells show sequencing as well as hierarchies. The Business Information Systems cell shows an increased quantity of detail.

The Database Object Class cell contains the discovered enterprise resources and their corresponding Resource Life Cycles. Resources are the fundamental components of the business that proceed through major states. The set of ordered states is called a Resource Life Cycle. Examples of resources are facilities, staff, reputation, intellectual property, real property, and the like.

A resource's life cycle includes its instigation, a set of state transforms, and then finally a dissolution. For example, employee requisition, employee candidates, employee new-hire, employee assigned, employee evaluated, and employee separated. These resources and Resource Life Cycles are important because they provide the lattice work through which the databases and business information systems are developed and evolved, and over which business information systems are created.

While related, Database Object Classes and resources are different. A Database Object Class is pure data that encapsulates states and processes. Resources, in contrast, are significantly more complex and may be related to many Database Object Classes, business information systems, and even whole databases.

Discovered in the Database Object Class cell also are the enterprise-level data elements, and the various data models of concepts that ultimately are employed as data model templates for building database designs. An enterprise-level data element is a business fact that may be employed in many business functions, databases and their tables, and business information systems.

This row also tells whole stories. Not only are there the mission, organizations, and functions along with their interrelationships, but there are also noun-intensive descriptions, that is, database domains of the data required by the missions. These noun-intensive descriptions are distilled into both Database Object Classes and also enterprise-wide data elements. The Database Object Classes are configured into a high level enterprise entity relationship diagram.

What is now conveyable are the missions, the data required to fulfill the missions, and the business information systems that cause the data to be entered, retrieved and manipulated.

From the right side of the row, staff through organization-based functions instigate business events that, in turn, employ the business information systems to fulfill their knowledge worker roles. These business events would be set within both business cycles and calenders so that from the first through the last column the analyst could really understand the scope and operation of the business.

## A1.1.3	System Row

The Systems row is the first row devoted to a "systems perspective." It presumes that the artifacts created for this row will be employed during the creation of a system. Not all systems are to be information technology systems, however. Some systems are just a systematic set of policies that guide the accomplishment of a highly engineered set of human activities, that is, functions.

For example, there might be a systematic manner through which attendees at a conference are given materials and/or badges. A line is formed, and an Id is presented. A box of registration materials is located and the registration entry is found. A conference badge is produced, and is given to the attendee along with any appropriate conference materials.

Conversely, an order entry system might be a combination of both human-functions and information technology system support. Finally, there might be an entire information technology "batch" system that obtains data from a database and stores it into a data warehouse database.

The cells in the Database Object Class, Business Information Systems, and Business Event for this system's row are created regardless of whether the system is IT-based or manual. In the conference registration example, if all the data are manual, it still has to be defined and entered on some engineered form so that it can be processed in a regular, repeatable, and a systematic manner.

The Mission cell would contain the policy hierarchies that govern the functions that are executed within the organizations and that might govern the rules executed by any system.

In the Database Object Classes cell, the full definitions of Database Object Classes would be found including the data structures, states, table-transformation processes, and entire database object transformation processes. Or, in the case of the manual system, the data and processes found on the forms.

The Business Information Systems cell would contain the design (versus implementation) specifications of any of the business information systems needed to transform the Database Object Classes. In the case of the manual system, these processes would not be in the business information system cell. Rather, they would be represented in more detailed levels of the Business Function specifications.

The Business Event cell would contain the business event models across the invocation protocols, and all the expected inputs and outputs. The Business Events would at this point be integrated with the Business Functions that invoke them and the Business Information Systems that they invoke.

The Business Function and the Business Organization models are clearly outside the scope of IT. The artifacts from these two columns have both an "as-is" and a "to-be" flavor about them. What is critical to know is how the "as-is" functions and organizations will change into the "to-be" functions and organization as a consequence of implementing a Business information system. If the culture of the enterprise, as evidenced in organizations and functions do not change as a consequence of a new way of conducting business then why have the new Business Information Systems?

Specifically for the Business Function's cell, there would be the creation of functional best practices, quality measures to ensure that the right processes were carried out, and then follow-through assessments on results over time. There's nothing like a "report-card" to keep one's attention. It would also be valuable to have the new functional descriptions evaluated by peer-level businesses, assuming of course that such peer-reviews would not compromise proprietary business practices.

In the Business Organization's cell, there may well be a need to recast job descriptions, methods of organizations that would remove stove-pipes, the ability to seek support through virtual support groups or communities of interest. These revised job descriptions would contain additional responsibilities, modifications to training, and possibly new organizational reporting requirements. All together, the quantity of time required to perform functions within the new organizations should go down because of increased efficiencies, and should show increased quality and effectiveness because of new assists provided by the new business information systems.

From Table 3, the sum of the percents across the Business Function and Business Organization columns from the System through the Operations rows is about 50%. Simply, that means that if all the other cells are done correctly, 50% of the reasons for failure still exist if there has not been a change in the way the enterprise is organized or the functions that are executed to then take advantage of the new business information system's environment. This could be a very expensive lesson indeed.

A1.1.4   Technology Row

The Technology row, is similar to the Systems row in that it represents a detailing and a new set of artifacts needed to support either policy specification, Business Organization and Business Function specification, or a furthering of the efforts in support of IT.

Thus, the cells in the Database Object Class, Business Information Systems, and Business Event for this technology row are really information technology cells. If there is not an information technology system, these cells would likely not be developed as their data would be represented through manual forms, and the detailed processes within the Business Functions column would completely dictate execution.

Given that there is an information technology system involved, the Database Object Class models are configured into actual database designs that are then implemented via database management systems. The Business Information Systems column artifacts are detailed into actual application information system designs.

The mission's cell focuses on the creation of the various enforcement mechanisms for policy execution. In the conference registration procedure above it might include a set of check boxes that require the production of a picture-id that could be used to match against the registration. If there is a Business information system that would be enforcing the registration, maybe the system would produce a picture of the registrant from an initial registration process that might have been on-line. In the case of a conference that would allow non-employees, then the enforcement might be to have a successfully executed fee payment transaction for the conference.

Analogously in the Business Organization and Business Function cells, there would be a further detailing of the various functions and organizations that would be created or revised. For Business Functions all the activity sequences would be set out and integrated with the various organizations responsible for their accomplishment. Similarly, the Business Organizations would have the various procedure manuals, task lists, quality measures and assessments engineered that would evaluate the organization as a whole.

In the Business Events cell, the actual presentation layers that represent the interfaces between Business Functions and the Business Information Systems exist and are designed to ensure that there are good human factors interfaces.

A1.1.5   Deployment Row

The Deployment row presumes that the new environments, from Mission through Business Organizations are ready to be deployed prior to operations. Essentially this overall row is a roll-out of all the artifacts so that they can be employed.

In the Mission cell, the various business policy procedures are installed and the various persons performing their organization-based functions are trained. Business Organizations and Business Function cells are similar in that what is installed, trained, and made operational are the office policy and procedures necessary to accomplish activities on a function by function basis, and with respect to Business Organizations, the daily shift schedules, personnel assignments and the like.

As to the Database Object Class cell, the various database designs are bound over to the specific DBMSs that are to operate the databases. In the Business Information Systems column, the systems are deployed on the various hardware. Included of course would have to be any hardware and computing environment procurement activities.

The Business Events cell is where the deployed functions meet the Business Information Systems. In this column's deployment, tests of ease of use and effectiveness would be accomplished to ensure that the projected functional and organization improvements are realized.

A1.1.6   Operations Row

The Operations row represents the new operating environment. The mission cell would be the operating business. Feedback mechanisms would occur from every set of organization-based functions. This will then enable a feed back cycle at least one row above. There would be a similar set of operations for the Business Functions and the Business Organizations.

It is very important to have feedback mechanisms including the gathering of operational and performance statistics.

The Database Object Class cell is finally defined in terms of SQL Views that interact with the various databases regardless of the form of data, that is, either fixed formats or XML. The Business Information Systems are set into operation so as to fulfill the needs of the various Business Functions. Finally, Business Events are the day-to-day activity interrupts that are ad hoc, set within business cycles or calendars.

A1.2   Knowledge Worker Framework Columns

The Knowledge Framework columns represent an unfolding and/or detailing of a collection of artifacts required over a common domain. These are described in the sections that follow.

A1.2.1   Mission Column

The mission column represents the rationale or basis for the knowledge worker environment. Missions include policies, policy execution enforcement, installed policies and procedures, and then the operations of those policies including feedback.

The first row, Scope, presents the list of missions. The sets of missions are those that form the basis of the enterprise. If a mission is missing then so too is an important aspect of the business. Missions are either external or internal. External missions are those that support the income of the business. Internal missions are those that employ the business's income to operate the business in support of its external missions. For example, if the external mission of the business is to sell a specific product line, then the internal missions are those that support sales, for example, human resource management, research and development, manufacturing, inventory and distribution, and sales management.

Missions are mechanisms for enterprise database partitioning. Once missions are listed, they become the criteria for including or excluding entries in the remaining 35 cells. Additionally, once missions are delineated, then one or more missions can be chosen to pursue through the remainder of the framework. Each mission may also be pursued by different analysis and design teams. The only real down side to this approach is the necessary integration once different subordinate mission Implementations are accomplished. If the top two rows (scope and business) are completed prior to breaking the work into separate projects, the end result is more easily integrated.

The business view of a mission contains mission hierarchies. Each mission, for example, product sales, or human resource management is represented as a hierarchy of text paragraphs and is presented in an "accomplished-form." That is, the mission is described as if it were completed in a completely ideal manner. Completely removed are any indications of either WHO or HOW.

The Systems cell contains hierarchies of the policies that must be present to accomplish various missions. Business policies must be present to accomplish an enterprise's mission. Each policy must be set out such that it can be easily understood, commonly rationalized, and its adherence must be easily assessed.

The Technology cell represents fully specified and implemented view of enterprise policies that are executed and/or enforced. When the policies are set within the organizations and then the functions to which they apply, they must represent common sense to the maximum extent possible. Confusion and misunderstanding lead to uneven execution and uneven results.

The Deployment view represents the actual "in the field" sets of policies whose execution result in data that is collected, updated, and reported. Data is executed policy. Deployment of policies must include all the necessary training, and if necessary the "hot-line" support to adjudicate the best and most efficient way of carrying out the policies. Of necessity, policy deployments are set within organizational and functional re-engineering efforts.

The Operations cell represents the ongoing and executing set of policies that carry out various aspects of the enterprise' missions. As operations occur it must be quickly and easily determine whether policies are being accurately carried out. Organizations and functions must exist to promote good policy execution, and the appropriate reporting and correction when established policies are being violated.

A1.2.2 Database Object Class Column

A Database Object Class is a collection of traditional (that is, formatted and structured data) and nontraditional (that is, video, sound, and unstructured text) data. Database Object Classes proceed through precisely defined states starting with the null state, and then a series of discrete business defined, interlinked non-null states, and finally a null state. Database Object Classes are squarely based on policy analysis for its data structure formulation, and on procedure specification for the proper valuation, modification, migration, and reporting of Database Object Classes.

The Scope cell contains the list of the major resources of the enterprise. Included for example would be organizations, assets, reputation, intellectual property, income and expenses. These resources are key indicators of the major classes of data that are to be discovered and designed into databases.

The Business cell contains three major items: Resource Life Cycles, Data Elements, and Specified Data Models. Not listed are database domains. The Resource Life Cycles are detailed from the Resources that are identified and described in the scope row. As already stated, a resource is a fundamental of the business about which information is collected, funds are expended, or is sold and expensed. Examples are people, contacts, fixed assets, and the like. All business resources are set squarely within the business' missions.

In the business cell, the resources are decomposed into their Resource Life Cycles. Resource Life Cycle (RLC) was developed by from Ron Ross.[19] Resource life cycles form the basis of the information system plans. Each Resource Life Cycle contains the major state names from the business

---

[19] *Resource Life Cycle Analysis, A Business Modeling Technique for IS Planning* (Database Research Group, Boston, 1992) is a technique for identifying the components of a business that is subject to information systems. The resource life cycles are the basis from which database objects are identified, designed, implemented and deployed.

---

resource's life cycle. From Ron Ross' book, the Resource Life Cycle for parts might be:

- Define part types
- Establish suppliers
- Acquire parts
- Accept part requests
- Ship parts
- Maintain parts

From a foundation of missions defined within the mission's column, database domains are identified from the mission leaves. Database domains are noun-intensive descriptions of the data necessary to accomplish the mission. From the database domains, the nouns, which are essentially undifferentiated entities are triaged into three groups: Database Object Classes, enterprise data elements, and classes of properties.

Enterprise data elements are the business facts important to the enterprise that may be represented in one or more data models that are created in the Business, System, Technology and Deployment models.

Database Object Classes are collections of data specifications about a single subject. For example, a Company database object would contain company identification information, company products, company locations, company staff assignments, and the like. Finally, a property class is collection of business facts about one simple topic. An example would be the business facts that are necessary to represent a company address.

The Business row also contains the Specified Data Models, which are data models of concepts. These concept data models[20] are employed in the creation of the data models in the subsequent rows.

Within the Business cell, the identified Database Object Classes and database domains need to be cross referenced. Having a database domain

---

[20]   Note: A data model of a concept is not a conceptual data model. The former is a fully defined data model, and the later represents a "fuzzy" form of a data model that, through data model "baking" becomes more well-formed, that is, a logical data model and then a physical data model. This is a critical difference. In Whitemarsh, Specified Data Models are data models of concepts. This is a difference with a real distinction.

without Database Object Classes or vice versa would be an analysis error. Similarly, not having a Resource Life Cycle node without one or more Database Object Classes would too be an analysis error.

The Technology cell represents Database Object Classes completely through Implemented Data Models within the persistent data language SQL. As ANSI SQL evolves, and as DBMS vendors implement greater quantities of the standards's features there should be fewer and fewer proprietary database facilities. Today, the majority of the database object processes and database object information systems are SQL vendor proprietary. Notwithstanding the quantity of vendor proprietary code, it is all commercial off the shelf (COTS) software, and firmly based on the technology independent Database Object Class specifications contained in the systems view.

The Deployment cell for Database Object Class represents the actual instances of distributed database data models. Most commonly, these data models operate through the SQL language under the control of a DBMS. If all the cells above the deployment cell have been accomplished carefully, there will be a great deal of interoperability across all the deployed databases. That is because many operational databases will share the same Implemented Data Model, which in turn will have been built using commonly constructed data models of concepts that finally, are based on enterprise-wide data elements.

The Operations cell, represent the running databases that interact with business information systems through views. Well engineered business information systems supported by quality database management systems will be able to share data across the databases. Alternatively, the data may be expressed from the business information systems not in terms of SQL views but as XML formatted schemas and instance streams. These in turn would be available for use by other business information systems.

A1.2.3   Business Information System Column

A business information system is a computer-based data processing system that accomplishes database object state transformations from within the context of business functions. Different business functions may cause the execution of the same business information system. If, in any of the business functions that employ a business information system, the database object value state transformation is not accomplished, the entire set of database object transformations is rolled back so that the database object returns to its prior state.

The Scope cell identifies the business information systems required to support the resources. The list is simple, one business information system per business resource[21]. If, for example, a business resource is people, the business information system would be the human resource management information system. Similarly identified and named are finance business information systems, customer management, facility's management, project management, and asset management.

The Business cell for business information systems contains the business information system hierarchies necessary to carry out the information system requirements of the database object transformations inferred by the business Resource Life Cycles. Named components within each detailed business information system clearly identify the nodes within each Resource Life Cycle. For the parts business resource, the necessary business information systems might be as depicted in Table 24.

Within the systems view, each identified business information system component, for example, Adjust Parts Inventory, is detailed in terms of its logic, windows, file accesses, and reports. Included at this level are the necessary connections to the specific aspects of each database object data structure. Identified and connected as well are the database object processes, and the necessary database object information systems that begin and structure the processes necessary to modify the database object's state from null to an allowed non-null state.

The critical difference between the database object information system and the business information system is that the database object information system is completely specified and totally implemented within ANSI standard SQL language while the business information system is completely specified and totally implemented within either an ANSI standard 3GL (e.g., COBOL, C) or a vendor proprietary 4GL (e.g., Clarion, FOCUS, and Power Builder).

---

[21] Within the Technology cell, each business information systems from the system's row may become multiple information systems that are implemented on different hardware, operating systems, and that operate through different DBMSs.

Parts Resource Life Cycle Nodes	Business information system Hierarchies
Part type definition	Create part type, Maintain parts (insert, maintain, and delete part)
Supplier establishment	Create supplier, Maintain suppliers (insert, maintain, and delete supplier)
Parts acquisition	Enter part receipt Adjust inventory
Order management	Reserve part for order Adjust order line item Report inventory status
Parts shipment	Build bill-of-lading Establish shipment Acknowledge shipment receipt
Parts maintenance	Adjust parts inventory Replace existing inventory

Table 24. Cross reference between Resource Life Cycle Nodes and Business Information Systems.

The reason that the database object information system is expressed entirely in ANSI/SQL syntax is so that it can be ported from one ANSI standard conforming SQL DBMS to another almost without regard to operating system, hardware platform, and presentation layer. In contrast, business information systems interface directly with end users. In client/server parlance that means that the business information systems include a "presentation layer."

Because of the business information system presentation layer, which is almost always operating system and computer platform dependent, porting business information systems can be problematic. It's even more problematic if the database-centric table processing rules have to be encoded in each business information system because not only are the presentation layer based business information systems bloated, the very same business rules have to be coded through a number of different languages. Database object information systems enable the table process rules to be encapsulated within the DBMS.

Within the technology cell, business information systems consist of traditional components, that is, detailed designs for windows, files, reports, processes, menus, and the like. To accelerate business implementation, business information system generators should be used whenever possible. Assuming they are, four benefits immediately accrue:

- Detailed design is quicker because the business information system generator builds so many of the system components.

- Coding errors within generated programs are virtually eliminated thus making unit test time close to zero.

- Generated system design documentation is commonly an automatic byproduct of business information system generators

- Long term maintenance is easier because of the three previous benefits.

Within the Deployment cell, business information system components are deployed. Included are equipment, acquisition of network support, and creation of an information technology support infrastructure for training and hotline. For example, the actual systems, programs, menus, and data files. When these components are generated, these only have to undergo normal configuration management.

Finally, within the Operations cell, the business information system components that take in data, produce reports and perform calculations execute. That is, accomplish the requirements of the business event that were instigated by a business function operating within a business organization.

A1.2.4   Business Event Column

Business Events are the interfaces between the two "machine" columns of the framework and the two "man" columns. The main reason there is a column formally dedicated to the interfaces between man and machine is to preserve their independence, and to set these events squarely within calendar and business cycles. The "man" columns are able to be crafted to fit different and individual functional styles within different and unique organizations.

The Scope cell contains the list of business events that are required to accomplish business information systems as they support business functions. For the "parts" example, above, the business events are: Perform parts acquisition and maintenance. Each listed business event acts as a surrogate for the set of business event sequences and if necessary, hierarchies. Each sequence or hierarchy is represented by one member of the business event list.

The Business cell contains the various business event sequences and hierarchies. For example, using the "parts" example from above, the information in the columns surrounding parts is presented in Table 25

The Systems cell contains the specifications of the invocation protocols, input and output data, and the various messages that must be exchanged between the business information systems and the business functions. In the example of parts, the input information is the specification of the data that must be submitted to establish a new part or supplier, or the specification of a report that is produced by a business information system in support of a particular business function.

Resource Life Cycle Node	Business Information System	Business Event	Business Function
Part type definition	Create part type	Invoke part creation	Create new part information for business
Supplier establishment	Create supplier,	Invoke supplier creation	Establish new supplier of parts
Parts acquisition	Enter part receipt	Invoke part receipt	Acquire parts from supplier

Table 25. Resource life cycle cross relationship with business information systems and business events.

The Technology cell contains the precise specifications of the man-machine interface for the different types of involved technology. For example, one business function may cause the creation of the data necessary to instigate a batch report. Another business function may have to create input data in a specific sequence and format. A final example might be the format and the mode of a generated report.

The Development cell of a business event contains the actual developed forms, computer windows, data entry instructions, and the instructions for acquiring and handling reports that ultimately form the operating environment.

The Operations cell embraces the day-to-day operational aspects of interfacing business functions and business information systems. This involves ensuring that there are enough data entry forms, sufficient paper for reports, computers, and telecommunications networks.

A1.2.5   Business Function Column

A Business Function is a procedure accomplished by someone within an organization to complete some aspect of a business' mission. Business functions almost always exceed the bounds of business information systems. For example, a business function to acquire a new part of a company's inventory might involve identification, gathering examples, analysis for engineering, durability, cost, and repair. Finally, a part is selected for inclusion. Then and only then is the information about the part encoded onto a data entry form as required by the appropriate business event, and then entered into a database through a business information system.

Business functions are commonly a matter of style. Different business organizations can have the same business function style, and the same business organization can have different business function styles. The greatest disaster that can befall a large scale information system is that its design is derived from a hierarchical decomposition of the business function's lowest levels. When that happens and there is the slightest change to the business functions, the business information systems must also change. The business information system gets whip-sawed. Or, stated differently, whenever the business functions get a *cold*, the business information system, at best gets a *pneumonia*, and at worst, *dies*.

The Knowledge Worker Framework is engineered to keep business information systems and business functions independent one from the other. Only when the business functions change to the extent that they need additional or different business information systems are business information systems impacted by business function changes. These changes typically occur only after there has been a business mission change.

The Scope cell of business functions is the list of the highest level business functions. These functions should closely parallel missions. Missions however, are different from business functions. Business missions are the ultimate targets of the enterprise. Not all missions are necessarily accomplished in the manner they are described. Business functions, however, are always accomplished else the business does not operate. Careful attention should be paid to any differences in business functions that need to be created once a new business information system's environment is put into place. The key questions are: What are the existing functions, what are the new functions, what functions have to be changed or even retired?

Business functions change over time far more frequently than do business missions. Consider for example any large insurance company. Clearly their missions deal with finding clients, offering insurance, performing underwriting, selling and administering policies, and paying claims. These missions have been the basis of insurance for several hundred years.

Business functions however, may change far more often. Insurance almost certainly was only sold through direct contacts with insurance agents. Today solicitations come in the mail almost every day and the agents call only during dinner. Payments formerly made through the agent who came to the door on a "debit" route can now be automatically deducted from checking accounts. Claimants used to await the individual insurance agent to inspect damage can now have their claims filed and adjudicated over the phone. Formerly, payments presented by the insurance agent can now be wire transferred or paid on-line to claimant accounts.

Sometimes however, the same business function is performed differently by different organizations. Another difference between mission and function is that missions are described independently from the *how* and *who* accomplish them. Business function is the *how* description. Within any business function, the missions are presumed, but the *who* is not known whenever business functions are performed by all business organizations. Whenever the same business function is performed by multiple organizations, but differently, then the business function description can be described in terms of the specific organization.

Within the Business cell, each business function is described in terms of the scenarios performed to accomplish some aspect of the business' mission. Each business function hierarchy is set down along with the sequencing of the steps within each hierarchy. If different business organizations perform the business function, the scenario descriptions can be different so long as the ultimate objectives of the function are clearly identified and are obvious to those who perform the function. As with the Scope cell, great care needs to be exercised to assess the current versus the new. Are functions going to be sequenced differently? What are the changes, and how will they affect the current staffing, current skill mixes, and the like? All these questions need to be asked and answered because any new information technology without corresponding human functions changes will only cause ultimate failure. The GAO study of the Reasons for information technology Failure prove that without question.

Within the System cell, each business function contains the exposition of the best practices, quality measure, and accomplishment assessments. These materials represent the idealized methods an organization can employ to accomplish business functions. Supporting each best practice is the various performance targets and assessments that judge satisfactory accomplishment. Whenever business functions are performed differently, there must be style independent assessments. Again, with the cells above, great care must be taken to discover the right set of new "best practices." Existing staff will not look too kindly on knowing that their current practice is now being replaced with "best practice." The staff will naturally ask, "haven't we been doing our best practice?" Time and care must be exercised as the new best practice may be subtly sabotaged by knowledge workers unwilling to change.

Within the Technology cell, business functions are detailed into their specific activity sequences that accomplish the business scenarios. Each set of activities is stylized to fit the specific organization carrying them out. The activity sequences are evaluated against the best practices and assessment criteria to ensure that the activities accomplish the desired result. As with the above cells, any new specific activity scenarios will have to be carefully worked out so that there is "buy-in" to the new procedures. All organizations will not work exactly the same way. Activity scenarios will likely be different because of different cultures, age groups, and other dynamics.

The Deployment cell represents the actual office procedures employed by organizations performing business functions. These deployed activities must be supported by necessary operational policies, procedures, and whatever technology supports that many be required. By this time in the process of unfolding a new business information systems environment, all must be ready and be willingly received or else the new business information system's deployment is in grave jeopardy. There must have been thorough testing in realistic laboratories of the new functions, new business events, new business information system presentation layers, and the like. If there is not marked improvement in productivity, data quality, ease of use, reporting, and the like, failure may well be right around the corner. It is critical to remember that 50% of the reasons for failure still exist once a business information systems is deployed.

The Operations cell represents the detailed instructions that exist within an office and a schedule to actually perform the business function's work. These office procedures should be taught, monitored, and constantly evaluated for maximum efficiency, effectiveness, and minimum cost and risk. At this point in the unfolding of new functionality, success or failure has been predetermined by the care taken in the above cells. No questions should remain when the business information systems are turned on.

A1.2.6   Organization Column

An organization is a formally constituted group of persons chartered to perform business functions to achieve some aspect of a business' mission. While small businesses often have the same organization from one location to another, large businesses do not. In fact, as businesses become larger and more diversified, organizations become different, stylized, and whenever management changes, business organizations often change in lock-step. Even when the mission of the enterprise fundamentally stays the same, there are business organizations. It is also quite common to change business function to match the new styles adopted by the business organization changes.

Business organizations are capable of change at a far greater rate than can the business information systems that support them. Thus, while organization changes might only cause mild disruptions, business information systems changes occur only after great expense and significant disruption. Because of these two dynamics, it's ideal not to have to change a business information system whenever a business organization and/or business function change.

To achieve this ideal, the Knowledge Worker Framework is engineered to keep business functions and business organizations independent one from the other, and both independent from business information systems. Only when the business organizations change to the extent that they need additional or different business functions are business functions impacted. The most common changes are those that cause business functions to be transferred from or into different business organizations. Those changes seldom ever impact business information systems. The only business organization changes that impact business information systems are those that typically occur after there has been a business mission change.

Within the Scope cell, the list of the business organizations performing the business functions is provided. It is critical to have a clear comparison between the "as-is" organizations and the "to-be" organizations. It is likely that the "as-is" organizations will have grown up over time to handle the existing set of business information systems, Database Object Classes, and business functions that may well be replaced. If these organizations are not analyzed to see how they might be reconfigured then the real benefits of the new business information systems may never be realized.

Within the Business cell, the various organization charts, jobs and their descriptions is provided. These provide an understanding of the types of persons who will be performing the business functions. In a manner similar to the Scope cell, the "as-is" organization charts, jobs, and descriptions need to be assessed and possibly massively reconfigured to then be the appropriate set of "to-be" organization charts, jobs, and descriptions. Resistance to change should never be under estimated. Great care and planning, and a large quantity of meetings may have to occur to convince the existing staff to change. This would especially be true if there's any hint of outsourcing and/or even "off-shoring" certain functions.

Similar with the two cells above, the System's cell would contain the detailed job roles, responsibilities and activity schedules are provided to better understand when and how the business functions are accomplished. It is likely that over the years there have been subtle changes to the formally constituted and written "as-is" versions of all the job descriptions. Consequently, the "as-is" job descriptions might have to be created from scratch to accurately reflect the current situation before any "to-be" versions of these materials can be created. Once the "to-be" versions are created then a "differences" assessment can be made that would then cause the creation of requirements for the development of new training materials, trainers, additional or different technology infrastructure, and the like that must be created prior to any new functionality deployment.

Within the Technology cell, the various new and/or revised procedure manuals are created along with their task lists, the quality measures that ensure that the activity is successfully accomplished by the specific organizational unit, and the specifications of exactly how the activities are assessed. These materials are created and then updated on an as needed basis.

Within the Deployment row, the daily schedules, shift and personnel assignments are created. These are integrated with the various business functions. Since organizations can vary there may be different configurations that perform business functions. The measures of equivalency are the best practices, measures, and assessment criteria created as part of the business function system viewpoint.

Within the Operations cell, organizations are deployed and accomplish the full set of business functions necessary to carry out the business' missions.

Attachment 2
Database Architecture Class Characteristics

Data Architecture Persistent Data Classifications and Characteristics				
Persistent Data Classification	**Persistent Data Characteristics**	**Process Characteristics**	**User Considerations**	**Technical Considerations**
Original Data Capture	Detailed atomic data Accurate as of the last update Well defined, long lasting database designs Normalized database designs Uses reference data No invalid data updates allowed	Tuned for transaction capture, storage and update Application oriented Transaction driven Processing supported by well known data integrity and business processing rules Understands, creates, and maintains TDSA databases through Original Data Capture business information system extracts Source data for TDSA	Original data source entry personnel High availability Supports day-to-day operations	Amount of data for processing is small Multiple vendor packages Package specific May or may not be controlled by SQL DBMS

Data Architecture Persistent Data Classifications and Characteristics				
Persistent Data Classification	**Persistent Data Characteristics**	**Process Characteristics**	**User Considerations**	**Technical Considerations**
TDSA: Transaction Data Staging Area	Transient data/short lived Foundation data source for all operational data business information systems Enterprise-wide standard semantics Package independent database designs Denormalized Full business transaction Does not use reference data	Accepts, stores, and then pushes forward function Only refreshed with changes from previous version Operations application data business information system daily update event driven Translation and transformation	Users cannot access	Multiple platforms Interface monitoring Applications insulation SQL DBMS controlled

Data Architecture Persistent Data Classifications and Characteristics				
Persistent Data Classification	**Persistent Data Characteristics**	**Process Characteristics**	**User Considerations**	**Technical Considerations**
ODS: Operational Data Store "Subject Area Data Store"	Detail level data May be lightly summarized Current or nearly current Rolling histories Broad subject area database scope Normalized database designs Redundant data from across enterprise May contain derived data from "outside" Uses reference data May receive and/or send data to databases within class Data source for all warehouse	Updated daily via TDSA data transaction files Accepts and stores data from TDSA Supports comprehensive reporting and generalized ad hoc query	End-user detailed level analysis Used for up to the minute decisions Used for detailed decision making	Requires fast response time Large volume SQL DBMS controlled

Data Architecture Persistent Data Classifications and Characteristics				
Persistent Data Classification	**Persistent Data Characteristics**	**Process Characteristics**	**User Considerations**	**Technical Considerations**
Warehouse: Wholesale	Summarized and some detail Rolling Histories Load/replace, no end-user update Enterprise-wide standard semantics Narrow/subset of one or more subject areas Redundant data from across enterprise May contain internal derived data Reference data fully embedded May receive and/or send data to databases within class Data source for all retail data warehouses	No end-user updating Regular, periodic updates Supports standardized, on-demand reports Supports general complex business data analyses such as trends and forecasting Views data from multiple subject areas	Supports managerial community Used for broad direction and positioning Used to formulate and assess long term decisions	Availability not on business' critical path User workstation access Large data volumes per query High processing power required SQL DBMS controlled

Data Architecture Persistent Data Classifications and Characteristics				
Persistent Data Classification	**Persistent Data Characteristics**	**Process Characteristics**	**User Considerations**	**Technical Considerations**
Warehouse: Retail	Light to highly summarized and some detail Rolling histories Load/replace, no end-user update Enterprise-wide standard semantics Denormalized and highly designed to specifically favor one or more reporting formats Redundant data from across enterprise May contain internal derived data Reference data fully embedded May receive and/or send data to databases within class	Availability not on business' critical path Regular, periodic updates Highly designed, end-user on-demand reports Supports very specific simple to complex business data analyses Views data from multiple subject areas	Supports managerial community Cannot update Used for direction and positioning Used for long term decision making Specific reporting need	Relaxed availability User workstations Large volume High processing power SQL DBMS controlled

Data Architecture Persistent Data Classifications and Characteristics				
Persistent Data Classification	**Persistent Data Characteristics**	**Process Characteristics**	**User Considerations**	**Technical Considerations**
Reference Data	Durable codes and long value alternatives with policy definitions and full descriptions Enterprise-wide standard semantics Source of all valid and invalid values Multiple group data field constructors for different countries and languages Definitive source for multi-use data Changed data history supported by conversion mappings Long lasting, seldom updated	Simple updates Update mappings required for reference data value migration	Needed by all levels in the organization Used by all business information systems Enables understanding and conversion of historical data	Supports the concept of single source Integration with all data store types

Table 26. Data architecture class descriptions.

Index